AF662131

Global Meltdown
Regional Impacts

GLOBAL MELTDOWN

Regional Impacts

Edited by

Nandita Sethi
A.V. Bala Krishna

Institute of Public Enterprise (IPE)
Hyderabad

in association with

New Century Publications
New Delhi, India

New Century Publications
4800/24, Bharat Ram Road,
Ansari Road, Daryaganj,
New Delhi – 110 002 (India)

Tel.: 011-2324 7798, 4358 7398, 6539 6605
Fax: 011-4101 7798
E-mail: indiatax@vsnl.com • info@newcenturypublications.com
www.newcenturypublications.com

Editorial office:
LG–7, Aakarshan Bhawan,
4754-57/23, Ansari Road, Daryaganj,
New Delhi – 110 002

Tel.: 011-4356 0919

Copyright © 2010 by the editors

All rights reserved. No part of this book may be reproduced, stored in a retrieval system, or transmitted in any form or by any means, mechanical, photocopying, recording, or otherwise without the prior written permission of the publisher.

First Published: **July 2010**

ISBN: **978-81-7708-235-7**

Published by New Century Publications and printed at Salasar Imaging Systems, New Delhi.

Designs: Patch Creative Unit, New Delhi.

PRINTED IN INDIA

Contents

Part II: Regional Impacts

About the Book

The financial turmoil which surfaced in August 2007 in the US financial system as a result of defaults of sub-prime mortgage loans has blown into an unprecedented financial crisis engulfing international money, credit, equity and foreign exchange markets. What started off as a sub-prime crisis in the US housing mortgage sector has turned successively into a global banking crisis, global financial crisis and now a global recession.

Though emerging market economies, including India, do not have direct or significant exposure to stressed financial instruments or troubled financial institutions, they are not immune to the adverse effects of the financial crisis.

Most of the crises over the past few decades have had their roots in developing and emerging countries, often resulting from abrupt reversals in capital flows, and from loose domestic monetary and fiscal policies. In contrast, the current ongoing global financial crisis has had its roots in the US.

Given the experience of the post-crisis period, the *decoupling hypothesis* stands invalidated. Reinforcing the notion that in a globalised world no country can be an island, growth prospects of emerging economies have been undermined by the cascading financial crisis with, of course, considerable variation across countries.

This book contains 16 analytical contributions gathered from various sources which give—with regional dimensions—deep insights into the origin, causes, consequences and remedial measures related to the crisis.

About the Editors

Nandita Sethi is currently Assistant Professor at the Institute of Public Enterprise (IPE), Hyderabad. She is a post-graduate in economics and scholarship holder in M. Phil. from Hyderabad Central University. She received the national level Indian Council of Social Science Research (ICSSR) scholarship for doctorate from Osmania University, Hyderabad. She has teaching and research experience of 19 years and has several published articles and 3 books. She is also the managing editor of *Journal of International Economics* published by IPE.

A.V. Bala Krishna is presently working as Editorial Associate at the Institute of Public Enterprise (IPE), Hyderabad. An MBA from Andhra University, he has about 15 years of industry and research experience. He has edited a few books in the areas of marketing, rural banking, branding and advertising and has published a number of articles in journals/ magazines.

Contributors and Organisations

Olivier Blanchard	International Monetary Fund (IMF)
José Viñals	International Monetary Fund (IMF)
Jorgen Elmeskov	Organisation for Economic Cooperation and Development (OECD)
Luci Ellis	Reserve Bank of Australia
Jack Boorman	Emerging Markets Forum
Eduardo Fernández-Arias	Inter-American Development Bank, US
Andrew Powell	Inter-American Development Bank, US
Alessandro Rebucci	Inter-American Development Bank, US
Sir John Gieve	Bank of England
Alejandro Jara	Bank for International Settlements, *BIS Quarterly*
Ramon Moreno	Bank for International Settlements, *BIS Quarterly*
Camilo E. Tovar	Bank for International Settlements *BIS Quarterly*
Sylvester C.W. Eijffinger	Centre for Economic Policy Research (CEPR), UK
Moussa Haddad	Oxfam, UK
Antonia Bance	Oxfam, UK
Amir Hadziomeragic	Centralna banka Bosne i Hercegovine; Oesterreichische National bank (OeNB)
Ljubinko Jankov	Hrvatska Narodna Banka; Oesterreichische National bank (OeNB)
Richard Pomfret	EU-Central Asia Monitoring (EUCAM)
Anwar Nasution	University of Indonesia
Jayati Ghosh	Jawaharlal Nehru University (JNU), India
D. Subbarao	Reserve Bank of India

Foreword

It is really a privilege and honour for me to introduce the book to the readers. Being a financial economist, I feel it becomes my moral responsibility to say a few words about the book. Many things have been said and written about the present crisis. However, books that deal with the causes, impacts, policy responses and recovery paths have not been many. This book is compiled exceptionally well covering what has driven the present crisis, how it is felt across the world, how various nations prepared themselves to contain the contagion, what are their policy responses and how the economies are responding to these remedial measures. The work of the editors in this regard is really commendable.

The financial crisis that began in the United States in the sub-prime mortgage market in 2007 spread quickly to other parts of the world and has become a global crisis in 2008. This crisis has affected both the financial systems and economic activity across the world; is being considered by many as the largest since the great depression and is coined as global meltdown in the current economic literature. The crisis affected both developed and developing countries alike though the severity varied between the two groups. The most affected are developed nations with falling currencies, closing manufacturing units, slumping markets, and reducing employment opportunities, while developing nations are facing difficulties mainly due to falling investment flows, declining exports and reducing tourism in the services sector. There have been many causes for the present crisis, some recent ones and some longstanding ones. Many economists believe that the most basic underlying driver of the present crisis is the changing human psychology around risk perceptions. The main driver of course was the unwinding of asset price hikes, financial leverage and risk appetite built up prior to the crisis. Responses of the nations are varied, timely and focused. Policymakers have provided fiscal stimulus and initiatives that support trade and financial flows which will help support global demand, with shared benefits. One of the major lessons from the recovery is the power of multilateralism—the success of working together to combat a crisis.

This book titled "Global Meltdown: Regional Impacts" consists of two sections: Section one focuses on the general causes of and the run up to the recession, its spread across the globe and some common impacts while section two captures the experiences of different countries and regions.

R.K. Mishra
Director
Institute of Public Enterprise, Hyderabad

Overview

Nandita Sethi and A.V. Bala Krishna

The year 2008 saw the world economy land itself in the midst of the most severe financial and economic recession since the Second World War. Global economic activity saw a collapse at a rate not seen since the Great Depression. The impacts felt are both wide in scope and depth worldwide and pose a major threat to the world economic and social development. While the crisis originated in developed countries, which are also leading the economic downturn, developing countries are also hit hard through capital reversals, rising borrowing costs, collapsing world trade and commodity prices, and subsiding remittance flows. The global meltdown has once again brought forth the fact that today we operate in a world that is highly connected and the good and bad contagion leaves no country isolated. As earlier episodes of financial crisis have shown, delays in tackling the underlying problem can lead to an even more severe and prolonged economic downturn and result in even greater costs, both in terms of taxpayer money and economic activity, most countries have been quick and proactive in dealing with the problem. Policymakers have provided fiscal stimulus and initiatives that support trade and financial flows which will help support global demand, with shared benefits. One of the major lessons from the recovery is the power of multilateralism—the success of working together to combat a crisis.

This book, ***"Global Meltdown: Regional Impacts"*** has been compiled with this recession of 2008 as the backdrop which began in the US and triggered a world-wide economic downturn. Through various articles written across various countries and regions, it goes into the origin of the crises, the causes of its spread, the multifarious impacts it had on different countries, the policy responses it evoked and the impact of those responses. The book has been categorised in two sections. Section one comprises of the general causes of and the run up to the recession, its spread across the globe and some common impacts. Section two is devoted to the experiences of different countries and regions – the channels of contagion, the impacts of the downturn, policy measures to combat the crises and some important lessons learnt.

The first article is the Executive summary of the IMF Report **World Economic Outlook** titled ***"Crises and Recovery"*** (April 2009). While giving the facts and figures of the global economy in a severe recession inflicted by a massive financial crisis and acute loss of confidence, the report projects the outlook and risks for the following year and the policy challenges in the short and medium term. Total expected write-downs on global exposures are estimated at about US$ 4 trillion, of which two-thirds will fall on banks and the remainder on insurance companies, pension funds, hedge funds, and other intermediaries. The Report projects that world output will recover only marginally in 2010 growing at around 1.9 percent. Achieving this turnaround will depend on stepping up efforts to heal the financial sector, while continuing to support demand with monetary and fiscal easing. The projections assume that financial market stabilization will take longer than envisaged, even with strong efforts by policymakers. Furthermore, in a highly uncertain context, fiscal and monetary policies may fail to gain traction, since high rates of precautionary saving could lower fiscal multipliers, and steps to ease funding could fail to slow the pace of deleveraging. On the upside, however, bold policy implementation that is able to convince markets that financial strains are being dealt with decisively could revive confidence and spending commitments.

This difficult and uncertain outlook argues for forceful action on both the financial and macroeconomic policy fronts. Initiatives that support trade and financial partners—including fiscal stimulus and official support for international financing flows—will help support global demand, with shared benefits. The greatest policy priority at this juncture is financial sector restructuring. In the short run, the three priorities identified are ensuring that financial institutions have access to liquidity; identifying and dealing with distressed assets and; recapitalizing weak but viable institutions. In advanced economies, scope for easing monetary policy further should be used aggressively to counter deflation risks. However, the challenge ahead will be to monitor the pace of this monetary stimulus so that it neither undercuts the recovery nor results in overheating. Fiscal policy must also play a crucial part in providing short-term stimulus to the global economy. However, the room to provide fiscal support will be limited if efforts erode credibility. Thus, governments are faced with a difficult balancing act, delivering short-term expansionary policies but also providing reassurance about medium-term prospects. The medium-run challenges will be with respect to financial policies, the task of regulation and making it more flexible to cover all systemically relevant institutions. In addition, regulation would need to include compensation structures that mitigate pro-cyclical effects, robust market clearing arrangements, accounting rules to accommodate illiquid securities, transparency about the nature and location of risks to foster market discipline, and better systemic liquidity management. Finally fiscal policymakers will need to bring down deficits and put public debt on a sustainable trajectory.

The second article titled "**The General Economic Background to the Crisis**" written by Jørgen Elmeskov of OECD is a paper presented at G20 Workshop on the Causes of the Crisis: Key Lessons Mumbai, 24-26 May, 2009. The article provides a backgrounder to the economic crisis. Origin of the crisis, symptoms and causes and its propagation are well detailed out in the article. It states that the three main drivers of the current crisis are unwinding of asset price hikes, financial leverage and risk appetite. The economic crisis has affected developed and emerging economies alike although it has not hit countries equally hard. Ironically it is not the countries where asset prices and financial leverage increased that where worst hit rather those with a heavy specialisation in durable goods and hi-tech manufacturing.

The article highlights that the origin of the crises lies in OECD countries. Falling bond yields coupled with shooting up real house prices lead to financial innovation. This resulted in evolution of sub-prime loans, rapidly expanded housing construction activity, enormous growth of bank credit and speedily rising share markets all of which bore the symptoms of a bubble. The article further highlights the causes of the bubble: Benign growth and inflation conditions gave a false sense of stability, rising saving rates in emerging economies, resulted in shift in global income distribution away from low-saving (typically OECD) countries towards high-saving (typically emerging Asian and oil exporting countries). Accommodative monetary policy with low interest rates helped to boost asset prices and the search for yield, and financial innovation allowed the emergence of the sub-prime market that led to greater leverage and generally higher levels of risks. The propagation of the crisis is manifested in OECD countries in the form of cutting back expenditure on consumption, reduced outlays and production, wealth losses on shares and housing, prospects of higher unemployment and general uncertainty. World trade was hit hard and was one of the essential transmission channels of the financial crisis to emerging economies. Reversal of capital flows from emerging economies was another major impact as enterprises sought safety in highly liquid assets.

The next article, **"The Global Financial Crisis: Causes, Consequences and Countermeasures"** are remarks by Dr. Luci. Ellis delivered at the conference on 'Australia in the global storm: A conference on the implications of the global financial crisis for Australia and its region' held on 15 April

2009. Dr. Luci Ellis goes into what caused the global financial crisis, the consequences and the countermeasures that governments and other policy-makers can take, to reduce the costs of the present crisis and to prevent a recurrence. The author focuses on three causes of the crises: the misperception and mismanagement of risk; the level of interest rates; and the regulation of the financial system. The most basic underlying driver of the crisis was the inherent human psychology around risk perceptions which diminishes in good times and gets bloated during crises. A second element that coincided with the perceptions of lower risk was the low level of interest rates in the early part of this decade. Also a lack of appropriate financial regulation in some countries is widely regarded as an important cause of the crisis. Many shortcomings have been identified in this area. These include: the capital requirements on complex financial products such as collateralised debt obligations (CDOs); the use of ratings provided by the private-sector rating agencies in the regulation of banks; the way credit rating agencies have themselves been regulated; and the structure of remuneration arrangements and the risk-taking incentives they create. Many internationally active banks failed to perceive, or appropriately manage, the risks involved in certain financial products and markets, and regulators did not make them do better on this front. The consequences were that projects that seemed likely to be profitable in the good times suddenly looked risky. Industrial output contracted sharply in much of the world. Commodity prices had been booming earlier in the year declined significantly towards the end of the year. This resulted in contraction in output and volume of world trade.

The author analyses the Australian financial system and draws some common conclusions. He says that Australia has withstood the shocks due to a number of factors. One of these is that it had not accumulated large exposures to securities in which losses at other banks have been concentrated. Rather, they were focused on their domestic lending business. As

Australia usually runs a current account deficit, so their banks were seeking offshore funding rather then casting around for foreign assets to invest in. Another reason is that in Australia the housing and mortgage markets did not become as over-extended and lending standards did not ease as much as in the United States because the regulatory arrangements, consumer protection laws concerning mortgage lending and foreclosure law are more stringent. For restoring the global banking system to health which is the immediate priority Governments can buy the assets outright and place them in an entity separate to the bank; they can insure assets remaining on banks' balance sheets against losses; or they can invest in joint investment funds that buy the assets. On top of these efforts to deal with the immediate problems, there is also considerable focus on reforms to the financial system architecture, to prevent a similar crisis from occurring again.

The next article titled **"The Impact of the Financial Crisis on Emerging Market Economies: The Transmission Mechanism, Policy Response and Lessons,"** written by Jack Boorman is from Emerging Markets Forum. The article provides an overview of the spread of the contagion to emerging economies, its impact, policy responses and lessons to be learnt by the emerging economies. The impact of the crisis is manifested in the form of declined growth rates of GDPs. The crisis was transmitted from the most developed regions of the world - U.S. and Europe to emerging economies mainly through five channels: fund withdrawal by financial institutions from their subsidiaries located in the emerging economies; reduced credit flows to emerging market countries; economic impact of reduced exports from emerging markets; uncertain prospects of remittances and the psychological impact.

The policy responses of various emerging market countries include capital reserve enhancing measures, strengthening of financial sectors, introduction of fiscal stimulus packages and trade protection measures. There are four major lessons that the emerging market countries should learn from the present financial crisis: inadequate financial sector regulation and supervision lead to the present crisis, a rethinking should be done on the effectiveness of reserve accumulation policies of the emerging market economies; fiscal stimulus should serve the purpose, be time framed and combined with a policy conducive to fiscal sustainability and; these economies should be more cautious in opening their capital markets.

The next article titled **"The Multilateral Response to the Global Crisis: Rationale, Modalities and Feasibility,"** written by Eduardo Fernandez-Arias, Andrew Powell and Alessandro Rebucci is from Inter-American Development Bank. This paper, as the title suggests, reviews the case for a strong multilateral response to the global crisis in emerging markets. It focuses first on the need for the multilateral intervention by emphasizing on the limitations of the individual countries' abilities to respond to the crisis by deliberating on fiscal policy and monetary policy flexibilities. The benefits of a multilateral response are: bridging the short-term financing needs, covering liquidity risks and guarding against trade protectionism thereby containing the damage to fundamentals that a full-blown liquidity crisis can provoke.
The study looks into the modalities of intervention and associated risks, specific role of multilateral development banks and the feasibility of such a multilateral response. The paper highlights that the multilateral response should be fast and decisive and it should aim at back-stopping liquidity, providing long-term finance and facilitating fiscal adjustment while preventing an increased risk of liquidity. Role of multilateral agencies in dealing with the ongoing financial and economic crisis is highlighted and discussed in detail under differing country scenarios. The paper concludes with a discussion on the international financial architecture issues and the strategic role of multilateral development banks

The next article titled **"Learning from the Financial Crisis,"** is the speech given by Sir John Gieve, Deputy

Governor, Bank of England at European Business School, London on November 19th, 2008. The author in his speech focused on three aspects of the crisis – the emergence of the crisis, the policy challenges and the lessons that can be drawn from the crisis. He emphasized that the roots of the crisis lay in global trade imbalances and capital flows between developed and emerging economies and its impact was felt in both the developed and emerging economies. The loss of confidence in financial markets and continued uncertainties about inflation pose major challenges to the policy makers.

Sir John Gieve draws out some lessons for the medium term: the importance of affecting a closer international co-ordination among various economies; the need for establishing a robust framework of rules to deal with cross-border financial crises in terms of capital, liquidity and legal structure; the need for filling-up the gaps and correcting the flaws in the regulatory and accounting conventions of the banks; and the need for bridging the gap between macroeconomic policy and the regulation of individual firms. He describe three ways to restrict banks from driving a cycle: (1) banks should build a general reserve that can be drawn on in downturns; (2) the risk weighting (and so, the capital requirement) of bank loans should include a growth-based component which could be linked either to the economy-wide growth rate of a particular type of business, or to the growth rate of an individual bank's lending relative to the market as a whole; or some combination of the two and (3) banks which are funding their expansion through risky funding should be required to match that expansion with an increasing stock of safer and lower-yielding assets.

The first article in the regional impacts section is titled **"The Global Crisis and Latin America: Financial Impact and Policy Responses"** in BIS Quarterly Review is written by Alejandro Jara, Ramon Moreno and Camilo E. Tovar. The article discusses about the impact of the ongoing economic crisis on the Latin American countries and delineates various policy responses undertaken by them. The article which starts by providing an introduction to the current global financial crisis highlights that though the initial impact of the crisis on the Latin economies was limited, it became intensified in the post-Lehman Brothers bankruptcy scenario. It discusses how the present crisis is different from the previous major crisis of Asia in 1997 and Brazilian and Argentinean crisis of 2000. The present crisis started in the developed financial markets and spread to the emerging economies; reduced Latin American public external debt gave governments more leeway to play a stabilising role for private markets, where external debt had remained high; and it was financial engineering rather than macroeconomic imbalances or banking sector weaknesses that caused new kinds of vulnerabilities in the system. Gross capital inflows to Latin America began to contract significantly in the third quarter of 2008. Several factors have contributed to the abrupt reversal in gross capital inflows: the increase in international risk aversion, efforts by financial institutions in developed countries to boost liquidity or shore up their balance sheets, high currency volatility, the terms-off-trade collapse and the derivatives exposure of some large corporations in Brazil and Mexico.

In terms of policy responses, most central banks in the region supplied foreign currency liquidity through intervention or operations in the foreign exchange market, including foreign exchange spot, repo and swap transactions and roll over of foreign debt. External resources have provided significant additional support to Latin American emerging economies during the current crisis especially the large reciprocal currency arrangements with the US Federal Reserve. The author concludes that there is a need to ensure that risks assumed in financial markets are well understood by market participants and policymakers to prevent bankruptcies and disruptions to local funding markets.

The next article titled "**Crisis Management in the European Union**" written by Sylvester C.W. Eijffinger is from Policy Insight brought out by Centre for Economic Policy Research (CEPR). The article is divided into five sections: The first section provides an introduction and captures various steps undertaken in crisis prevention and management by European Union. Section two deals with the development of the crisis by focusing on the denial, discovery and disposal phases of the crisis. The denial phase was characterized by different executives not willing to acknowledge that the crisis has set in, while the discovery phase was marked by loan write-offs, lack of confidence in the markets and contagion of the sub-prime crisis becoming a reality and, the disposal phase is marked by governments resorting to rescuing operations of the financial systems. Section three highlights the bailout phase and describes the conditions to make the bailout as unattractive as possible. The bailout phase was marked by nationalization of banks and insurance companies. Section four draws the four key lessons that could be learnt from the credit crises based on the expcriences that caused the crisis: Asymmetric reward structure of the top executives with no downward risk was not sustainable in bad times, risk management models bases on Basel II were inadequate, financial supervision was less involved in risk management, and the fragmented and ineffective US framework of financial supervision has failed and needs improvement. The article concludes by delineating the benchmarks for a new financial system that meets the **criterion** of sustainability, integrity and transparency.

The next article titled **"UK Poverty and the Economic Downturn"** written by Moussa Haddad and Antonia Bance is from Oxfam International. The authors discuss how this recession is going to hit hard particularly the poor sections of the society and how the government can make use of these challenges to ensure a fair and sustainable society. Despite UK being the sixth richest country of the World, about 22% of the country's population is living in poverty. These poor sections of the society are faced with rising cost of living, housing problems, employment problems apart from such other problems as volatile inflation, increasing gap between income and cost of living etc.,. The impact of the ongoing recession is likely to impact the poor the most. Rising unemployment rates, growing risk of insecurity at work, vulnerability to poverty, housing insecurity are likely to be some of the recession manifestations. The author suggests that decisions that determine who loses most in a downturn must be made in the light of who benefited from the preceding period of growth. As the poor neither benefited much from the previous growth nor was responsible for the present crises they should not be made to bear the brunt of the economic crisis.

A few steps have been suggested for the government that may protect the poor from its worst impact such as, promoting economic stability, curbing market excesses, redistributing wealth, tackling inequality etc.,. It argues for the prevention of cutting expenditure on public services and social protection measures which benefit the poor especially on the economic logic that they have higher marginal propensity to consume, and money put into their hands will spur consumption and re circulate money into the wider economy. The article enumerates a few measures that could prevent the country's economic system being run into chaos. Introducing a fairer tax policy that immunes poorest from paying major chunk of their income in the form of taxes, making use of fiscal stimulus packages to ensure a sustainable economy from all perspectives, strictly enforcing employment rights, regulating the credit market so as to enable affordable credit, providing secure housing that prevents people from falling into homelessness and promoting social cohesion and solidarity among the people

The next article titled **"The Current Crisis – a Challenge as well as a Chance to Implement Needed Reforms?"** is written by Amir Hadziomeragic. The article opens up with a brief introduction about Bosnia and Herzegovina economy by focusing on the various facets of their economy. Its growth dynamics as seen by macroeconomic indicators such as GDP growth, inflation, current account balance (CAB), capital flows and share of FDI in CAB, external deficits, government balance, export performance, exchange rate, external debt, credit operations, etc, have been captured concisely in the introduction part. The economy has grown at an annual rate of 6% per annum between 2003 and 2008. The current account deficit was very large and FDI became an important source of financing the current account deficit. With an exception in 2007, FDI accounted for about 33 percent to 73 percent of the current account deficit and credit grew at an average of 19 percent between 2004 and 2008. The article further highlights that the monetary regime was successful in keeping the inflation low. The privatization and huge capital inflows led to increase in credit flows to private sector. In order to control negative macroeconomic consequences that may result due to rapid credit expansion, the central bank tightened reserve requirements to slow down credit growth. The banking sector witnessed a steady growth during the period and the central bank emphasized on financial stability of the whole system.

The financial crisis hit all the industries and the affected industries witnessed decline in output, price, demand and exports. Exports of automobile industry declined, metal prices fell steeply, construction sector suffered due to credit crunch and the retail sector experienced slowdown. The FDI inflow is likely to decline relatively to previous years. Moreover, the private sector is finding it increasingly difficult to borrow from abroad. Consequently, a larger portion of CAB financing may put pressure on foreign exchange reserves. The banking sector is likely to face a further deterioration and shocks on both sides of its balance sheet. The fiscal position has been very strained after the crisis started. The robust growth of tax revenue that was seen in recent years will not continue for some time. The article highlights the need for structural changes and different growth patterns by focusing on monetary and exchange rate regime. Securing the financial stability, improvement in banking supervision, prevention of real appreciation of domestic currency, maintenance of wage rate flexibility, reliance on external sources of capital to boost domestic demand, securing additional funds to finance projects, etc., have been emphasized in this regard. The author feels that the ongoing crisis is an opportunity to accelerate reforms to address several deficiencies, which were frequently neglected during the periods of economic prosperity.

The next article titled **"Spillovers of the Crisis: How different Is Croatia?"** is written by Ljubinko Jankov, Executive Director of Hrvatska Narodna Banka (HNB). The article discusses about the impact of the crisis on Croatia and how it has been able to manage the crisis successfully so far. The article discusses in detail the role of the Central Bank in controlling the negative effects of the crisis on the Croatian Banking system. The Central Bank (HNB) focused on price stability and tight control of exchange rate of Croatian Kuna against Euro since 1993 which proved to be very successful in controlling the inflation. The article highlights that the Central Bank recognized that high inflow of foreign funds in the short run and granting of bank loans to house holds were occurring as the seeds of the future crisis for the economy and started to act against these trends by focusing on soft monetary policy and various administrative and prudential measures. In the year 2003, the Central Bank imposed a speed limit on the bank lending by different Banks and also on the minimum retained earnings if bank lending exceeds a certain threshold. It was later replaced by marginal reserve requirement in the year 2004 in order to improve the banks' liquidity position against risks and the minimum foreign exchange liquidity requirement. Taken together, these three requirements reached their peak at the end of 2005, and—although there were some minor variations in the minimum foreign exchange liquidity requirement—remained there until October 2008. Banks were required to place 72 percent of the increase in foreign liabilities with the HNB, or in liquid foreign assets, while the remaining 28 percent was disposable for lending to clients.

The exchange rate pressures were successfully contained by HNB providing liquidity in foreign and tightening liquidity in domestic currency. The article stresses that the episode of Lehman Brothers showed a negative impact on the capital flows to the countries of Central and Eastern Europe and Croatia is no exception. The article further states that the position of money and foreign exchange markets stabilized by March 2009. It concludes by highlighting the future challenges for the Croatian economy by stressing on structural weaknesses: low total factor productivity, low labour participation, a smaller share of goods exports in GDP than in peer countries, etc. These present a challenge for their international competitiveness and implementation of economic policy in the long run and should be reversed by launching more structural reforms that increase their economy's long run growth potential.

The next article titled "**Central Asia and the Global Economic Crisis**," written by Richard Pomfret is from EU-Central Asia Monitoring (EUCAM). The article highlights that though, the impact of the present global economic crisis is benign on the region, the respective character of the individual economies of the Central Asia bears influence on the extent of impact of the crisis on them. The economies which are more liberalized are more vulnerable to the shocks of the crisis than the economies which are relatively closed. Of the five Central Asian republics, Kyrgyz Republic and Kazakhstan have been the more liberal economic reformers while Uzbekistan and Turkmenistan were more cautious reformers. Tajikistan's economic transition fell between these two pairs

The article discusses the impact of the global economic crisis on the region under three different heads - the financial sector, trade and migration and remittances. The financial sectors of the central Asian countries are relatively less exposed to turmoil in global financial markets but, the impact on trade is likely to be considerable as the region's exports are concentrated in a few commodities and fall in demand and price changes have impacted these countries differently. In terms of migration and remittances hundreds of thousands of workers from Tajikistan and to a lesser extent the Kyrgyz Republic and Uzbekistan are working abroad and their prospects will be directly influenced by economic conditions in Russia and elsewhere. The article further discusses about the implications for EU policy towards Central Asian countries by stressing on encouragement to imports from Central Asian countries, promotion of regional cooperation, commitment to poverty alleviation in the region and long-term strategy towards energy security.

The next article titled "**Measuring the Pulse of Africa in Times of Crisis**," is a policy brief from Organization for Economic Co-operation and Development (OECD) that focuses on the impact of the present global crisis on major African Economies. (It analyses 47 African economies, accounting for 97 percent of Africa's population and 99 percent of its economic output). The African economies which recorded 5 percent growth consecutively for four years are expected to fall down to 2.8 percent in the year 2009-2010 as a result of thc ongoing economic crisis. The crisis has manifested itself in the fall of commodity prices, persistence of high prices for the internationally traded food items; rising inflation etc. The hardest hit African economies are those that are heavily reliant on commodity exports as commodity prices have fallen. Net oil importing African countries face a different set of challenges, with GDP growth in many of them expected to continue its fall in 2010. Official development assistance to Africa, which was driven largely by debt relief and emergency assistance, fell by 18 percent in real terms in 2007, mostly due to the end of exceptional debt relief operations. However, global aid reached a record high in 2008, and may well grow, albeit slowly, in 2009 and 2010. The article highlights the importance of nurturing an economic environment that would be conducive to private-sector development and fostering progress in governance. However, the article ends on a positive note by highlighting that, with the right mix of policy reforms and donors' willingness to compensate for drops in trade revenues, foreign private capital flows and government revenues, the continent is in a better position to survive the present economic crisis and lay a stronger basis for future growth and development.

The Global Financial Crisis and its impact on the Asia-Pacific Region by Anwar Nasution discusses the impact of the recession on the economies of the Asia Pacific region which are affected through falls in commodity prices, declining trade, capital outflows and lower remittances from abroad. Mostly being export oriented economies they neither have a sufficiently robust domestic demand, nor large intra-regional trade to offset the impact of falling exports to the United States and Europe. The study analyzes the evolution of the global financial crisis and contrasts it with the Asian financial crisis of 1997-98. It examines the current economic situation in the Asia Pacific region, global and regional responses, and sets out recommendations for policy coordination in the region aimed at promoting global economic recovery. The author proposes that these countries should adopt a two-way approach to the crisis, i.e., internally, they should make better use of the region's financial resources and relatively large domestic markets and globally, they should work with other regions, particularly with their main export markets in the US and Europe, to promote world economic growth. All of these require closer cooperation on monetary, fiscal and exchange rate policies, both regionally and globally.

The Asia-Pacific economies can implement five forms of economic cooperation and coordination in order to achieve common goals. Firstly, national economies should be stimulated through the expansion of both public sector spending and private consumption expenditures and in the long-term, the export-led development strategy can gradually be replaced by a domestic oriented growth strategy especially in countries with potentially large domestic demand. Part of the economic stimulus should be for the building of modern infrastructure. Secondly, bilateral currency swap arrangements under the Chiang Mai Initiatives should be used for expanding the intra-regional private sector investment and trade in the region. Thirdly, financial resources should be provided to emerging countries in this region, in order to limit the adverse effects of the global crisis, through bilateral mechanisms and/or through multilateral financial institutions such as the ADB, IMF and the World Bank. Fourthly, closer regional economic cooperation on financial issues can be started by encouraging closer cooperation between banks and financial market regulators in terms of sharing information on the management of liquidity by banks, total leverage and assessment of risk-weighted assets. Lastly, policy coordination should also be strengthened through close coordination on issues such as exchange rate management, the environment, state aid, agriculture, trade and investment.

"The Global Financial Crisis, Developing Countries and India" by Jayati Ghosh discusses how this financial crises is different from the various financial crises in that it originated in the core of capitalism; made healthy institutions look fragile and how its global spread effected sectors and economies perceived to be relatively immune. The author argues that the financial sector has stopped playing its basic role of intermediating between savings and investment, and transferring resources from capital-rich to capital poor economies. Instead, financial liberalisation has resulted in directing credit to non-priority and import-intensive but more profitable sectors which adversely affects employment-intensive sectors such as agriculture and small-scale enterprises, where transaction costs and risks are high. The author discusses the implications the crisis has had on the developing world in general and on India in particular. A medium-term implication is the likely reduction in private capital flows (which however is not so worrisome, as these flows were not accompanied by a net transfer of financial resources, rather resulted in accumulating foreign exchange reserves which counter-flowed from South to North in the form of central bank investments in safe assets and sovereign wealth funds of developing countries). The Official Development Assistance and remittances will also decline as they flow from countries which are themselves in crises. Exports of goods and services are going to be affected as, for most developing countries the US and the European Union remain the most important destination for export. Another detrimental effect is likely to be the postponement or cancellation of large investment projects which will have negative multiplier effects, as cancelled orders and lost jobs further reduce demand. Progressive change will require fundamental changes in the system of organising global finance and the institutions that govern trade and finance.

For India it is clear that important elements of the balance of payments and the domestic financial sector have been affected. In domestic banking the credit crunch has dramatically affected access to credit especially for small and medium enterprises. There are effects on some important macro economic prices–in particular the exchange rate. Also there are effects on employment, with falling export employment generating negative multiplier effects. Three macroeconomic indicators which have deteriorated since the crises are: the decline in the foreign exchange reserves; the fall in the external value of the rupee, especially vis-à-vis the US dollar; and the decline in stock market indices. Expansionary fiscal stance to create more economic activity and demand is the need of the hour. A longer view clearly requires a new system, where there is systematic state regulation of finance and where there is some degree of socialisation of banking and public control over the direction of credit. Fiscal stimulation is essential in both developed and developing countries to prevent economic activity and employment from falling. Finally, the international economic framework must support all this, which means that capital flows must be controlled and regulated so as not to destabilise any of these strategies. Adequate public spending is required which will be more effective and welfare-improving if it is directed towards employment schemes, social spending and rural and urban infrastructure.

The next article titled **"Risk Management in the Midst of the Global Financial Crisis,"** is a speech delivered by Dr. D. Subbarao, Governor, Reserve Bank of India (RBI) at the Financial Management Summit held in Mumbai on May 22, 2009. The author articulates that the global economy has been going through a very difficult phase precipitated by global economic downturn and in these circumstances, protecting the Indian economy from the crisis impact becomes a major challenge for Indian government as well as RBI. Though the financial sector in India has had no much direct exposure to tainted assets and its off-balance sheet activities are limited; and also because India's merchandise exports are less than 15 per cent of GDP, yet the crisis hit India underscoring the rising two-way trade in goods and services and financial integration with the rest of the world. The Government of India in close coordination with RBI responded to the crisis strongly with some policy initiatives that are aimed at *'containing the contagion from the global financial crisis while maintaining comfortable domestic and foreign exchange liquidity.'* He further highlighted that the government, in order to stimulate the demand, launched three fiscal stimulus packages between December 2008 and February 2009 in the form of safety-net programme for the rural poor, the farm loan waiver package and payout following the Sixth Pay Commission report.

The RBI Governor in his speech is quite optimistic about the future turnaround of the Indian economy during the latter part of 2009, once the remedial measures taken show their impact and the restoration of confidence in the global financial markets takes place. The main challenge for the Indian economy however would be to manage the economic recovery with the prevailing risks of uncertainties which continue to persist both in the domestic and global economy. He focuses his discussion further on the three areas of monetary and fiscal policy and financial stability in order to define the contours of uncertainty. On the monetary front, managing the risk calls for maintaining ample liquidity in the system ensuring that economic growth gathers momentum and the excess liquidity does not get inflationary. The challenge for fiscal policy is to balance immediate support for the economy through stimulus with the need to get back on track on the medium term fiscal consolidation process. And finally maintaining a sound and resilient banking sector, well-functioning financial markets, robust liquidity management and payment and settlement infrastructure are the pre-requisites for financial stability. He concludes on a hopeful note that with the right mix of macroeconomic policy and corporate strategy, Indian economy would emerge stronger from the crisis.

Hyderabad
April 2010

1

World Economic Outlook, April 2009

Crises and Recovery

Executive Summary

(International Monetary Fund)

Recent Economic and Financial Developments

Economies around the world have been seriously affected by the financial crisis and slump in activity. The advanced economies experienced an unprecedented 7½ percent decline in real GDP during the fourth quarter of 2008, and output is estimated to have continued to fall almost as fast during the first quarter of 2009. Although the U.S. economy may have suffered most from intensified financial strains and the continued fall in the housing sector, Western Europe and advanced Asia have been hit hard by the collapse in global trade, as well as by rising financial problems of their own and housing corrections in some national markets. Emerging economies too are suffering badly and contracted 4 percent in the fourth quarter in the aggregate. The damage is being inflicted through both financial and trade channels, particularly to east Asian countries that rely heavily on manufacturing exports and the emerging European and Commonwealth of Independent States (CIS) economies, which have depended on strong capital inflows to fuel growth.

In parallel with the rapid cooling of global activity, inflation pressures have subsided quickly. Commodity prices fell sharply from midyear highs, causing an especially large loss of income for the Middle Eastern and CIS economies but also for many other commodity exporters in Latin America and Africa. At the same time, rising economic slack has contained wage increases and eroded profit margins. As a result, 12-month headline inflation in the advanced economies fell below 1 percent in February 2009, although core inflation remained in the 1½–2 percent range, with the notable exception of Japan. Inflation has also moderated significantly across the emerging economies, although in some cases falling exchange rates have dampened the downward momentum.

Wide-ranging and often unorthodox policy responses have made limited progress in stabilizing financial markets and containing the downturn in output, failing to arrest corrosive feedback between weakening activity and intense financial strains. Initiatives to stanch the bleeding include public capital injections and an array of liquidity facilities, monetary easing, and fiscal stimulus packages. While there have been some encouraging signs of improving sentiment since the Group of 20 (G20) meeting in early April, confidence in financial markets is still low, weighing against the prospects for an early economic recovery.

The April 2009 *Global Financial Stability Report* (GFSR) estimates write-downs on U.S. originated assets by all financial institutions over 2007-10 will be US$ 2.7 trillion, up from the estimate of US$ 2.2 trillion in January 2009, largely as a result of the worsening prospects for economic growth. Total expected write-downs on global exposures are estimated at about US$ 4 trillion, of which two-thirds will fall on banks and the remainder on insurance companies, pension funds, hedge funds, and other intermediaries. Across the world, banks are limiting access to credit (and will continue to do so) as the overhang of bad assets and uncertainty about which institutions will remain solvent keep private capital on the sidelines. Funding strains have spread well beyond short-term bank funding markets in advanced economies. Many non-financial corporations are unable to obtain working capital, and some are having difficulty raising longer-term debt.

The broad retrenchment of foreign investors and banks from emerging economies and the resulting buildup in funding pressures are particularly worrisome. New securities issues have come to a virtual stop, bank-related flows have been curtailed, bond spreads have soared, equity prices have dropped, and exchange markets have come under heavy pressure. Beyond a general rise in risk aversion, this reflects a range of adverse factors, including the damage done to advanced economy banks and hedge funds, the desire to move funds under the "umbrella" provided by the increasing provision of guarantees in mature markets, and rising concerns about the economic prospects and vulnerabilities of emerging economies.

An important side effect of the financial crisis has been a flight to safety and return of home bias, which have had an impact on the world's major currencies. Since September 2008, the U.S. dollar, euro, and yen have all strengthened in real effective terms. The Chinese renminbi and currencies pegged to the dollar (including those in the Middle East) have also appreciated. Most other emerging economy currencies have weakened sharply, despite the use of international reserves for support.

Outlook and Risks

The *World Economic Outlook (WEO)* projections assume that financial market stabilization will take longer than previously envisaged, even with strong efforts by policymakers. Thus, financial strains in the mature markets are projected to remain heavy until well into 2010, improving only slowly as greater clarity over losses on bad assets and injections of public capital reduce insolvency concerns, lower counterparty risks and market volatility, and restore more liquid market conditions. Overall credit to the private sector in the advanced economies is expected to decline in both 2009 and 2010. Meanwhile, emerging and developing economies are expected to face greatly curtailed access to external financing in both years. This is consistent with the findings in Chapter 4 that the acute degree of stress in mature markets and its concentration in the banking system suggest that capital flows to emerging economies will suffer large declines and recover only slowly.

The projections also incorporate strong macroeconomic policy support. Monetary policy interest rates are expected to be lowered to or remain near the zero bound in the major advanced economies, while central banks continue to explore ways to use both the size and composition of their balance sheets to ease credit conditions. Fiscal deficits are expected to widen sharply in both advanced and emerging economies, as governments are assumed to implement fiscal stimulus plans in G20 countries amounting to 2 percent of GDP in 2009 and 1½ percent of GDP in 2010. The projections also assume that commodity prices remain close to current levels in 2009 and rise only modestly in 2010, consistent with forward market pricing.

Even with determined policy actions, and anticipating a moderation in the rate of contraction from the second quarter onward, global activity is now projected to decline 1.3 percent in 2009, a substantial downward revision from the January *WEO Update*. This would represent by far the deepest post–World War II recession. Moreover, the downturn is truly global: output per capita is projected to decline in countries representing three-quarters of the global economy, and growth in virtually all countries has decelerated sharply from rates observed in 2003-07. Growth is projected to reemerge in 2010, but at just 1.9 percent would be sluggish relative to past recoveries, consistent with the findings in Chapter 3 that recoveries after financial crises are significantly slower than other recoveries.

The current outlook is exceptionally uncertain, with risks weighed to the downside. The dominant concern is that policies will continue to be insufficient to arrest the negative feedback between deteriorating financial conditions and weakening economies, particularly in the face of limited public support for policy action. Key transmission channels include rising corporate and household defaults that cause further falls in asset prices and greater losses across financial balance sheets, and new systemic events that further complicate the task of restoring credibility. Furthermore, in a highly uncertain context, fiscal and monetary policies may fail to gain traction, since high rates of precautionary saving could lower fiscal multipliers, and steps to ease funding could fail to slow the pace of deleveraging. On the upside, however, bold policy implementation that is able to convince markets that financial strains are being dealt with decisively could revive confidence and spending commitments.

Even once the crisis is over, there will be a difficult transition period, with output growth appreciably below rates seen in the recent past. Financial leverage will need to be reduced, implying lower credit growth and scarcer financing than in recent years, especially in emerging and developing economies. In addition, large fiscal deficits will need to be rolled back just as population aging accelerates in a number of advanced economies. Moreover, in key advanced economies, households will likely continue to rebuild savings for some time. All this will weigh on both actual and potential growth over the medium run.

Policy Challenges

This difficult and uncertain outlook argues for forceful action on both the financial and macroeconomic policy fronts. Past episodes of financial crisis have shown that delays in tackling the underlying problem mean an even more protracted economic downturn and even greater costs, both in terms of taxpayer money and economic activity. Policymakers must be mindful of the cross-border ramifications of policy choices. Initiatives that support trade and financial partners—including fiscal stimulus and official support for international financing flows—will help support global demand, with shared benefits. Conversely, a slide toward trade and financial protectionism would be hugely damaging to all, a clear warning from the experience of 1930s beggar-thy-neighbor policies.

Advancing Financial Sector Restructuring

The greatest policy priority at this juncture is financial sector restructuring. Convincing progress on this front is the sine qua non for an economic recovery to take hold and would significantly enhance the effectiveness of monetary and fiscal stimulus. In the short run, the three priorities identified in previous GFSRs remain appropriate: (1) ensuring that financial institutions have access to liquidity, (2) identifying and dealing with distressed assets, and (3) recapitalizing weak but viable institutions. The first area is being addressed forcefully. Policy initiatives in the other two areas, however, need to advance more convincingly.

The critical underpinning of an enduring solution must be credible loss recognition on impaired assets. To that effect, governments need to establish common basic methodologies for the realistic valuation of securitized credit instruments, which should be based on expected economic conditions and an attempt to estimate the value of future income streams. Steps will also be needed to reduce considerably the uncertainty related to further losses from these exposures. Various approaches to dealing with bad assets in banks can work, provided they are supported with adequate funding and implemented in a transparent manner.

Recapitalization methods must be rooted in a careful evaluation of the long-term viability of institutions, taking into account both losses to date and a realistic assessment of the prospects of further write-downs. Subject to a number of assumptions, GFSR estimates suggest that the amount of capital needed might amount to US$ 275 billion–US$ 500 billion for U.S. banks, US$ 475 billion–US$ 950 billion for European banks (excluding those in the United Kingdom), and US$ 125 billion–US$ 250 billion for U.K. banks. [1] As supervisors assess recapitalization needs on a bank-by-bank basis, they will need assurance of the quality of banks' capital; the robustness of their funding, business plans, and risk management processes; the appropriateness of compensation policies; and the strength of management. Supervisors will also need to establish the appropriate level of regulatory capital for institutions, taking into account regulatory minimums and the need for buffers to absorb further unexpected losses. Viable banks that have insufficient capital should be quickly recapitalized, with capital injections from the government (if possible, accompanied by private capital) to bring capital ratios to a level sufficient to regain market confidence. Authorities should be prepared to provide capital in the form of common shares in order to improve confidence and funding prospects and this may entail a temporary period of public ownership until a private sector solution can be developed. Nonviable financial institutions need to be intervened promptly, leading to resolution through closures or mergers. Amounts of public funding needed are likely to be large, but requirements are likely to rise the longer it takes for a solution to be implemented.

Wide-ranging efforts to deal with financial strains will also be needed in emerging economies. The corporate sector is at considerable risk. Direct government support for corporate borrowing may be warranted. Some countries have also extended their guarantees of bank debt to firms, focusing on those associated with export markets, or have provided backstops to trade finance through various facilities—helping to keep trade fl owing and limiting damage to the real economy. In addition, contingency plans should be devised to prepare for potential large-scale restructuring in case circumstances deteriorate further.

Greater international cooperation is needed to avoid exacerbating cross-border strains. Coordination and collaboration is particularly important with respect to financial policies to avoid adverse international spillovers from national actions. At the same time, international support, including from the IMF, can help countries buffer the impact of the financial crisis on real activity and, particularly in the developing countries, limit its effects on poverty. Recent reforms to increase the flexibility of lending instruments for good performers caught in bad weather, together with plans advanced by the G20 summit to increase the resources available to the IMF, are enhancing the capacity of the international financial community to address risks related to sudden stops of private capital flows.

Easing Monetary Policy

In advanced economies, scope for easing monetary policy further should be used aggressively to counter deflation risks. Although policy rates are already near the zero floor in many countries, whatever policy room remains should be used quickly. At the same time, a clear communication strategy is important—central bankers should underline their determination to avoid deflation by sustaining easy monetary conditions for as long as necessary. In an increasing number of cases, lower interest rates will need to be supported by increasing recourse to less conventional measures, using both the size and composition of the central bank's own balance sheet to support credit intermediation. To the extent possible, such actions should be structured to maximize relief in dislocated markets while leaving credit allocation decisions to the private sector and protecting the central bank balance sheet from credit risk.

Emerging economies also need to ease monetary conditions to respond to the deteriorating outlook. However, in many of those economies, the task of central banks is further complicated by the need to sustain external stability in the face of highly fragile financing flows. To a much greater extent than in advanced economies, emerging market financing is subject to dramatic disruptions—sudden stops—in part because of much greater concerns about the creditworthiness of the sovereign. Emerging economies also have tended to borrow more heavily in foreign currency, and so large exchange rate depreciations can severely damage balance sheets. Thus, while most central banks in these economies have lowered interest rates in the face of the global downturn, they have been appropriately cautious in doing so to maintain incentives for capital inflows and to avoid disorderly exchange rate moves.

Looking further ahead, a key challenge will be to calibrate the pace at which the extraordinary monetary stimulus now being provided should be withdrawn. Acting too fast would risk undercutting what is likely to be a fragile recovery, but acting too slowly could risk overheating and inflating new asset price bubbles.

Combining Fiscal Stimulus with Sustainability

In view of the extent of the downturn and the limits to the effectiveness of monetary policy, fiscal policy must play a crucial part in providing short-term stimulus to the global economy. Past experience suggests that fiscal policy is particularly effective in shortening the duration of recessions caused by financial crises. However, the room to provide fiscal support will be limited if efforts erode credibility. Thus, governments are faced with a difficult balancing act, delivering short-term expansionary policies but also providing reassurance about medium-term prospects. Fiscal consolidation will be needed once a recovery has taken hold, and this can be facilitated by strong medium-term fiscal frameworks. However, consolidation should not be launched prematurely. While governments have acted to provide substantial stimulus in 2009, it is now apparent that the effort will need to be at least sustained, if not increased, in 2010, and countries with fiscal room should stand ready to introduce new stimulus measures as needed to support the recovery. As far as possible, this should be a joint effort, since part of the impact of an individual country's measures will leak across borders, but brings benefits to the global economy.

How can the tension between stimulus and sustainability be alleviated? One key is the choice of stimulus measures. As far as possible, these should be temporary and maximize "bang for the buck" (for example, accelerated spending on already planned or existing projects and time-bound tax cuts for credit constrained households). It is also desirable to target measures that bring long-term benefits to the economy's productive potential, such as spending on infrastructure. Second, governments need to complement initiatives to provide short-term stimulus with reforms to strengthen medium-term fiscal frameworks to provide reassurance that short-term deficits will be reversed and public debt contained. Third, a key element to ensure fiscal sustainability in many countries would be concrete progress toward dealing with the fiscal challenges posed by aging populations. The costs of the current financial crisis—while sizable—are dwarfed by the impending costs from rising expenditures on social security and health care for the elderly. Credible policy reforms to these programs may not have much immediate impact on fiscal accounts but could make an enormous change to fiscal prospects, and thus could help preserve fiscal room to provide short-term fiscal support.

Medium-Run Policy Challenges

At the root of the market failure that led to the current crisis was optimism bred by a long period of high growth and low real interest rates and volatility, along with policy failures. Financial regulation was not equipped to address the risk concentrations and flawed incentives behind the financial innovation boom. Macroeconomic policies did not take into account the buildup of systemic risks in the financial system and in housing markets.

This raises important medium-run challenges for policymakers. With respect to financial policies, the task now is to broaden the perimeter of regulation and make it more flexible to cover all systemically relevant institutions. In addition, there is a need to develop a macro-prudential approach to regulation, which would include compensation structures that mitigate pro-cyclical effects, robust market clearing arrangements, accounting rules to accommodate illiquid securities, transparency about the nature and location of risks to foster market discipline, and better systemic liquidity management.

Regarding macroeconomic policies, central banks should also adopt a broader macro-prudential view, paying due attention to financial stability as well as price stability by taking into account asset price movements, credit booms, leverage, and the buildup of systemic risk. Fiscal policymakers will need to bring down deficits and put public debt on a sustainable trajectory.

International policy coordination and collaboration need to be strengthened, based on better early-warning systems and a more open communication of risks. Cooperation is particularly pressing for financial policies, because of the major spillovers that domestic actions can have on other countries. At the same time, rapid completion of the Doha Round of multilateral trade talks could revitalize global growth prospects, while strong support from bilateral and multilateral sources, including the IMF, could help limit the adverse economic and social fallout of the financial crisis in many emerging and developing economies.

Source: World Economic Outlook, April 2009, *Crises and Recovery* World Economic and Financial Surveys, www.imf.org
© International Monetary Fund, IMF. Reprinted with Permission.

Note

1. The lower end of the range corresponds to capital needed to adjust leverage, measured as tangible common equity (TCE) over total assets, to 4 percent. The upper end corresponds to capital needed to raise the TCE ratio to 6 percent, consistent with levels observed in the mid-1990s (see the April 2009 GFSR).

2

The General Economic Background to the Crisis

Jørgen Elmeskov

1. Introduction

The financial crisis that broke in mid-2007 and intensified following the Lehman Brothers bankruptcy in September 2008 has triggered a world-wide economic downturn. Quite apart from its amplitude, many other features of the current cycle are unusual:

- The recession was not to any material extent caused by monetary policy tightening in response to rising inflation. Rather, the main driver was the unwinding of asset price hikes, financial leverage and risk appetite built up prior to the crisis.
- The economic crisis has affected developed and emerging economies alike. Indeed, the slowdown in growth between the second half of 2007 and end-2008 seems to have been of broadly similar magnitude in the two regions (Figure 1). Hence, earlier talk of *decoupling* has proved unfounded.
- Still, the economic crisis has not hit countries equally hard. The particular propagation pattern of the crisis appears, ironically, to have allowed some of the countries where asset prices and financial leverage increased the most to escape relatively lightly in terms of GDP loss. By contrast, countries with a heavy specialisation in durable goods and hi-tech manufacturing appear to have been badly affected.

A main theme of the current paper is that the rapid process of globalisation over the past two decades can explain some of these features and has played a main role in both the run-up to and propagation of the current crisis. This is not to deny that other factors played important roles. As concerns the financial crisis, for example, ill-designed regulation and misguided incentives in financial markets were main factors contributing to excessive leverage and risk taking. However, that is not the focus of this workshop. Here, the focus will be on the broader macroeconomic environment leading up to the crises and its subsequent propagation. Specifically, the paper will deal with the benign inflation and growth environment over recent decades, sometimes referred to as the great moderation"; the rise in world-wide saving; the role of monetary policy; and the role of global integration in propagating the crisis.

2. The Symptoms of a Bubble

The origin of the crisis clearly lay in OECD countries. A number of developments in these countries over the past decade can, with the benefit of hindsight, be seen to have had a bubble character. In some cases, the potential bubble character of developments was even discussed and warned against in real time. However, as often, it proved hard to call a bubble. A number of developments are worth highlighting.

- Bond yields in many countries fell to unusually low levels in historical comparison, both in nominal and real terms (Figure 2). While a substantial part of the fall seems to have derived from expectations that short-term interest rates were to remain relatively low, some portion also represented a reduced term premium. Concern was expressed about the risk of a back-up in bond yields and its potential implications for financial institutions (e.g. Brook, 2003; Ahrend et al., 2006). In the event, however, the onset of the crisis, monetary policy easing and the flight to safety have resulted in even lower government bond yields.
- Reflecting the low interest rate environment, real house prices shot up in most OECD countries (Figure 3). While expectations of permanently lower mortgage interest rates could justify some run-up in house prices, the development

went well beyond what could be rationalised on this basis. Again, warnings of over-valuation were given and, in this case, proved accurate (e.g. OECD, 2005). Rising house prices in countries with liberal and competitive mortgage markets gave rise to mortgage equity withdrawal, fuelling consumption over and above any wealth-type effects. Financial innovation allowed the market for sub-prime loans to evolve, primarily in the United States, with many of the mortgage holders unable to service their debt unless house prices continued to increase.

- Against the background of rising house prices, and generally good economic conditions, housing construction also expanded rapidly to reach historical highs in terms of GDP in many countries (Figure 4).
- Low interest rates across the yield curve together with rapid development in financial innovation led to bank credit growing at rates more than usually in excess of GDP (Figure 5). Over and above this, and related to financial innovation and the general increase in leverage, liquidity creation outside the banking sector (principally through securities markets) proceeded rapidly (Ahrend et al., 2008). Following the on-set of the crisis, and until central bank intervention re-established some activity, liquidity provision through securities markets came to a halt.
- Share prices in OECD countries increased from their troughs in early 2003, but at the peak were at most moderately above the levels reached during the dot-com bubble. As earnings had significantly expanded in the mean-time, price-earnings ratios were in most cases well below the peaks of the dot-com bubble and not out of line with historical averages (Figure 6). This does not exclude a bubble to the extent earnings themselves may have been flattered by bubble-related earnings in the financial sector and, in any event, share prices plummeted after the onset of financial crisis.

The following sections review a number of the factors that

contributed to the outcomes described above. Basically, these are factors that led to real interest rates all along the yield curve being unusually low earlier in the current decade and boosted asset prices. Some part of the hikes in asset prices may have been warranted but some also represented over-shooting in conditions where incentives were skewed towards excessive risk taking and leverage.

3. Causes of the Bubble

3.1 Benign Growth and Inflation Conditions: It is well established that, prior to the current crisis, cyclical fluctuations in both activity and inflation had tended to trend down (e.g. Dalsgaard et al., 2002). The greater stability is likely to have been one of the factors reducing risk premia in financial markets (Figure 7). The sense of reduced risk may have been strengthened as a number of potentially destabilising events (the Russia and South—East Asia crises; the LTCM collapse; Y2K; the bursting of the dot-com bubble; and the 11/9 attack) were overcome fairly rapidly. Lower perceived and observed risk is likely to have increased the appetite for leverage and risky investment in financial and other asset markets (including via misleading proxies for risk in models used to determine portfolio choices).

Among the factors generating greater stability of activity were:

- A shift of economic activity towards services and a correspondingly smaller role for the stock building cycle. At the same time, better inventory management also contributed to reducing the destabilising influence of stocks (their contribution to the downturn at end-2008/early-2009 notwithstanding).
- Greater openness of economies and thereby greater international diffusion of idiosyncratic shocks.
- The smaller role of common shocks, notably oil shocks. Oil intensities of developed economies are much reduced compared with the early 1970s and at the same time, oil

prices moved up in a fairly steady way until the second half of 2007.

- Less policy-induced instability in an environment where inflation seemed durably low and stable. More generally, economic policy in emerging economies became set to a much larger extent within a framework emphasising medium-term stability.
- Greater financial depth and competition diminishing the role of liquidity constraints and allowing households (and possibly firms) to better smooth demand. Thus, evidence suggests that depth of mortgage markets is associated with greater resilience to economic shocks (Duval et al., 2007). This implies a positive feed-back between greater economic stability and financial depth (which has obviously gone into reverse after the financial crisis broke).

On the inflation side, a number of factors have also contributed to greater stability. Indeed, among developed countries it appeared that the link between activity and inflation had weakened almost to the point of insignificance (Figure 8). Main factors behind these outcomes included:

- Greater international competition is likely to have made enterprises more wary of raising their prices relative to those of competitors and, hence, more reluctant to grant wage increases against the background of local demand pressures.
- Internationalisation of production and more scope for delocalisation is likely to have made wage earners more reluctant to press for higher wage increases even at times of demand pressure. Thus, OECD evidence points to labour demand elasticities having increased in recent decades (Figure 9). The flipside of this development might have been thought to be a greater role for world-wide demand pressures in driving wage developments but the empirical evidence on this point is not strong (Pain et al., 2006).

- More independent and transparent monetary policy geared towards price stability is likely to have better anchored inflation expectations. Hence, deviations from price stability have become less likely to feed on themselves.
- A number of reforms in labour and product markets could also have weakened the ability of producers and wage earners to press for higher prices and wages. However, the evidence on the impact of such reforms on cyclical inflation patterns is limited.
- The absence (until mid-2007) of strong pressures in commodity markets also helped to preserve a stable level of inflation.
- In a number of OECD economies international migration increasingly acted as a cushion against local labour market over-heating.

Over and above greater stability, benign developments on the supply side also implied that monetary policy, for a period, could stabilise inflation at lower policy interest rates than normal (see below under monetary policy).

3.2 Rising Saving Rates: Observed trends in saving are endogenous outcomes. Hence, based on observed data it is difficult to say to what extent ex ante saving developments contributed to lowering real interest rates and boosting asset prices. Nonetheless, it seems likely that positive shocks to saving contributed to these developments.

Emerging and developing economies as a group experienced rising saving rates over the past decade (Figure 10). With asset price and interest rate developments tending to put downward pressure on saving, it seems reasonable to treat this increase as a positive saving shock. While investment rates also increased, this did not happen to the same extent, as reflected in the combined current account position of this group of countries, and may at least partly have reflected an endogenous response. Part of the rise in saving in emerging and developing economies reflected fiscal consolidation (Figure 11). It may also be the case that some of the rise in saving reflected a slow catch-up of perceptions of permanent income to high growth rates. High saving in the enterprise sector in some countries may also raise questions about corporate governance (including for state-owned enterprises). Overall, it is likely that following the Asian crisis a number of countries deliberately pursued a policy of boosting current account surpluses to accumulate substantial exchange reserves.

Aggregate saving rates declined slightly in OECD countries. Given an environment of low interest rates and rising asset prices this could still have resulted from some ex ante increase in saving but this argument is somewhat tenuous. That said, fiscal balances were slightly worse in 2007 than a decade earlier (also on a cyclically-adjusted basis), mainly reflecting the deteriorating US budget position while Japan and the euro area saw significant improvements. Overall, then, aggregate OECD saving changes probably did not contribute much to interest rate and asset price changes over the past decade. US fiscal profligacy and low and declining household saving, while problematic developments in their own right including through this contribution to global imbalances, if anything must have provided an offset.

An additional factor putting upward pressure on saving is likely to have been the shift in global income distribution away from low-saving (typically OECD) countries towards high-saving (typically emerging Asian and oil exporting countries). Part of this shift reflected changing shares in world output as between high-saving and low-saving countries (Figure 12). Another part of the shift was driven by the terms-of-trade improvements experienced by oil exporting countries given the run-up in oil prices.

It is very hard to translate the ex ante rise in saving to effects on interest rates and the cost of capital. As a possible benchmark, a recent review of the sensitivity of government bond yields to budget balances (OECD, 2009) suggests that a sustained government deficit of 1 percent of GDP could push up bond yields by some 10-50 basis points. These estimates relate to effects within individual countries, where some of the interest rate effect may leak abroad. Nonetheless, using these numbers and assuming that they are representative of saving effects more generally, the impact of a 2-3 percentage point rise in the world saving rate could be in the order of ½-1 percent on bond yields.

3.3 Easy Monetary Policy: Low actual and expected policy interest rates in some OECD countries also helped to boost asset prices and the search for yield. There were a number of reasons for policy interest rates being low, some of which were captured in Taylor-rule type relationships (Figure 13) while others may be seen as justifying deviations from such rules. The uncertainty associated with Taylor-type rules needs to be underlined but, nonetheless, they may provide a useful benchmark for discussion and, furthermore, analysis has suggested that a number of conclusions drawn on the basis of these rules are invariant to smaller changes in numerical assumptions (Ahrend et al., 2008).

Since the mid-1990s, inflation outcomes in OECD countries have been importantly affected by globalisation. Lower prices of manufactured imports resulted both from falling export prices in emerging market producer countries and from greater penetration of producers with low cost bases (implying a shift in sourcing towards emerging market economies). OECD estimations suggest that during the first part of the current decade, these effects reduced annual inflation by some 2-4 percentage points (Figure 14). Some offset came from the fact that rapid and commodity-intensive growth in emerging economies put upward pressure on commodity prices but the net result was still a dis-inflationary effect in OECD countries. Over and above these effects, greater competition in product markets and structural reform in labour markets may also have put some transient downward pressure on inflation. As a result, the policy interest rates required to achieve a given target inflation rate were reduced. While some degree of undershooting of inflation targets for some time could have been defended it would have been politically difficult for central banks, in the prevailing regime, not to pass through this favourable supply shock in lower interest rates.

At the same time, two factors militated for interest rates below those predicted by Taylor rules. First, the bursting of the dot-com bubble led to lower share prices with negative wealth effects on growth, something which a Taylor rule does not pick up. This effect was compounded for a while by corporate scandals which temporarily increased risk premia. Second, and at least in the United States, deflation was seen as a relevant risk. Given the zero floor on interest rates, this was seen as implying an asymmetric distribution of risks and, hence, a separate reason for maintaining interest rates below Taylor-rule levels. Whatever the merit of these arguments on an ex ante basis, it is clear that rates seem to have been overly low when assessed on an ex post basis. Indeed, even on an ex ante basis rates may have been raised at too "measured" a pace during 2004-5. Cross-country evidence suggests that mortgage lending, housing investment, construction investment and house prices all are correlated with deviations from a Taylor rule (Figure 15) [Ahrend et al., 2008].

3.4 Financial Innovation: On a more speculative note, and at the margin of the remit of this paper, financial innovation may have played an independent role in the run-up to the crisis. In particular, financial instruments that allowed the emergence of the sub-prime market and which facilitated housing equity withdrawal, in some cases also encouraged through tax breaks for mortgage interest payments, may have boosted demand for housing and helped to drive up its price (especially in conditions of inflexible supply). While monetary policy was generally set so as to stabilise inflation, with the potential mistakes in this regard described above, financial innovation could have implied a higher level of housing prices for any level of interest rates. The impetus to housing prices coming from this channel could have been followed by some overshooting. Indeed, with housing supply more flexible in the long term than in the short term, some degree of overshooting is likely.

Financial innovation also implied greater, real and perceived, opportunities to transfer and thereby manage risk. Again, for given interest rates and given aversion to risk, this may have led to greater leverage and generally higher levels of risks before hedging.

4. Propagation of the Financial Crisis

The development that triggered the financial crisis was the turnaround in the US housing market. As the prospects of continued house price increases dimmed, defaults on sub-prime mortgages began to rise and the value of mortgage based, and often non-transparent, securities fell. This again led to losses among banks and other financial actors, concerns about their solvency in conditions of high leverage, runs on individual institutions, rising prices of insuring against default and a general seizing up of securities and interbank markets and a hardening of lending attitudes among banks.

OECD country consumers cut back on consumption in response to tighter financial conditions, wealth losses on shares and housing, prospects of higher unemployment and general uncertainty. Enterprises also reduced outlays in response to more difficult financing conditions, expectations of declining sales and higher uncertainty. They also reduced production drastically towards the end of 2008 but not sufficiently to avoid a run-up in inventories that is having to be worked off in 2009.

Given the nature of the set-back, OECD demand for durable goods has been hit particularly hard. With manufacturing sectors having undergone a substantial internationalisation of their value chain (Figure 16), world trade was hit hard (Figure 17). OECD estimations suggest that the tightening in financial conditions may have had an additional negative influence on trade growth, presumably reflecting difficulties with respect to trade finance. The decline in world trade was one of the essential transmission channels from countries directly affected by the financial crisis towards others, including emerging economies. In addition to this channel, emerging economies were also affected by a reversal of capital flows as lending and FDI flows were cut back and OECD financial and non-financial enterprises sought safety in highly liquid assets.

5. Conclusions and Policy Issues

The description above suggests that a number of developments that were in themselves desirable contributed to generating an environment of high asset prices, low risk premia and appetite for leverage. A number of questions suggest themselves against this background:

- Inflation targeting monetary policy may, in conditions of positive supply or saving shocks, lead to low interest rates which are likely to translate into higher asset prices. If the positive shocks turn out to be temporary or if an impetus to asset prices leads to over-shooting, a painful adjustment period may sometimes follow. This raises the question whether changes to the inflation targeting framework may allow better dealing with such developments (e.g. through longer time horizons and greater tolerance of short-term deviations from target); whether the objective of monetary policy needs modification (e.g. to include some target related to financial stability); or if additional instruments are required (e.g. macro-prudential regulation affecting lenders or borrowers)?
- At current levels of explicit or implicit inflation targets, a monetary policy that leans against a wind of higher asset prices might lead to unduly low current inflation rates. At the same time, experience following the bursting of the Japanese asset price bubble, the dot.com bubble and, now, the financial bubble have shown that bursting bubbles may entail a substantial risk of deflation. Once the current crisis

is over, should this influence the objectives set for monetary policy? In particular, should inflation targets be higher or should a (rising) price-level target be set?

- During the recent bubble episode, fiscal policy at the level of the OECD countries at large did not contribute much to saving developments in either direction. It may also be argued that to the extent a tighter fiscal stance would have put downward pressure on bond yields, it could have contributed to an unsustainable asset price boom. By contrast, greater fiscal discipline would have provided a better starting point for addressing the fall-out from the bursting of the bubble. Are there any strong conclusions to be drawn as to the appropriate role of fiscal policy during asset price bubbles?
- The rise in saving in emerging economies may have reflected the interaction between rapid growth in income and the need to build-up precautionary saving in conditions where social safety nets, including health and pension systems, are weak and where access to financial markets is limited. While such recommendations would not be standard fare for developed economies, could liberalisation of financial markets and extensions of social safety nets in emerging economies help avert unwarranted increases in domestic saving and associated international payments imbalances?

Source: www.oecd.org
© Jørgen Elmeskov, OECD (2009). Reprinted with Permission from OECD.

This paper was originally presented in the session 1 on — How the global economy headed into crisis at the G20 Workshop on the Causes of the Crisis: Key Lessons, Mumbai, 24-26 May, 2009. The paper does not necessarily reflect the position of the OECD.

Bibliography

Ahrend, Rudiger, Boris Cournède and Robert Price (2008), "Monetary Policy, Market Excesses and Financial Turmoil",

Economics Department Working Papers, No. 597, OECD, Paris.

Ahrend, Rudiger, Pietro Catte and Robert Price (2006), "Monetary Policy, Market Excesses and Financial Turmoil" Economics Department Working Papers, No. 490, OECD, Paris.

Brook, Anne-Marie (2003), "Recent and Prospective Trends in Real Long-term Interest Rates: Fiscal Policy and Other Drivers", Economics Department Working Papers, No. 367, OECD, Paris.

Dalsgaard, Thomas, Jørgen Elmeskov and Cyn-Young Park (2002), "Ongoing Changes in the Business Cycle – Evidence and Causes", Economics Department Working Papers, No. 315, OECD, Paris.

OECD (2009), "The Effectiveness and Scope of Fiscal Stimulus", Chapter 3, OECD Economic Outlook: Interim Report, OECD, Paris, March.

OECD (2005), "Recent House Price Developments: The Role of Fundamentals", Chapter III, OECD Economic Outlook, Vol. 2005/2, No. 78, OECD, Paris, December.

Pain, Nigel, Isabell Koske and Marte Sollie (2006), "Globalisation and Inflation in the OECD Economies", Economics Department Working Papers, No. 524, OECD, Paris.

Figure 1. The economic downturn is global

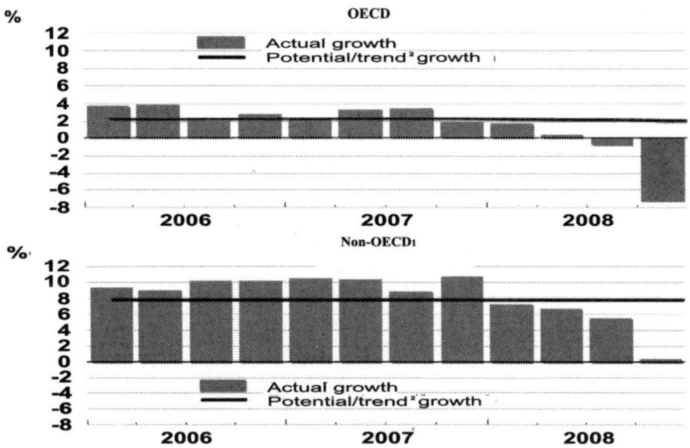

1. The non-OECD region is a weighted average, using 2000 GDP weights and PPPs, of Brazil, China, the Russian Federation and India, which together accounted for about half of non-OECD output in 2000.

2. Trend growth for the non-OECD region is the average over the period 2000-2007.

Source: OECD.

Figure 2: Government bond yields fell to low levels
(10-year maturity)

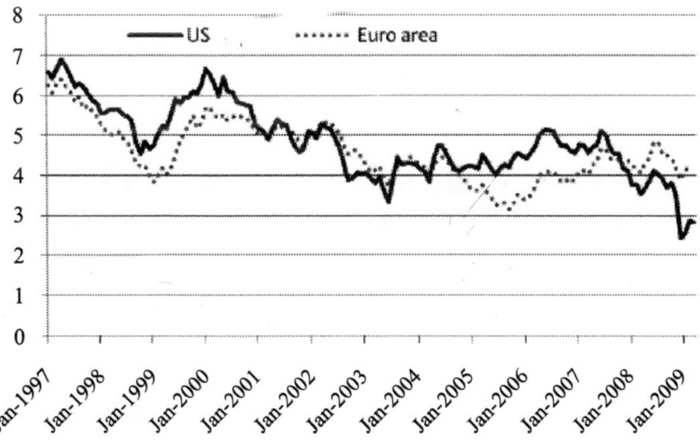

Source: OECD

Figure 3: OECD house price and economic cycles became desynchronised

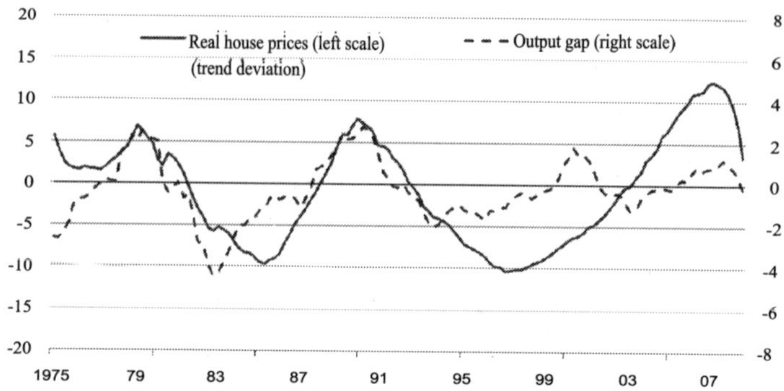

Note : Real house prices have been detrended using a linear trend. The OECD real house price index is an agreegate of the 17countries for which time sereis start in the early1970's Computed using purchasing power parity-adjusted GDP weights.

Source : OECD.

Figure 4. Housing investment reached high levels

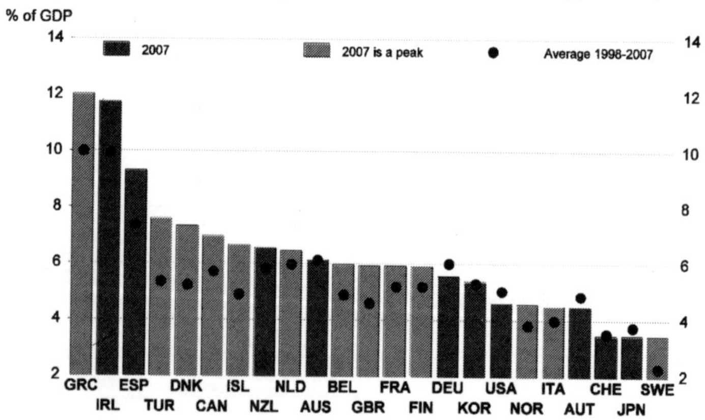

Source: OECD Economic Outlook 82.

Figure 5. Credit increased above its trend in the US and euro area

(Excess credit level1)

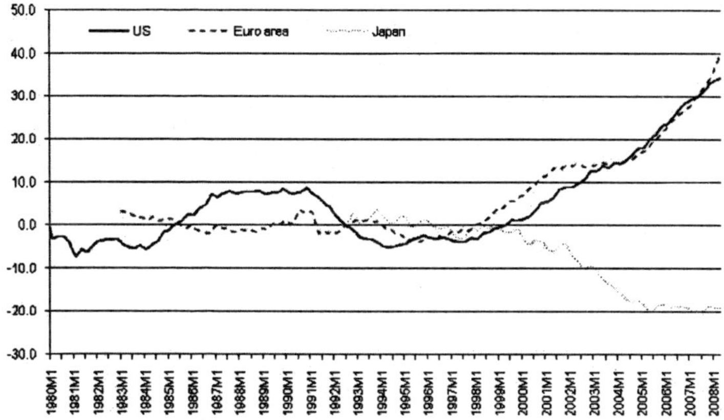

1. Deviation of domestic bank lending to the private non-financial sector as a share of GDP from long-term trend. 3-month moving average.

Source: OECD.

Figure 6. Price-to-earning ratios were below those of the dot-com years

Last observation: April 2009

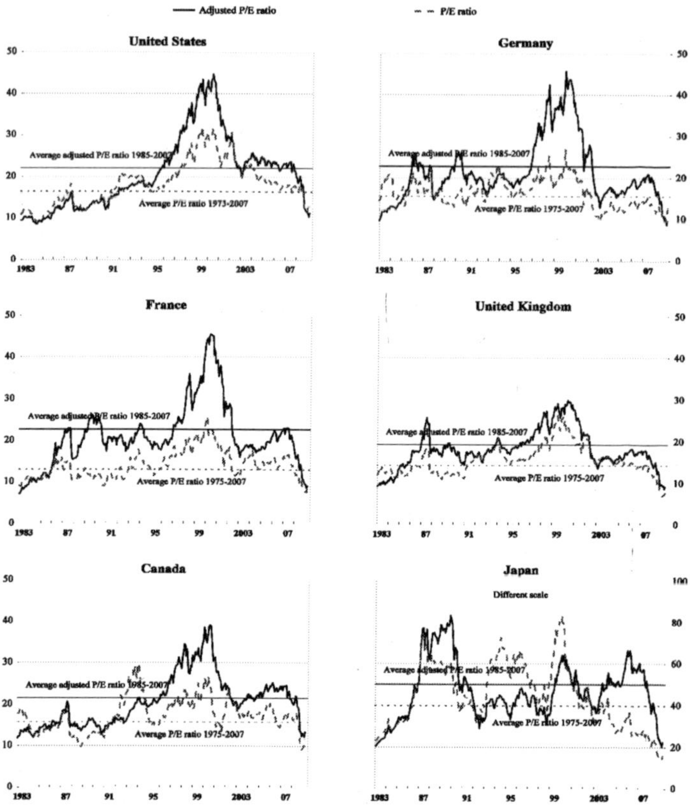

Note: Adjusted P/E ratios are calculated as the ratio of stock prices to the moving average of the previous 10 years' earnings, adjusted for nominal trend growth.

Source: Datastream, OECD calculations.

Figure 7: Bond market risk premia were low until the crisis

OECD synthetic indicator of bond risk, actual and predicted values

Deviation from average (in terms of standard deviations of synthetic indicator)

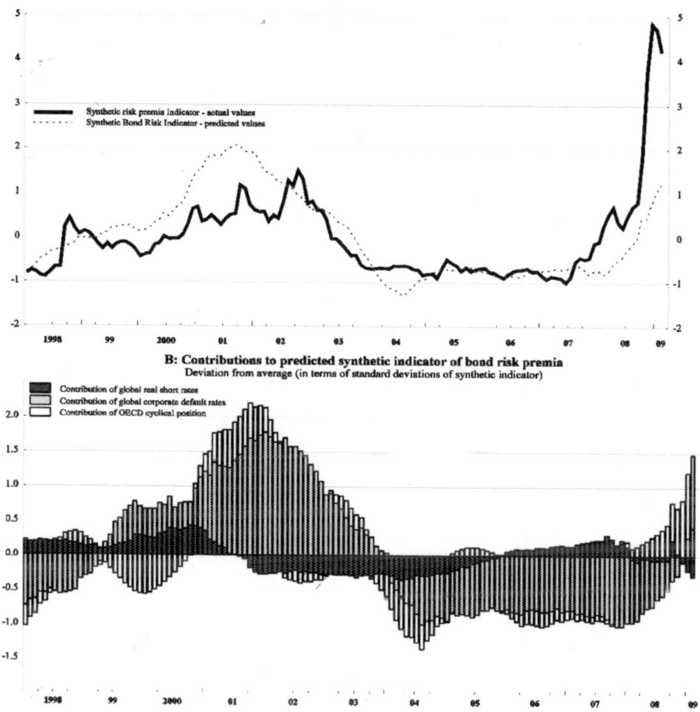

Note: The synthetic measure is derived from risk proxies of various securities, including corporate and emerging market bonds. In regression analysis it is well explained by global short-term interest rates and liquidity, corporate default rates and OECD's leading economic indicators, a proxy for expectations of the near-term outlook for the OECD cyclical position.

Source: OECD calculation.

Figure 8. The relationship between inflation and the unemployment gap has weakened

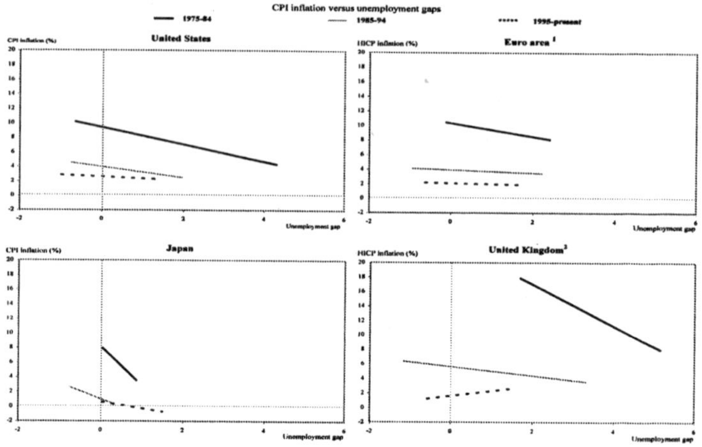

Note: The unemployment gap is the difference between the unemployment rate and the NAIRU (as estimated by the OECD). The chart shows regression lines over the periods in question.

1. In calculating the euro area aggregate, Western Germany is used in place of unified Germany prior to 1991.

2. The slope of the trend line in the United Kingdom from 1995 to the present period should not be interpreted as indicating that more economic slack is associated with higher inflation. The granting of operational independence to the Bank of England in May 1997 has noticeably modified the relationship between UK inflation and unemployment. This change implies that the regression line on data covering the 1995-to-present period is biased.

Source: OECD.

Figure 9. The wage elasticity of labour demand has increased

(Rolling window estimates, 5-year span)

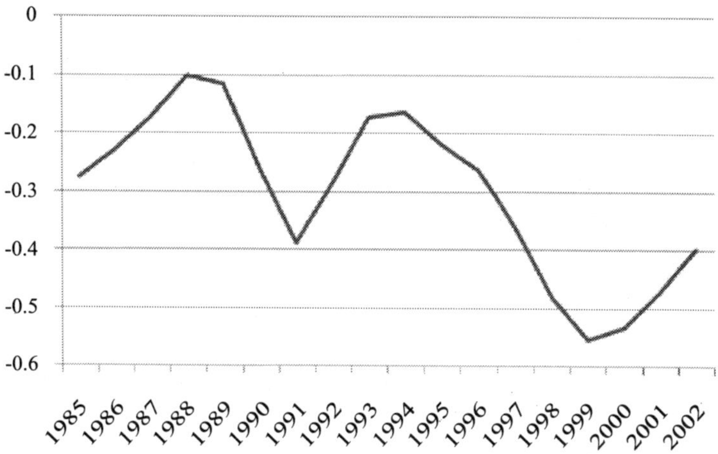

Note: **Elasticities have been estimated from a static model of labour demand across countries and over rolling 5-year time periods.**

Source: OECD, Employment Outlook 2007.

Figure 10. Saving rates have diverged between advanced and emerging economies

(Total economy % of GDP)

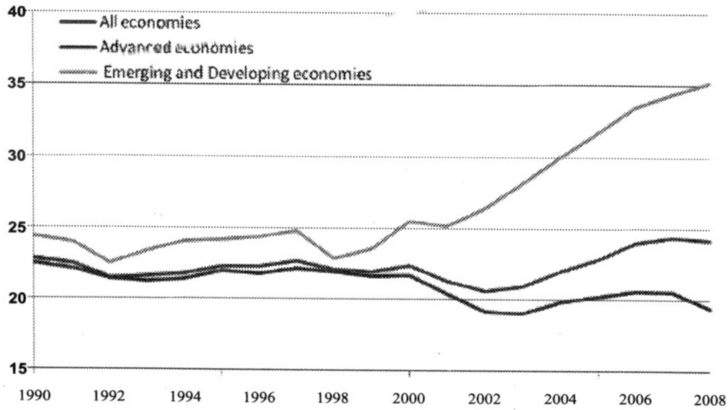

Source: IMF, ***World Economic Outlook.***

Figure 11. The position of public finances in selected countries

(General government net lending, % of GDP)

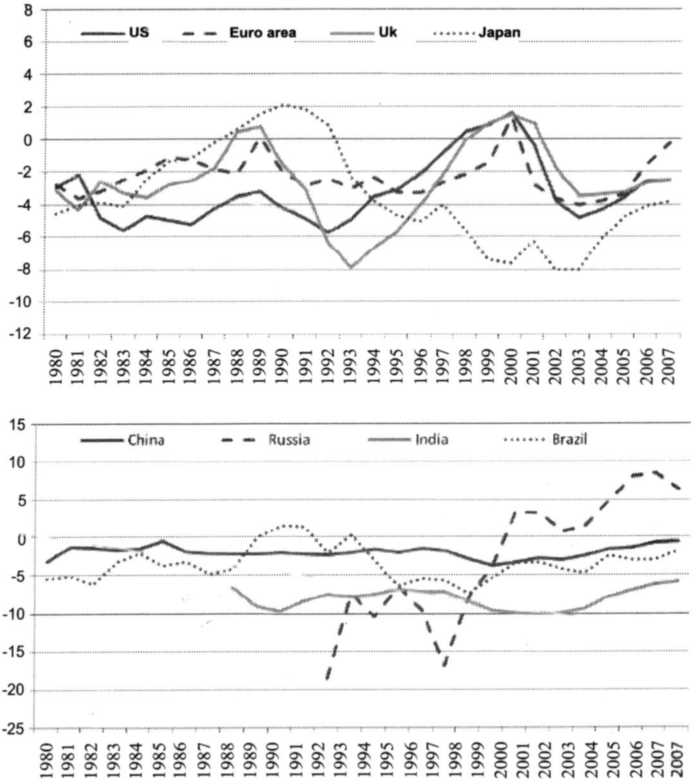

Source: IMF, *Government Financial Statistics.*

Figure 12. Income has shifted from low saving to high saving economies

(Change in the share of world GDP over the period 2000 -2007, % points)

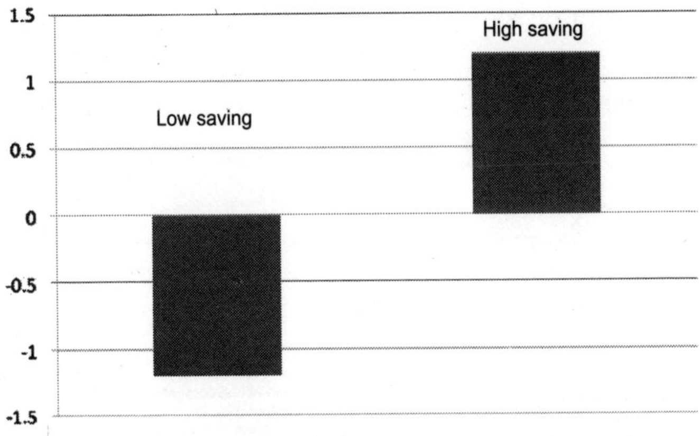

Note: Low saving countries are those with a saving rate lower than 30% in year 2000, and high saving countries are those with a saving rate higher or equal to 30%.

Source: World Bank, World Development Indicators.

Figure 13. Monetary policy has been accommodative

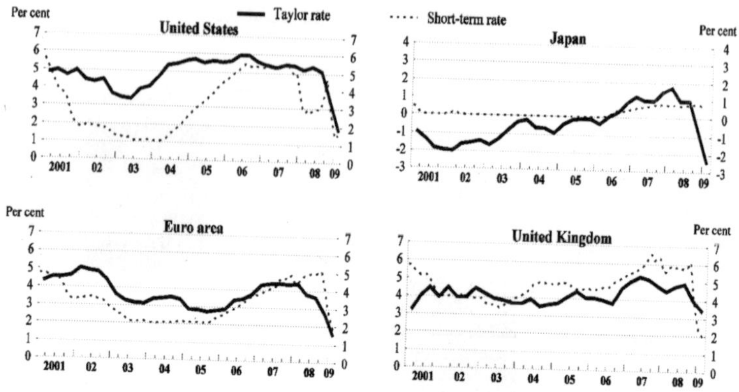

Note: The Taylor rule rate is a function of the equilibrium real interest rate (short term), the (implicit) inflation target, the average output gap and the gap between actual core inflation and the implicit inflation target. Equal weight is given to the inflation gap and the output gap. For the United States, the assumed price stability target is for inflation of 1.9% and the assumed equilibrium real interest rate is 2.85%. For Japan, the assumed price stability target is for inflation of 1.9% and the assumed equilibrium real interest rate is 2.1%. For the euro area, the assumed price stability target is for inflation of 1.9% and the assumed equilibrium real interest rate is 2.1%. For the United Kingdom, the assumed price stability target is for inflation of 2.0% and the assumed equilibrium real interest rate is 3.0%.

Source: OECD.

Figure 14. Without globalisation inflation would have been boosted

(Simulation inflation impacts of removing globalisation, average % point difference over 2000-05)

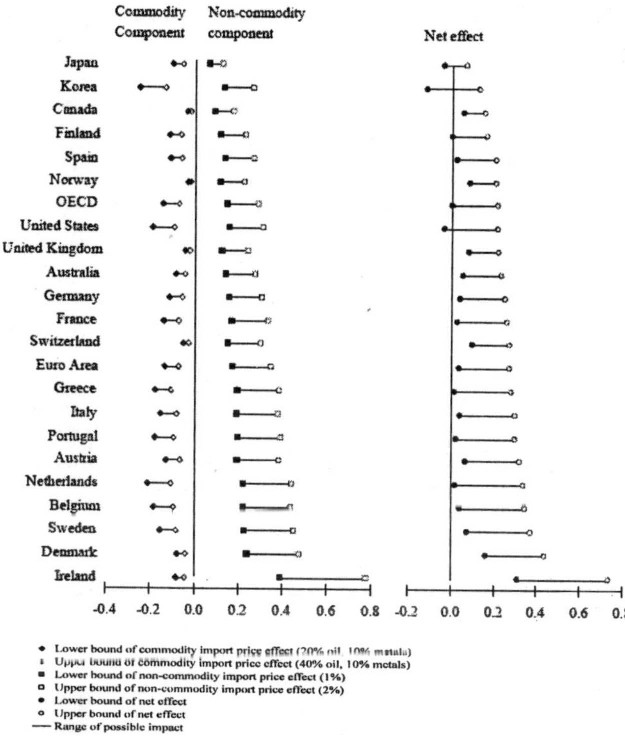

Note: Simulations are based on the estimated impact of globalisation on non-commodity and commodity price inflation in each country. The lower (upper) bound estimate of the impact of globalistion on non-commodity import price is 1% (2 %). The lower (upper) bound estimate of the impact of globalistion on oil price is 20% (40 %). The estimate of the impact of globalistion on metal is 10%.

Source: Pain *et al.* (2006).

Figure 15. Housing and construction investment are correlated with low interest rates

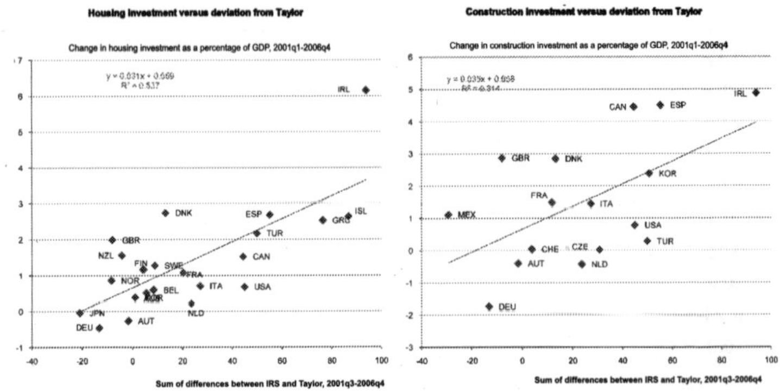

Note: The Taylor rule rate is a function of equilibrium real interest rate (short term), the (implicit) inflation target, the average output gap and the gap between actual core inflation and the implicit inflation target. Equal weight is given to the inflation gap and the output gap. For the United States, the assumed price stability target is for inflation of 1.9% and the assumed equilibrium real interest rate is 2.85%. For Japan, the assumed price stability target is for inflation of 1.9% and the assumed equilibrium real interest rate is 2.1%. For the euro area, the assumed price stability target is for inflation of 1.9% and the assumed equilibrium real interest rate is 2.1%. For the United Kingdom, the assumed price stability target is for inflation of 2.0% and the assumed equilibrium real interest rate is 3.0%.

Source: OECD.

Figure 16. Production chains have become more international
(Share of imported inputs in manufacturing production)

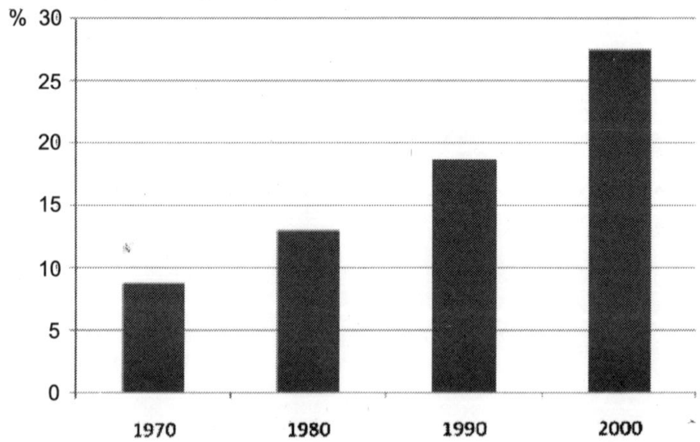

Source: OECD, Structural Analysis database.

Figure 17. World trade growth has collapsed

(Quarterly growth rates annualised)

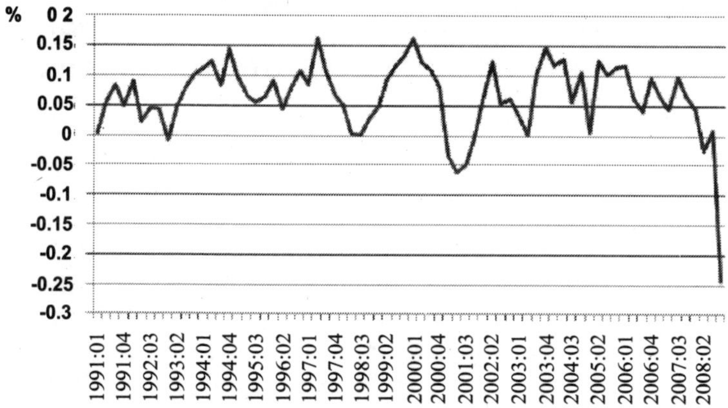

Source:: OECD.

3

The Global Financial Crisis: Causes, Consequences and Countermeasures

Luci Ellis

I would like to thank Victoria University of Technology and the organisers of this conference for the opportunity to speak to you today. The conference is concerned with an important and highly topical subject: what was at first called a 'sub-prime crisis', then later 'financial turmoil', and is now being called the Global Financial Crisis. Indeed, many financial systems around the world have been under extraordinary strain for the past year and a half. The macroeconomic and human consequences of that crisis are becoming all too clear.

These events have raised many questions for policy-makers and for market participants. What caused this global financial crisis? Why did it develop in the way it did? What have been the consequences, both for the global economy and the financial system itself? And are there any countermeasures that governments and other policy-makers can take, to reduce the costs of the present crisis, and to prevent a recurrence?

These are all good questions and will no doubt keep many of us busy in the period ahead. This morning, I would like to suggest a few answers to at least some of these questions.

Causes

As with any large event in any field of human endeavour, it is never about just one thing. There were many causes of the financial crisis, some recent and some longstanding. I would like to focus on three of those causes today: the misperception and mismanagement of risk; the level of interest rates; and the regulation of the financial system.

Perhaps the most basic underlying driver of the crisis was the inherent cycle of human psychology around risk perceptions. When times are good, perceptions of risk diminish. People start to convince themselves that the good times will go on forever. Then, when the cycle turns, risk aversion increases again, often far beyond normal levels, let alone those seen during the boom.

Graph 1

Bond Spreads

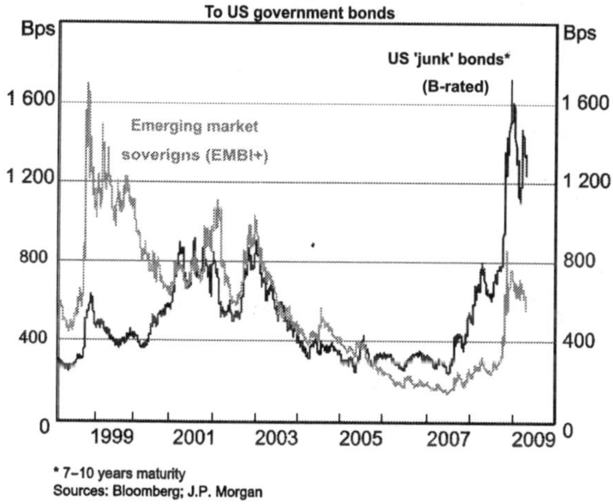

We can see in Graph 1 how investors' perception of risk changed in the years up to the crisis. Yields on emerging market bonds or US companies at the riskier end of the spectrum all narrowed relative to those on US government bonds and other securities that are seen as very safe. More recently, those spreads have widened out dramatically, as investors became more risk-averse, and the 'search for yield' turned into a 'flight to safety'.

The effects of this boom-bust cycle of psychology are amplified when investors use leverage. Borrowing to purchase assets is lucrative when asset prices are rising, because all the upside beyond the interest costs goes to the investor, not the lender. But when times are bad and asset valuations are falling, investors' losses are magnified by leverage.

Graph 2

Policy Interest Rates

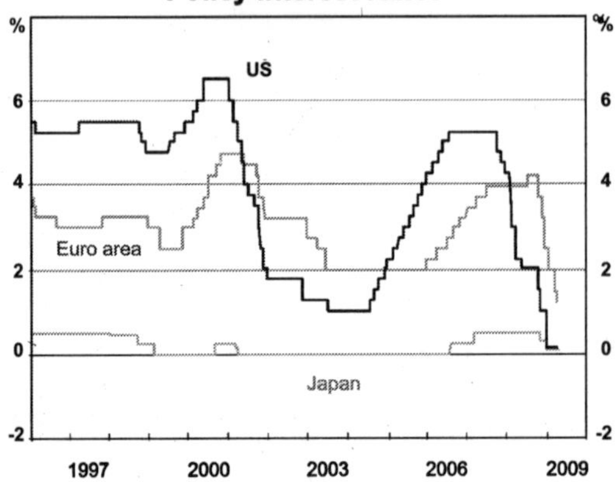

Source: central banks

A second element that coincided with the perceptions of lower risk was the low level of interest rates in the early part of this decade. At the short end, policy interest rates in the major economies reached levels that were unusually low compared with history, as shown in Graph 2.

At the longer end, bond yields in the major economies were also unusually low over this period. As Graph 3 shows, this remained the case even once policy rates started to rise in 2004. At the time, the low level of long rates was considered somewhat puzzling —a 'conundrum', as former Fed chairman Greenspan put it. Over time, though, many observers have come to the view that unusually strong investor demand had pushed long rates down. Among those investors were central banks and other government agencies in emerging and industrialised economies, which were accumulating foreign reserves.

Graph 3

10-year Government Bond Yields

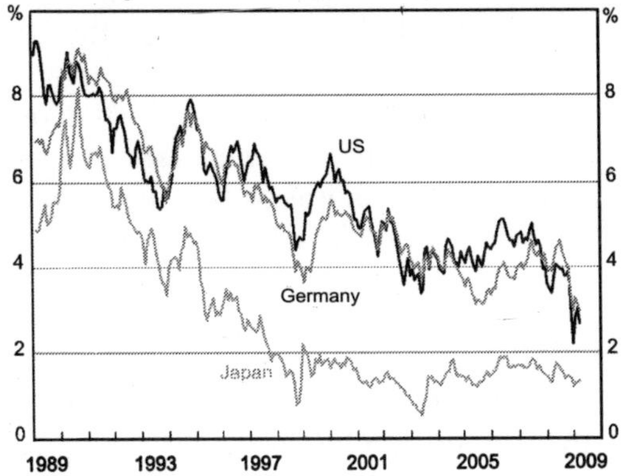

Many observers were concerned about the way the low level of interest rates made higher leverage so attractive. Inflation pressures were quite subdued at that time, so the macroeconomic situation didn't necessarily warrant much higher interest rates. There has been plenty of debate, inside and outside central banks, on whether monetary policy should also respond to financial stability concerns. But there is also recognition in many quarters that low interest rates were not—and shouldn't be—enough to cause such a crisis on their own.

A lack of appropriate financial regulation in some countries is widely regarded as one of the important causes of the crisis. Many shortcomings have been identified in this area. These include: the capital requirements on complex financial products such as collateralised debt obligations (CDOs); the use of ratings provided by the private-sector rating agencies in the regulation of banks; the way credit rating agencies have themselves been regulated; and the structure of remuneration arrangements and the risk-taking incentives they create. Perhaps most crucially, many internationally active banks failed to perceive, or appropriately manage, the risks involved in certain financial products and markets, and regulators did not make them do better on this front.

The Build-up to the Crisis

With this background in mind, I'd like to turn to the specifics of the build-up of tensions that finally broke as this financial crisis. Appetite for risk had been strong for some years; that risk was priced cheaply; and as a result, credit markets were booming and some measures of leverage were rising. The low price of risk was in fact regularly cited in the Bank's *Financial Stability Reviews* as a potential source of vulnerability for the global financial system.

One sector that took particular advantage of low long-term interest rates was the US mortgage market. American households traditionally took out fixed-rate mortgages, often guaranteed by the government-sponsored enterprises, Fannie Mae and Freddie Mac–the GSEs. As rates fell, households refinanced in large numbers, but this extra origination business dried up once rates started to rise again. Rather than shrink their business, US mortgage lenders pursued riskier segments of the market that the GSEs did not insure, as Graph 4 shows. This included thc sub-prime segment, but also so-called 'Alt-A' and other non-standard loans involving easier lending terms. At the time, this was considered a positive development, because it was thought that it allowed more people to become home owners. Products requiring low or no deposit, or with a low introductory interest rate were known as 'affordability products'. They allowed households to pay the very high housing prices that their own stronger demand was generating.

As the US housing boom wore on, lending standards eased further. As Graph 5 shows, up until 2006 the sub-prime market segment increasingly allowed mortgages with very high loan-to-valuation ratios: that is, borrowers did not need much deposit. Low-doc loans became more common across the board. Negative amortisation loans, sometimes called 'Pay-option ARMs', also became more common. These are mortgages where the borrower can pick a repayment level that is so low that the loan balance actually rises for a while—something that is essentially unheard of in other countries.

Graph 4

US Mortgage-backed Securities Issuance

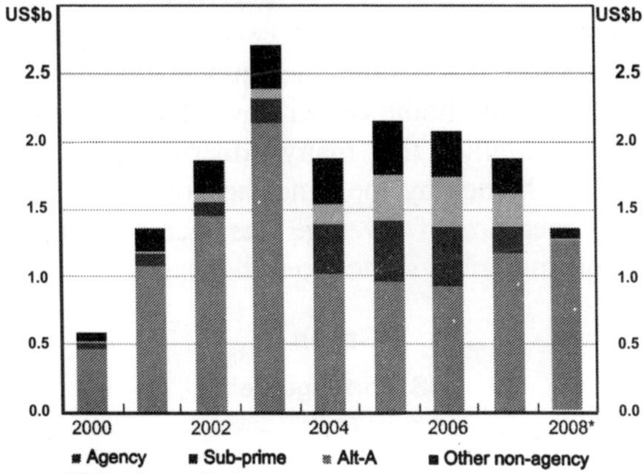

* First quarter, annualised
Source: UBS

Graph 5

Sub-prime Lending Standards

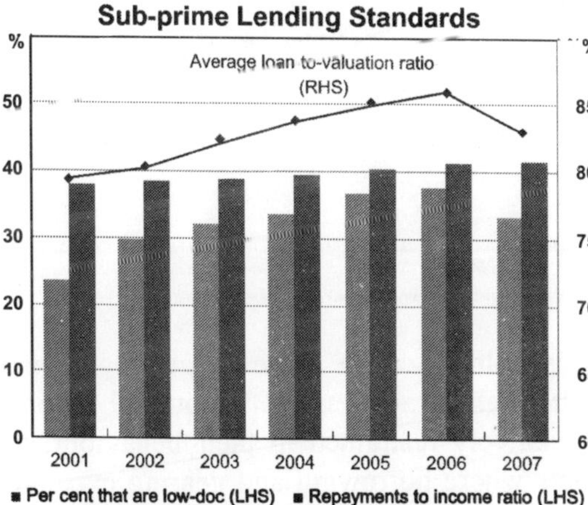

Source: Demyanyk YS and O Van Hemert (2008), 'Understanding the Subprime Mortgage Crisis', Federal Reserve Bank of St. Louis Supervisory Policy Analysis Working Paper 2007-05, rev Aug 2008.

The result of all that mortgage borrowing was, as shown in Graph 6, an increase in leverage, defined to be the ratio of home mortgage debt to the value of the housing stock. This measure had been quite stable in the United States for a number of years. But it increased in those last couple of years of the boom, reaching around 45 per cent by the time prices peaked sometime in 2006. (The exact date depends on the price series used.) In Australia, the equivalent ratio is below 30 percent. Since many home owners own their homes outright, the US figure implies that many Americans had very little equity in their homes by the time the boom peaked. And of course, this measure of leverage has increased a great deal since US housing prices started to fall.

Graph 6

US Mortgage Debt

Per cent of real estate assets

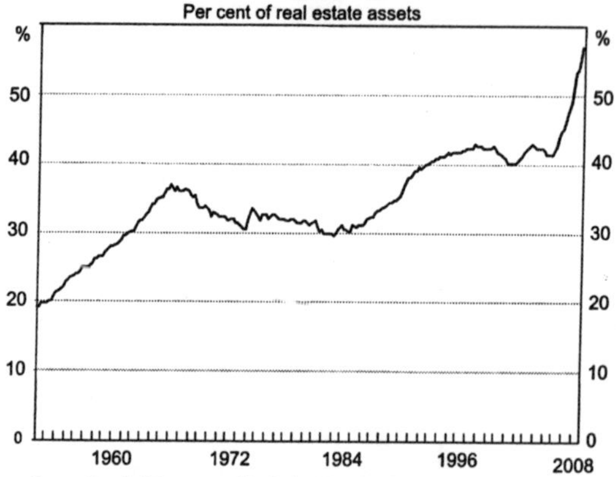

Source: Board of Governors of the Federal Reserve System

US households weren't alone in gearing themselves up like this. Although corporate sectors around the world were by and large relatively restrained in their behaviour, there were some pockets where borrowing and gearing expanded a great deal. Some examples include the asset-backed commercial paper market, which is often used to finance entities that invest in other securities, and the leveraged loan market, often used to finance buyouts of companies. And as Graph 7 shows, leveraged buyout activity boomed, especially in North America and Europe. As with the mortgage market, the excesses built up most where the financing structures were most opaque, and the underestimation of the risks was greatest.

Graph 7

Global LBO Activity

Announced and completed

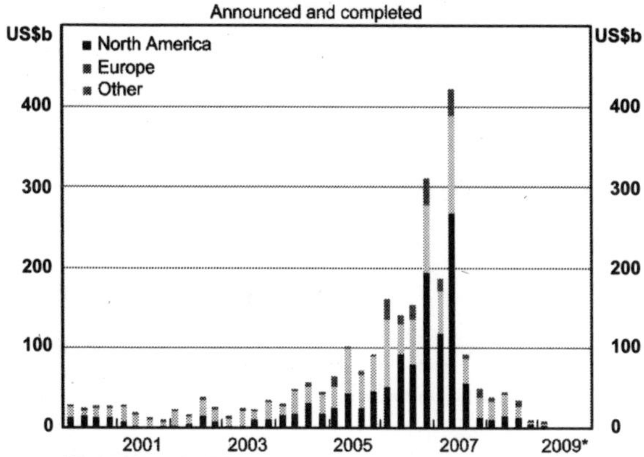

* Deals announced to date
Source: Thomson Reuters

The Onset of the Crisis

But you can't borrow your way to a good time forever, and this recent example of a credit-fuelled boom was no exception. The first signs of trouble were in the US mortgage market. Lending standards had eased so far—and outright fraud had gotten to be such a problem—that arrears rates started to rise more than lenders and investors expected. Graph 8 shows that, the rise started in around 2006 for both prime and sub-prime mortgages, but became more obvious through 2007. The extraordinary thing was that, unlike in every other housing bust, arrears rates increased significantly before the labour market started to weaken.

The first consequence of this was the failure of a number of US mortgage lenders. Some of these were brought down by early defaults, where the borrower didn't even make the first payment. If a loan is securitised and sold, the lender typically has to compensate the buyers of the securities if the loan defaults soon afterwards.

Graph 8

US Mortgage Delinquency Rates

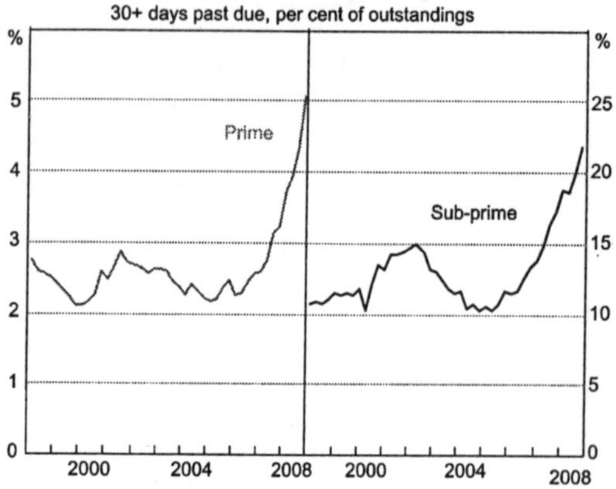

Source: Mortgage Bankers Association

But not all of these losses on mortgages could be pushed back on the original lender or broker, especially if these had already gone out of business. After years of underestimating risks on mortgage-related and other complex securities, banks and other investors started to realise just how risky these securities were. They also started to realise that they didn't know how exposed their counterparties were to these losses. Following a series of loss announcements and suspensions of some bank-sponsored investment funds in mid 2007, market participants began to hoard liquidity. They were worried about their counterparties, but they were also worried about their own future liquidity needs.

As a result, the asset-backed commercial paper market froze in several countries. The rates at which banks would lend to each other in overnight and term money markets started to widen. Normally these money market rates sit close to the policy rates set by central banks, but that relationship broke down in August 2007, as Graph 9 shows. Investor demand for certain kinds of mortgage-backed securities also dried up in the following months. Lenders that had depended on short-term money markets or securitisation therefore started to find it very difficult to obtain funding.

Graph 9

3-month LIBOR to Swap Spread*

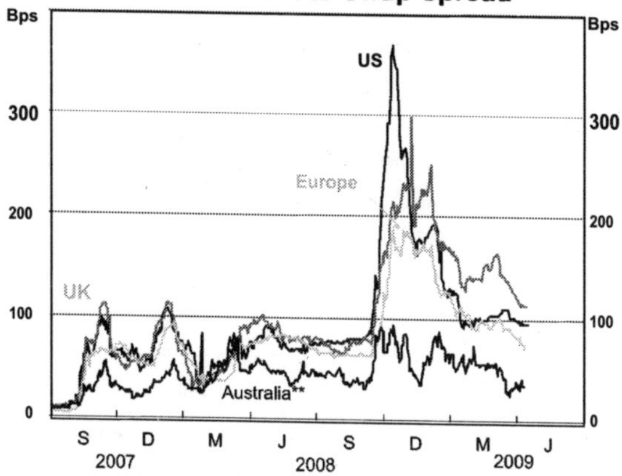

* Spread is to: OIS in Australia and US; EONIA in Europe; and SONIA in UK
** Bank bill to OIS
Sources: Bloomberg; Tullett Prebon (Australia) Pty Ltd

The easing of lending standards during the boom was especially marked in US mortgage markets, and so were its consequences. Compared to loans in most other countries, US mortgages are more likely to be packaged into securities. And if the market price of these securities should fall, accounting treatment often requires that the loss be recognised immediately, which is not the case for a traditional loan portfolio. For these reasons, it should not be surprising that banks' losses have been concentrated in securities holdings rather than traditional on-balance sheet lending. This meant that investment banks and others with large securities trading and investment books have been especially affected. The first major firm that had to be rescued was Bear Stearns, but many others had already declared losses by then. As shown in Graph 10, total profits in several banking systems started to turn negative.

Graph 10

Banks' Profits

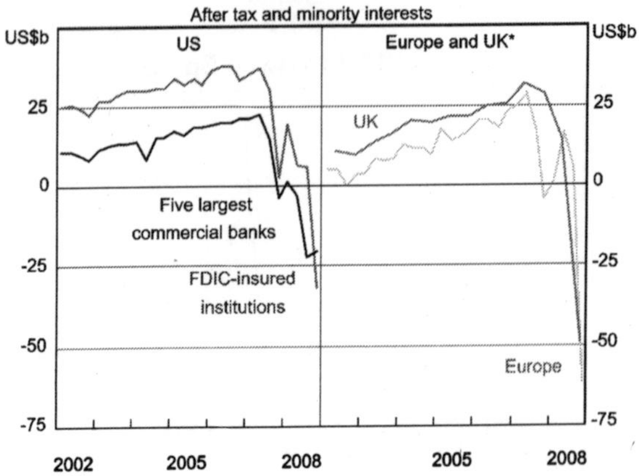

* 10 largest European and 5 largest UK banks

Sources: Bloomberg; Federal Deposit Insurance Corporation; banks' annual and interim reports

In this environment, banks' perceptions of risk increased, and they started to tighten lending standards. A feedback loop started to develop. Banks were becoming more risk-averse, but so were their customers, who started to pull back on spending. The major industrialised economies of the United States, euro area and Japan were already experiencing economic contractions by the first half of 2008.

As investors and others began to realise the macroeconomic consequences of the turmoil, other asset markets were also affected. Share prices fell sharply all over the world, especially for banks, as shown by the indices in Graph 11. Prices fell even further when Lehman Brothers failed.

Lehman had been an important player in many of the securities and derivative markets that were freezing up. It even had a sub-prime mortgage subsidiary, which it shut down in August 2007. Lehman had already incurred substantial losses in the quarters prior to its failure. And once people start to become concerned about a bank's solvency, it becomes very hard to prevent the loss of counterparty confidence that can bring that insolvency on.

Graph 11

Banks' Share Prices

2 July 2007 = 100

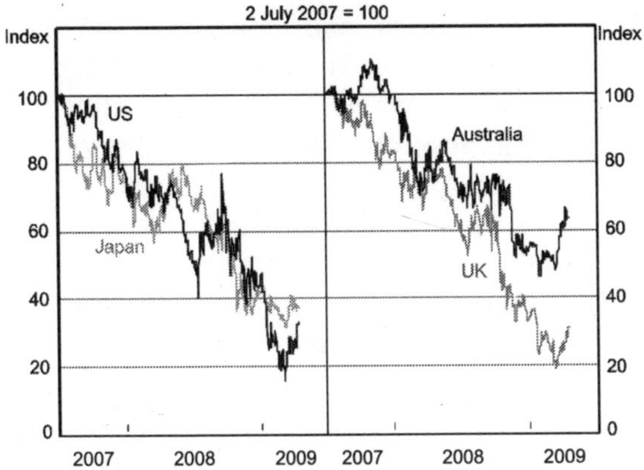

Source: Bloomberg

When Lehman failed, it triggered a further increase in risk aversion. There was a flight to the safety of government bonds, and away from emerging market and other assets. Yield spreads on traditionally risky assets widened further, as well as those on newer kinds of derivatives and securities such as credit default swaps or collateralized debt obligations.

Those newer classes of assets were especially affected by the increase in the price of risk. They didn't have much history to use to measure their riskiness in the upswing, so the subsequent surprise factor in the downswing was greater. Also weighing on confidence is the fact that it is not clear if those asset classes can even survive. When markets are very liquid and risk premiums are low, the financial system can approach the textbook, complete-markets ideal, where every possible pattern of pay-offs can be created and every individual risk can be hedged. But when risk appetite returns to a more normal, lower level, markets become less complete again. Some of the more exotic structured products might not survive as viable asset classes outside of a credit-market boom.

Consequences

When risk aversion rises like this, the macroeconomic consequences can be severe. Since at least Keynes' day, it has been recognised that economies run in large part on confidence. When firms and consumers no longer feel confident, they pull back from spending. When banks and other financial institutions no longer feel confident, they pull back from lending. Projects that seemed likely to be profitable in the good times suddenly seem risky and less attractive. Bank regulation and behaviour might explain how a US mortgage crisis propagated into essentially a North Atlantic banking crisis. But trade and confidence effects explain why that North Atlantic banking crisis has escalated into a global problem.

The intensification of the current crisis following the Lehman failure in September saw the deterioration of many macroeconomic indicators. Industrial output contracted sharply in much of the world. Commodity prices had been booming earlier in the year, but declined significantly towards the end of the year. There was a sudden contraction in the volume of world trade. In this environment, forecasters have had to scale down their forecasts for output growth repeatedly. As Graph 12 shows, the IMF is now forecasting that global output will contract in 2009. This would be the first annual contraction in output since at least the Second World War.

The weak global macroeconomic outlook implies that borrowers have become riskier. Some are likely to face greater difficulty servicing their debts. Bad loans normally rise relative to total lending when economies turn down, and the current global downturn will be no exception to this pattern. In the current environment, this could weigh on the profitability of already weakened banking sectors in the major economies.

Graph 12

World GDP

Year-ended percentage change

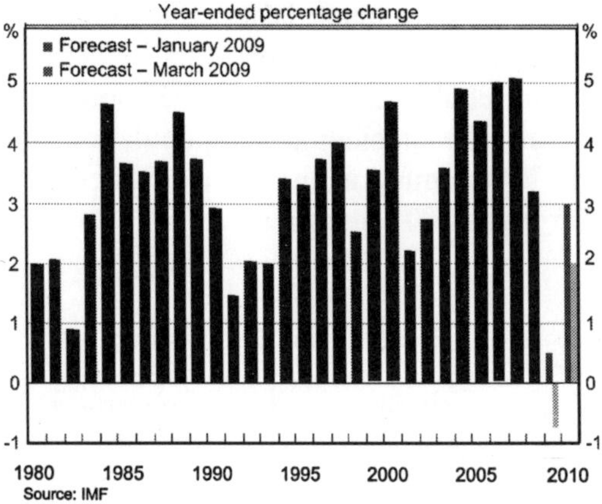

The Australian Scene

The Australian financial system has withstood the shocks coming from overseas better than many others. Australian-owned banks have recorded solid profits over the past year. Unlike banks in many other countries, they have been able to raise additional capital where required from private investors, at only modest discounts to the market price of their equity at the time.

There are a number of reasons for their relatively good performance during a period of considerable turbulence. One of these is that they had not previously accumulated large exposures to the kinds of tradable securities in which losses at other banks have been concentrated. Rather, Australian banks were focused on their domestic lending business. Australia usually runs a current account deficit, so our banks were seeking offshore funding for their domestic activities, not casting around for foreign assets in which they could invest their domestic surpluses.

Another reason is that housing and mortgage markets did not become as over-extended as in the United States. For a start, the underlying position of the household sector was better in Australia. Graph 13 shows, two aspects of this point. First, in the left panel, the real earnings of average Australian workers were growing much faster than in the United States. Second, in the right panel, the total incomes of typical Australian households have been further boosted by the tight labour market. The employment-to-population ratio has been rising here; by contrast, in the United States, it never really recovered from its 2001 recession.

Graph 13

Earnings and Employment

* Private sector. For Australia, includes non-farm ordinary-time weekly earnings; US data are for non-farm, non-supervisory workers.
Sources: ABS; Bureau of Labor Statistics; Thomson Reuters

The housing market in Australia also wasn't so over-extended, and in any case it had already had its boom. As the left panel of Graph 14 shows, the truly rapid growth rates in national housing prices had ceased around the end of 2003, especially for apartments. The Australian market was going through a period of consolidation when the US market melted down. Prices were still rising in Australia, especially in Perth and other areas affected by the mining boom. But unlike in the United States, housing supply had not boomed in the same way for the past five years. There simply has not been an overhang of supply built up that would subsequently weigh on prices.

In thinking about the sustainability of a particular level of housing prices, we must take many things into account. Theory and experience suggest that average inflation, credit constraints, tax rates and the distribution of income all matter to the so-called user cost of housing, and thus equilibrium housing prices. Just looking at one thing—say the ratio of prices to household incomes—is really not enough. In addition, looking at one type of housing in isolation—say, detached houses—gives only a guide about movements, not a level that can be compared across countries. So it's best to use prices of all dwellings, houses and apartments together, and assess the whole market. The right-hand panel of Graph 14 shows, overall dwelling prices as a ratio to post-tax income is not a measure of sustainability or equilibrium housing prices, because all those other determinants of equilibrium user cost also change over time. But even taking this crude measure as a guide, since 2003, dwelling prices have been rising more slowly than household incomes in Australia.

Graph 14

Dwelling Price Indicators

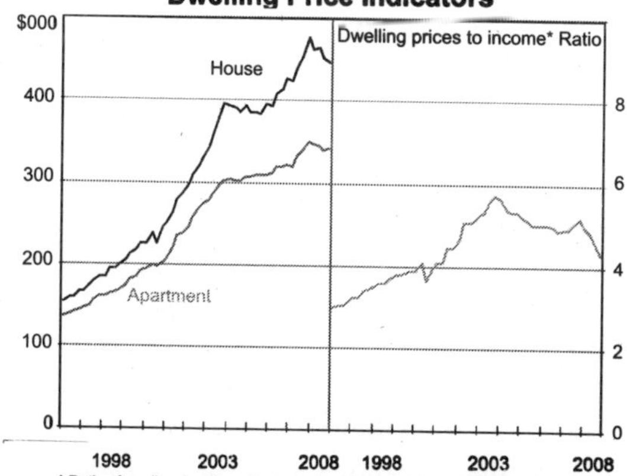

* Ratio of median dwelling price to average household disposable income; disposable income is after tax and before the deduction of interest payments

Sources: ABS; APM; RBA; REIA

Another reason the Australian housing market was less over-extended was that lending standards did not ease as much as in the United States. Sitting on the other side of the world, it's easy to lose sight of just how far lending standards did decline in the US mortgage market. Low-doc loans exist in Australia but they are less common. And in contrast to common practice in the United States, low-doc didn't mean providing no documentation at all. No-deposit mortgages are also less common in Australia than they were in the United States over the boom period.

One reason for the more moderate easing in standards here is that the regulatory arrangements concerning mortgage lending are different. For example, Australia's prudential regulator, APRA, raised capital requirements on certain kinds of riskier mortgage products. There are also important differences in consumer protection laws concerning lending, and in the way foreclosure law affects lenders' decisions, as was detailed in the Bank's *Financial Stability Review* released last month.

The tax systems also differ between the two countries. Australian households cannot deduct the interest on their own home's mortgage against their tax, so they are not effectively encouraged to keep their mortgage balances high. Many Australian households pay off more than they have to. In doing so, they accumulate potential redraws that serve both as precautionary saving and an additional buffer of equity against falls in housing prices.

Partly as a result of these tax and regulatory differences, Australian households by and large have more of a financial buffer against falls in housing prices than their American counterparts did. Timely data are hard to come by, but we can look at current loan-to-valuation ratios based on households' own assessments of their mortgage balance and the current value of their home, using the HILDA survey. The distribution of these loan-to-valuation ratios, as seen in Graph 15, saw an increase in the proportion of households with high ratios between 2003 and 2007. Overall, though, that proportion remained low compared with the United States. It seems that relatively few households in Australia face going into negative equity, even if housing prices do fall somewhat. By contrast, in the United States, some private-sector estimates suggest that more than 10 percent of mortgage borrowers are already in negative equity, perhaps as many as one in six. Thus, a much greater proportion of US home owners risk defaulting if they get into repayment difficulty, because they cannot easily sell or refinance if the mortgage is worth more than the home.

Graph 15

Self-reported Loan-to-valuation Ratios*

Per cent of all households with owner-occupier mortgages

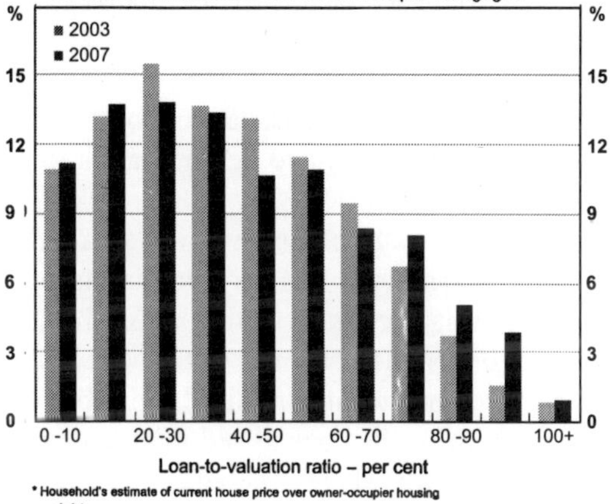

* Household's estimate of current house price over owner-occupier housing debt

Source: HILDA Release 7.0

As the crisis has unfolded, there are signs that Australian banks and other lenders have become more risk-averse and they have tightened lending criteria somewhat. However, it appears that good quality borrowers can still obtain and roll over credit. The Australian household and business sectors have also become much more risk-averse than in recent years. Some indicators of this change include higher household saving, and a shift from debt to equity funding by some firms. Their demand for credit has weakened as they have become more cautious. Together with those tighter lending standards, this has contributed to a slowdown in credit growth.

Counter Measures

At this stage, policy-makers around the world are focusing on solving the immediate problems in the banking system. Governments and central banks are also providing macroeconomic stimulus through fiscal and monetary policy easing. Restoring the global banking system to health is a precondition for a recovery in credit supply and economic activity. As such, it has to take priority over longer-term reforms.

In this environment, the need for credible steps to restore the health of the financial system is crucial. Governments in the most-affected countries have provided substantial support to financial institutions and markets, especially since the Lehman failure. Most have ensured banks' access to funding by guaranteeing wholesale debt issuance; some have injected capital into banks; and a few have helped banks to reduce the risk in their balance sheets.

There are several ways of undertaking this de-risking of balance sheets. Governments can buy the assets outright and place them in an entity separate to the bank; they can insure assets remaining on banks' balance sheets against losses; or they can invest in joint investment funds that buy the assets. Each of these approaches has been used in at least one country in the recent crisis. At this stage it is hard to say if there is one right way to deal with these issues. The important thing is that they are dealt with.

Despite these considerable efforts, confidence in the financial system remains fragile. Some market-based indicators of confidence have nonetheless improved in recent weeks. Money market spreads have retraced much of the increase that occurred following the Lehman failure. Equity markets have also staged a partial recovery, especially after the US Government released further details about its own programs for de-risking bank balance sheets.

On top of these efforts to deal with the immediate problems, there is also considerable focus on reforms to the financial system architecture, to prevent a similar crisis from occurring again. Policy initiatives under discussion include changes to the regulation of credit rating agencies, the pay incentives faced by financial institutions and their staff, and the regulation of bank capital and liquidity.

Many of these initiatives have been developed under the auspices of international groupings of central banks and bank regulators, such as the Financial Stability Forum, now known as the Financial Stability Board, and the Basel Committee on Bank Supervision. Both groupings have expanded their memberships in the past few weeks, in particular to include major emerging economies. Australia was already represented on the Financial Stability Forum, and is one of the countries that have just joined the Basel Committee.

Central banks and other authorities around the world are working together to deal with the crisis and finalise these initiatives. Some of the reforms being considered will take a couple of years to be introduced. The global financial system is therefore facing a period of change. The present financial crisis has followed a period in which the price of risk was unusually low and conducive to the build-up of excesses in credit markets. These easier conditions are unlikely to return any time soon. What happens over the next few years, at least, is highly uncertain. For the time being, credit conditions will probably still be tighter than had been the case a few years ago. There will probably be less financing available for asset acquisition. Among the important open questions are: how quickly the banking systems in major economies can repair their balance sheets; and how quickly confidence can be restored.

Source: www.rba.gov.au
© Reserve Bank of Australia. Reprinted with Permission.

This speech was delivered at the conference on 'Australia in the global storm: A conference on the implications of the global financial crisis for Australia and its region' held at Victoria University, Melbourne on 15 April 2009.

4

The Impact of the Financial Crisis on Emerging Market Economies: The Transmission Mechanism, Policy Response and Lessons

Jack Boorman

Impact of the Crisis

The financial crisis that began in the United States in the sub-prime mortgage market in 2007 and that spread quickly to Europe has become a global crisis, affecting both financial systems across the globe and economic activity in virtually all countries. Emerging market countries have been hit hard. Even those countries that had strengthened their policies and built defenses to withstand a less benign global environment than that which existed for much of the previous decade have not been spared.

The serious nature of this still-unfolding crisis is evident in the increasingly pessimistic picture painted by forecasts for economic growth. Since the beginning of the crisis in 2007, forecasts for growth rates in 2008 and beyond have been repeatedly revised downward. As of this writing, this monotonic pattern of downward revisions has yet to be reversed. The latest projections from the IMF World Economic Outlook are shown in Table 4.1.

The global economy is now expected to contract this year by 1.3 percent—the first such contraction since the Second World War. However, this figure hides significant differences among countries and regions. The worst affected regions include emerging Europe, the CIS countries and the newly industrialized Asian economies, each of which is expected to see contractions in GDP in 2009 near or even above five percent. Some other regions are expected to do much better, including the emerging market countries of South Asia, Africa and the Middle East, most of which are expected to avoid recession. But there is a wide range of projections even within regions.

Table 4.1: GDP Growth Projections (percent)

	2008	2009	2010	2011
World	3.2	-1.3	1.9	4.3
Advanced Economies	0.8	-3.8	0.01	2.6
US	1.1	-2.8	-0.05	3.5
EU	1.1	-4.0	-0.3	1.7
Japan	-0.6	-6.2	0.5	2.2
Emerging Market Economies	5.2	0.01	3.2	5.7
Emerging Asia	6.3	2.5	5.0	7.6
Emerging South Asia	7.0	4.3	5.3	6.6
Emerging Europe	4.0	-4.8	0.7	3.6
Emerging Americas	4.0	-1.7	1.6	3.5
Emerging Middle East	5.3	0.5	2.4	3.9
Emerging Africa	4.8	1.5	3.7	5.2
Newly Industrialized Asia	1.6	-5.6	0.8	4.4
Developing Asia	7.7	4.8	6.1	8.3
China	9.0	6.5	7.5	10.2
India	7.3	4.5	5.6	6.9

Source: IMF, World Economic Outlook, April, 2009

Most notably, while emerging Asia as a whole is projected to grow by 2.5 percent this year, the developing countries within the region are set to grow at near five percent, while the newly industrialized countries are projected to contract by 5.6 percent. The worst hit counties are expected to include Singapore (-10 percent), Taiwan-China (-7.5 percent), Hong Kong-China (-4.5 percent) and Korea (-4 percent). China and India, the largest emerging economies in the region and in the world, are projected to grow by 6.5 percent and 4.5 percent, respectively. While surprisingly good in the current environment, these growth rates are, of course, below those registered by these countries in recent years. Some of the reasons for this diverse performance will be touched upon in subsequent sections of this paper.

The global contraction is forecast to give way to renewed growth next year, with world GDP increasing by almost two percent. Again, however, the performance in the advanced economies is expected to be markedly different from that in the emerging market economies; and growth rates within regions are also expected to vary substantially. The major industrial economies are expected to see little or no growth year-on-year in 2010, and, at best, to return to potential only at the end of the year. The emerging economies, however, are projected to grow by over three percent, with Asia leading the way at about five percent. Once again, the developing countries in Asia are expected to register the best performance. As always, there are significant caveats about these projections. However, there are recent signs that the bottom may have been reached in a number of countries, including in Asia, so that the next revision of these projections may see at least a halt to the repeated worsening of the picture seen over the last two years. For example, the most recent data from China indicate that investment spending, bolstered by the stimulus package introduced late last year, has risen to record highs, bank lending is already ahead of the government's target for all of 2009, industrial production is expanding significantly, and retail sales have recovered.

That said, there are well known lags in the recovery process–including in the recovery of employment. This is particularly the case in the advanced economies where employers commit to new hiring only after clear signs of a rebound in activity. Thus, in most of the industrial world, unemployment is expected to continue to increase throughout most of 2010, causing continued pain. Moreover, there will be a critical question about the sustainability of any recovery. A return to the global imbalances of the past decade will threaten that sustainability. Renewed global growth will be secure only if the macroeconomic structures of a number of economies—especially the savings balances in the United States and China—emerge as significantly different from what they were in the lead up to the current crisis.

The Transmission Mechanism

The transmission of the crisis from the U.S. and Europe to the rest of the world came through a number of channels. The financial institutions in most emerging market economies had not engaged in the kind of practices seen in the institutions that populate the financial centers in the major industrial countries. Balance sheets were typically not exposed to the toxic assets that increasingly dominated positions in the major institutions. Derivatives were employed much less frequently and were generally limited to the more traditional instruments employed to hedge against currency and other risks associated with trade. Financial institutions in the emerging economies either shied away from the more exotic instruments, including such things as credit default swaps and collateralized debt obligations, or were prevented by regulation from holding or trading such instruments. Banking was generally of the more "boring", old fashioned kind!

But, in the end, this did not protect these countries. Five major channels brought the crisis home to these economies:

First was the withdrawal of funds by some of the major financial institutions from their subsidiaries located in the emerging economies. The general contraction of the balance sheets of the major institutions and the need to rebuild their capital base has constrained the funding available to other institutions in both the industrial countries (e.g., hedge funds) and in the emerging world that rely on dollar (or even Euro) funding. This has been the case notwithstanding the massive support injected into banking systems in the financial centers that are home to most of the major international banks.

Second was the seizing-up of the international credit

markets. Credit flows through the international banks and global bond markets to emerging market countries all but dried up. This has created significant financial stress in some of those countries—especially those in central and Eastern Europe—that ran up dangerously large current account deficits and took on substantial international debt. For example, BIS data show that consolidated claims of BIS-reporting banks on all emerging market economies decreased from a peak of US$ 5.4 trillion in June, 2008 to US$ 4.6 trillion by December—a decline of over 14 percent. No emerging market regions were spared, and all of them saw similar declines. Recent anecdotal evidence suggests that this withdrawal has continued in most regions. Data on capital flows show an even more dramatic picture. Net private flows to emerging market countries peaked at about 5 percent of GDP in 2007. However, all categories of inward flows to emerging market countries have registered significant declines from 2007 to 2008 and are projected to decline further in 2009. The cumulative decline in the major categories of flows to emerging market countries between 2007 and 2009 are currently expected to be very large: 62 percent for international bond issues; 61 percent for commercial bank loans; and 54 percent for inward direct investment. (Table 4.2) The flow of export credits to the emerging market countries as well as inward portfolio investment all but collapsed in 2008. The withdrawal of portfolio investment was a key factor behind a decline in emerging stock markets that exceeded the sharp declines in advanced economy markets. [1]

In total, emerging market economies—especially those that are heavily indebted and face large financing requirements both from current deficits as well as from the need to refinance maturing debt—have seen a substantial decline in all major categories of capital inflows. Some of the worst affected countries have also recorded significant capital flight and sharp depreciations of their currencies. All of this has been reflected in a substantial fall in international reserves, with emerging market countries in all regions of the world other than East Asia recording significant declines; emerging countries in Europe were the most seriously affected.

Table 4.2: Capital Flows, Export Financing and International Reserves (US$ billions)

	2006	2007	2008	2009	2010
Emerging Market Countries:					
Export Credits	37.4	48.7	62.6	-100.8	13.5
International Bond Issues	133.8	189.0	142.4	71.4	100.6
Commercial Bank Loans	403.9	505.1	453.0	195.6	254.7
Inward Portfolio Investment	156.0	231.4	-214.3	-55.2	76.9
Inward FDI	487.6	656.8	674.0	299.1	399.6
Change in International Reserves	724.2	1248.5	458.5	-393.3	135.4
Emerging Asia:					
Export Credits	13.1	16.5	28.0	-42.0	7.5
International Bond Issues	46.1	46.5	39.4	23.5	30.4
Commercial Bank Loans	100.8	102.3	81.5	37.3	52.0
Inward Portfolio Investment	106.9	184.0	-159.8	-68.1	29.3
Inward FDI	215.6	303.1	317.2	127.2	165.1
Change in International Reserves	416.6	711.3	423.1	-37.7	110.8
Emerging South Asia:					
Export Credits	3.6	3.2	6.8	-6.1	2.1
International Bond Issues	5.9	6.2	5.8	4.7	5.2
Commercial Bank Loans	10.2	9.8	9.2	7.0	8.2
Inward Portfolio Investment	6.9	36.5	-15.6	5.5	16.1
Inward FDI	25.1	31.2	47.7	32.6	38.3
Change in International Reserves	43.2	102.7	-25.1	-37.6	-15.0

Source: The Economist Intelligence Unit

Third, was the impact of the crisis on economic activity - in the first instance, in the United States and Europe, and subsequently in Japan. Initially, this manifested itself in a sharp contraction in exports from those emerging market countries that had become the largest exporters to the industrial world. Quite rapidly, however, exports declined from the other emerging economies, i.e., those whose exports consisted of raw and intermediate goods shipped to those larger emerging market countries, particularly China that had become key providers of final manufactured goods in the increasingly complex supply chains that came to populate world trade.

This fall in exports—at a virtually unprecedented rate of collapse—created an internal feedback loop wherein the initial reduction in trade weakened the domestic economies of the emerging market countries, with further negative feedback on the financial sectors in those countries as the quality of domestic credit deteriorated.

Fourth, are the still uncertain prospects for remittances–an important source of income and foreign exchange in many emerging market economies. Total remittances to emerging market countries were over US$ 206 billion in 2007 and are estimated to have reached more than US$230 billion in 2008 (Table 4.3). Like unemployment figures, remittances tend to lag the decline in economic activity–and will likely lag in the recovery. While recent data are sketchy, remittances to emerging market countries appear to be falling significantly and are estimated to total only about US$ 170 billion this year before recovering somewhat to about US$ 195 billion in 2010. [2] Such projections are subject to a wide margin of error and are dependent on an assumed recovery in the global economy. Interestingly, the transfer of domestic remittances, i.e., those remittances that go from individuals who have moved to urban areas in search of employment and higher income to those left behind in the rural or less developed regions of a country, have also declined. This is helping to transfer the weakness in the export and service sectors in emerging economies to parts of those countries that otherwise would have been less affected.

The return of workers from abroad could put additional pressure on these regions as those workers seek employment in already depressed economies.

Table 4.3: Workers Remittances (US$ billions)

	2006	2007	2008	2009	2010
Remittance inflows to: Emerging Market Countries	172.3	206.2	231.7	170	195
Emerging Asia	86.3	111.8	132.9	95	115
Emerging South Asia	38.7	50.4	63.3	46	57
India	25.7	35.0	45.0	30	40
China	22.5	32.0	37.0	26	34
Philippines	14.9	15.6	16.8	12	11
Vietnam	4.8	7.6	9.3	7.8	7.9
Bangladesh	5.5	6.9	8.5	6.7	7.8
Pakistan	5.4	6,0	7.1	6.8	6.9

Emerging Markets Countries are classified as Algeria, Angola, Argentina, Bahrain, Bangladesh, Bolivia, Botswana, Brazil, Bulgaria, Cameroon, Chile, China, Colombia, Costa Rica, Cote d'Ivoire, Croatia, Czech Republic, Czechoslovakia, Ecuador, Egypt, Estonia, Ethiopia, Ghana, Hong Kong (China), Hungary, India, Indonesia, Iran, Israel, Jordan, Kazakhstan, Kenya, Korea, Kuwait, Latvia, Lithuania, Madagascar, Malaysia, Mauritania, Mauritius, Mexico, Morocco, Nigeria, Pakistan, Peru, Philippines, Poland, Romania, Russia, Saudi Arabia, Senegal, Serbia, Serbia and Montenegro, Sierra Leone, Singapore, Slovak Republic, South Africa, Sri Lanka, Taiwan (China), Tanzania, Thailand, Togo, Trinidad and Tobago, Tunisia, Turkey, Uganda, Ukraine, United Arab Emirates, Uruguay, Venezuela, Vietnam

Source: The Economist Intelligence Unit

Fifth, and finally, is the psychological factor. The world has become all too familiar with financial crises. But a financial crisis originating in the United States and spreading quickly to other industrial countries took most of the world by surprise. So did the severe worsening of the crisis in September and October, 2008 which saw the collapse of some of the world's most prized private financial institutions and extraordinary—and untested—policy actions by industrial country governments. This was quickly followed by a seizing-up of financial markets around the world, a massive loss in asset values, and a virtually unprecedented collapse of exports. It is fair to say that no one was prepared for this, and that it undermined the business plans and expectations of almost everyone. The decline in asset values, especially of equities and houses, and the rapid rise in unemployment brought that insecurity and its accompanying fear to consumers. Financial systems and economies are driven by confidence. These events thoroughly shook consumers' confidence, causing a self-aggravating feedback to the rest of the economy. This experience may well affect the nature of any recovery in ways as yet not fully understood.

The Policy Response

Reserve-Enhancing Measures: Virtually all emerging market countries have been affected by these developments. However, the policy responses have been very different and go some way to explain the diversity of growth prospects pointed to above. In light of the impact of the crisis on the availability of capital through the international financial markets, a number of countries have entered into swap arrangements so as to strengthen their reserve positions. The largest such operations have involved the U.S. Federal Reserve Bank entering into temporary reciprocal currency arrangements for the provision of dollar liquidity with Brazil, Mexico, Singapore and South Korea. Other bilateral swap arrangements have been agreed or increased, and a number of multilateral arrangements have been discussed, e.g., through the G7 and through the Chiang Mai Initiative. A significant number of emerging market countries have turned to the International Monetary Fund (IMF) for support. Since mid-2008–after a steady decline in both the number of countries borrowing from the IMF and in the outstanding claims of the institution on member countries –

fourteen emerging market countries have secured IMF financial support totaling more than US$ 53 billion. The largest financing arrangements have been with Hungary, Pakistan, Ukraine, Belarus and Iceland. Most recently, Mexico has availed itself of the IMF's new Flexible Credit Line (FCL) in an amount of about US$ 47 billion. This arrangement, the first under the IMF's new crisis prevention facility, is intended to be precautionary and the Mexican authorities have indicated that they do not intend to draw on those resources. With the absence of a quick recovery in international credit markets, the IMF is likely to see increasing demand from emerging market countries facing declining exports and the need to roll-over substantial amounts of international debt.

Measures to Strengthen Financial Sectors

Measures taken by some countries have attempted to address the impact on the banking sector and the financial sector more generally of both the direct effects of the financial crisis and the emerging effect of weakening domestic economies. In at least twenty emerging market countries, existing deposit insurance schemes have been modified to broaden the kinds of deposits covered or to increase the maximum amount covered. A number of countries in Asia that had not previously had deposit insurance schemes have introduced them as a means of bolstering public confidence in their banking systems.

Other measures directed at the banking and financial systems have included capital injections and other support mechanisms for domestic banks, both to assist banks in meeting minimum capital adequacy standards and to support bank lending operations, especially in the critical area of trade credit. Many of the measures taken have been ad hoc and have confronted the same problem that surfaced in the more advanced economies, i.e., the consistency and coordination across borders of measures to support domestic banking systems. (See the section below on lessons from the crisis for more on this issue.)

Fiscal Stimulus Packages

Along with most of the world's more advanced economies, a large number of emerging market countries have also introduced ambitious fiscal stimulus packages. For example, the emerging market countries that are members of the G20 have taken significant measures to bolster domestic activity. Of those 11 countries, only Turkey has chosen not to introduce a special stimulus package. The largest such initiative by far has been undertaken by China. A package comprised solely of expenditure measures is estimated by the staff of the IMF to amount to US$ 93.3 billion in 2009 and an additional US$ 102 billion in 2010-over two percent of China's GDP in each of those years. The packages announced by the other countries in the group total over US$ 80 billion, with India accounting for US$ 6.8 billion. On average these stimulus packages are estimated to add almost 1.5 percent to the GDP of most of these economies. In a number of countries, automatic stabilizers that lower the tax burden or increase public spending will add to the impact of these discretionary measures. However, the impact of those stabilizers is generally minor and varies significantly across the emerging market countries.

There is considerable variation across these countries in the composition of these stimulus packages. On average, about one-third of the measures comprise direct government tax cuts and other revenue measures to spur private spending and about two-thirds comprise expenditure measures. In virtually all countries the expenditure measures are heavily weighted towards infrastructure spending. In China, for example, the stimulus package is comprised solely of expenditure measures. In India, on the other hand, about one-third of the measures are temporary indirect tax reductions. Some of these emerging market countries that are taking these measures are those that have built up sizeable international reserves and have run significant fiscal surpluses in recent years. These policies have created both fiscal space and the reserves needed to manage large stimulus packages. Other countries, India included, have been more constrained in their capacity to employ fiscal stimulus to help counter the impact of the crisis. Still other countries, especially in Eastern Europe, have had no scope to take such actions and, indeed, have had to take measures to tighten expenditures. [3]

For some other countries, stimulus packages–along with the impact of declining levels of activity in their economies–will worsen both fiscal positions and debt profiles in the short run. These realities have led a number of countries to hesitate in announcing further stimulus measures for 2010. This caution is warranted, not least as the global conditions for securing new financing that confront these countries—and the private sectors in these countries—may deteriorate further. That will depend on the extent to which the contraction of international capital flows to these countries since early 2008 will be reversed. That, in turn, will depend on how the unprecedented levels of borrowing by many of the major industrial countries affect conditions in the global markets, including interest rates. [4]

Protectionist Measures

Unfortunately, and in contrast to the generally constructive measures described above, protectionist trade measures have also been part of the response to the crisis. Recalling the experience of the 1930's, the leaders of the G20 signed a pledge at their November 15, 2008 summit to avoid protectionist measures. That pledge notwithstanding, by February 2009, 17 members of the G20 had implemented 47 restrictive trade measures. According to the World Bank's monitoring list of trade and trade related measures, 66 trade-restrictive measures have taken effect since the beginning of the crisis. [5] Developed countries have relied solely on subsidies and other support packages. Developing countries have employed a variety of measures, including subsidies, import duties, import bans and non-tariff measures. In the developed countries, and particularly in the high income countries, subsidies to the auto industry have proliferated and are estimated to total US$ 48 billion worldwide. But the emerging market countries have also been active in the automotive sector, especially in protecting their component suppliers. Protectionist tendencies have also been evident in the financial sector: virtually all nations have focused their financial sector subsidies on domestically owned banks rather than subsidiaries of foreign banks.

While many of these protectionist measures, thus far, are relatively minor, they are of significant importance for particular exporters. They also reflect a trend that contradicts the pledges made by the countries in the G20, both developed and emerging economies. This is a matter of concern and warrants close monitoring and publicity to help stem this tide. There is no need to learn again the lessons of the 1930's!

Decoupling

The impact of the crisis in the US and Europe on the emerging market economies has surprised some analysts. A proposition had been put forward that the emerging economies had "decoupled" from the industrial world to a degree that would permit them to more easily absorb the impact of a slowdown in economic activity in those countries. The serious global impact of this crisis would seem to put the lie to that proposition. The evidence is growing that decoupling has not occurred to anything like the extent that would be needed to isolate the emerging economies from a weakening of activity in the industrial world. [6] Indeed, it could be argued that the explosion of global trade—the major force in the rapid growth of many of the emerging economies over the last few decades, together with the design of the world's supply chains, as well as the ever-increasing integration of financial markets has, in fact, increased the coupling of the emerging market economies–and many of the poorer developing countries - with the industrial world.

Perhaps even more important, beyond trade, other inter-linkages have developed that increase the dependency among various groups of countries and, in some ways, reverse the direction of influence. For example, for years it was the developing world and the emerging market countries, in particular, that were dependent for their financing on the global financial markets centered in the industrial countries. Large current account deficits in the emerging market countries were financed through capital flows from the industrial world. Much of that financing took the form of bank loans until the mid 1980's; and then increasingly took the form of flows through the bond markets. That story ended in the financial crises in Latin America in the 1980's and in Asia and elsewhere in the 1990's and the first few years of this millennium. Important lessons were learned in those crises and many of the emerging market countries fundamentally changed the management of their economies. Macroeconomic policies became more orthodox; policy-making institutions were strengthened; and the flow of capital shifted dramatically. Together with the rise in crude oil and other commodity prices, the rapid growth of emerging market countries with high savings rates, and the shift in the United States to negative savings by both the government and consumers, fundamentally changed the nature and the flow of capital–and dependency–among the world's economies.

The increase in commodity prices was further evidence of the shift in influence that was taking place. It was the rapid growth of many of the emerging market countries themselves that led to the sharp rise in commodity and raw material prices. That development, in turn, became the dominant influence on inflationary pressures in the industrial world, limiting the power of traditional central bank policy instruments to control domestic inflation. Thus, the interlinkages between the industrial and emerging world have become far more complex and multi-dimensional—and the very concept of decoupling seems almost quaint! The framework of analysis can no longer be limited to the impact of the level of activity in the industrial world—or the impact of a single market, such as that for equities-on the emerging market economies. As important are the influence of high savings rates and capital flows from the emerging economies to the industrial world—and especially to the United States.

Thus, rather than a decoupling, an increased inter-dependence has emerged. Policy in the industrial countries needs to anticipate the impact of growth in the emerging world (through the effects on commodity prices, for example), and the impact of changing savings rates and portfolio investment preferences on interest rates and exchange rates. In turn, policy in the emerging market countries needs to anticipate the impact of changing levels of activity in the industrial world on exports and on foreign direct investment, and changing savings rates, especially in the US.

Notwithstanding the apparent power of these arguments, the proposition that emerging market countries have de-coupled from the industrial world still finds some favor. In a recent issue of the Economist (May 22-29, 2009) it is argued that (1) "...the biggest emerging economies are less dependent on American spending than commonly believed;" and (2) "...they have proven more able and willing to respond to economic weaknesses than many feared.". The first of these propositions may turn out to be correct. That will be tested if the recent increase in savings by the American consumer persists and the spending rate does not recover to earlier levels. [7]

Perhaps more important, it is not clear that the second point made above has much to do with the basic concept of decoupling. Decoupling is a proposition about the impact of a slowdown in activity in the industrial or developed world on the level of activity and growth in the emerging, and developing world. If the emerging economies have shown that they have the capacity to offset that impact to some degree through their own countercyclical policies, that is to be welcomed. But one should not confuse that with decoupling. That is, instead, a matter of the extent to which emerging economies can offset the impact of changing levels of activity in the countries to which they are coupled. So long as they remain coupled, the important questions will be to what extent they have the capacity to take such offsetting action. It is not a matter of taking solace in the possibility that there will be no impact.

This interpretation of what may now be happening is important. It leads to questions about what emerging market countries need to do to keep themselves ready to respond to a slowdown in the industrial world. It does not suggest that they need not be so prepared because they have decoupled! The reason that many emerging market economies were prepared to design and implement policies to help counter the impact of the current recession in most of the industrial world was the result of the fundamental shift in the practice of economic management that took place in those countries in the wake of the financial market crisis that hit so many of them from the mid 1990's until the early 2000's. Far more responsible fiscal policies were introduced in many countries; inflationary risks were taken more seriously and monetary policy was more singularly focused on that objective; better regulation—and greater transparency—was introduced into banking systems; many governments got out of businesses that are better left in the hands of the private sector; international reserves were increased by substantial amounts—in some cases excessively; and so on. These were hard won achievements, but they have paid off in faster growth and in a capacity to counter contractionary forces originating elsewhere. If some of the emerging market countries succeed in their efforts to stabilize their economies and to maintain or restore growth, they should ask which policies allowed them to do that and how they can maintain that readiness in the future. Other emerging economies that skated closer to the edge with weak fiscal positions, over-borrowing, lax regulations, unsustainable borrowing, weak debt management policies, and mistaken capital market liberalization polices should learn from the success of the others.

Lessons from the Crisis

Against this background, a number of critical policy questions now confront the emerging market countries. Much work will be needed to sort through the lessons of this crisis. This paper will raise only four of the questions that need to be addressed—both individually by these countries, and collectively by both the emerging and the more developed countries. These include:

- What has been learned about financial sector regulation and supervision in the current crisis? More 1. generally, what is the appropriate model for emerging market countries to look to in designing their financial regulatory systems?
- Did the accumulation of large stocks of international reserves by many of the emerging market 2. countries put them in a better position to confront the current crisis? Was it beneficial from a longer term cost/benefit perspective, or was it overdone? Related to the question of the appropriate level of reserves, are there lessons to be learned about the dominant role of the U.S. dollar as the primary reserve asset in the global system?
- What preliminary lessons have been learned about the capacity of the emerging market economies to engage in stimulative domestic monetary and fiscal policies in the face of a softening or a contraction of global demand? What conditions are necessary for such measures to be both feasible and effective and how powerful can the impact of such measures be on the global economy? And
- A number of countries, in Eastern Europe and elsewhere, have been severely damaged by the 4. reversal of capital

flows in the past year. In many cases, the fault has been seen to lie, at least in part, in the policies pursued in opening their capital markets. What are the lessons that have been learned? What should be done to avoid a repeat of this experience in these and, as importantly, in frontier emerging economies? Is there a greater role for the IMF here?

These are all difficult questions. In the remainder of this paper, the first three questions will be elaborated upon to begin a discussion of the issues they raise. The last question is addressed in separate papers and may be an element in the discussions to take place in subsequent days regarding the reform of the IMF and of the global economic and financial architecture.

Financial Sector Regulation

One of the major factors leading to the current crisis was what many consider to have been inadequate regulation and supervision both within and across those countries that host the global financial centers and the major international financial institutions. It was facilitated by the extraordinarily weak performance of many of the credit rating agencies which failed in their most fundamental fiduciary responsibilities. Much of this stemmed from the persistent trend towards deregulation in the U.S.—driven more by ideology than by evidence; from an almost blind faith in the efficient markets hypotheses; from the competitive pressures that undermined prudent financial risk management in some of the major global financial centers; from the possibilities that existed to arbitrage regulations across jurisdictions; and from the complexity of some of the financial innovations of this period.

Notwithstanding the increased complexity of the global financial markets, much of the regulatory failure resulted from ignoring the basics. It was a failure to demand basic transparency in the financial system from the special investment vehicles (SIVs) that have come to plague the banking system in the U.S., and in the trading of credit default swaps and other exotic—and, it might noted, formerly illegal—instruments. It was reflected in inadequate capital and liquidity requirements that failed to keep up with the innovations that were taking place in the banks and in the financial system more generally. But perhaps most importantly —and most inexcusably—many of the problems that developed stem from a simple lack of attention to the incentives that were permitted to build in the system. The result was that the system went from "exotic" to "toxic" in short order!

Take just the example of the sub-prime mortgage market in the United States.

- Mortgage originators held virtually none on the debt they created; they sold it off as fast as possible after the mortgage was signed and got their fees. As a result, they had little interest in the quality of the credit; they had, as is said, "no skin in the game"!
- The mortgages were then quickly sold to Wall Street to bundle with other mortgages into securitized instruments to be sold to investors. Those doing the bundling received their fees and, like the originators, had little interest in the quality of the credit. Wall Street profited enormously from this business and quickly developed a voracious appetite for mortgages to slice and dice into more and more exotic instruments, putting further pressure on the originators to deliver more and more mortgages.
- The compensation structure in the banks and other institutions was based on the short term payoff to activities such as this. It was divorced from the longer term risks that the institutions were taking on especially as they began to hold these instruments themselves on their own balance sheets or off-balance sheet in the SIVs.
- The rating agencies which should have cared about the quality of the credit, and had a fundamental responsibility to have such concerns received their fees from those who

had bundled the mortgages and were trying to market them. If a particular rating agency did not provide the rating wanted by the issuers, it would lose the business to a more willing agency. This represented a clear conflict of interest; but nothing was done to halt the process.

- The target investors, who were searching for yield in a low interest rate environment that was allowed to persist for far too long, failed in their own due diligence. If those investors saw some risk in the instruments they were purchasing, there were other institutions that happily sold the credit default swaps to insure against default. But those latter institutions saw virtually no risk of default and failed to provision anywhere near sufficiently against those losses. They even sold insurance to investors who did not own the underlying instrument they were betting against. This is a big part of the AIG story!

Where were the regulators and supervisors while all this was going on? They were apparently blinded by the deregulation mantra that had developed, by the priority to home-ownership that became policy in the United States and in some other countries, and by the view that central banks could not, in any case, do anything to prevent bubbles. [8] And so they let the party continue! Unfortunately, regulators in some other jurisdictions were also paying too little attention. In the end, the crisis spread to other countries and to other markets from mid 2007 to mid-2008, mostly through banks and other financial institutions that had taken on risks similar to those taken on by the large banks in the U.S.

Fortunately, there is now significant public pressure in both the United States and Europe for a reform of the financial regulatory framework. Fortunately, as well, most regulatory regimes in emerging market countries never adopted the deregulation fervor that affected the United States. But still there are lessons to be learned from the experience in the United States and Europe. There is a very large agenda to be covered in considering the reforms needed to better regulate and monitor financial systems. A paper prepared in the IMF earlier this year set out that agenda rather clearly. [9] The main elements were listed as follows:

- Instituting a macro-prudential approach to supervision and assigning a clear mandate to a systemic stability regulator.
- Expanding the perimeter of financial sector surveillance to ensure that the systemic risks posed by unregulated or less regulated financial sector segments are addressed.
- Ensuring that prudential regimes encourage incentives that support systemic stability and discourage regulatory arbitrage, and assure effective enforcement of regulation.
- Addressing the pro-cyclicality of existing capital requirements and other prudential norms, preferably in a manner that is rules based and counters the cycle.
- Filling the information gaps, especially with regard to lightly regulated financial institutions, and ensuring that both supervisors and investors are provided more disclosure and a higher level of granularity in information provided.
- Resolving the political and legal impediments to the effective regulation of cross-border institutions; developing special insolvency regimes to be used for large cross-border financial firms; and harmonizing remedial action frameworks.
- Strengthening the capacity of central banks to provide liquidity and respond to systemic shocks.
- Improving the capacity of national authorities to respond to systemic crises, including by establishing mechanisms for coordination both within and across borders.
- Establishing the basis for fiscal support during the crisis containment and restructuring phase, and an exit strategy for withdrawing public support and for a transition to a new and more stable financial market structure.

An additional item could be added to this list that should be on the agenda of every financial sector regulator in the world. Should financial institutions be prevented through regulation and supervision from ever becoming too large to fail?

This is an ambitious agenda and will require the active engagement not only of national regulators and supervisors but also of the relevant regional and international bodies such as the Basel Committees, the international standard setting agencies, the Financial Stability Board, and others. It will also require a broadened surveillance mandate for the IMF, especially to widen the focus of its Financial Sector Assessments (FSAPs) and to make them mandatory.

Considerations on the Accumulation of Reserves

When considering the policies of emerging market countries that warrant re-thinking, the reserve accumulation policies of some of those countries over the last decade must be near the top of the list. This is, of course, related to the undue reliance on exports as a source of growth for many emerging market countries and the associated trade and current account surpluses that resulted. The global imbalances of the past decade are an integral element of the tapestry that led to the explosion of credit that took place across many corners of the global economy and, ultimately, to the financial crisis in the United States. In turn, those imbalances were made possible by the decline in savings in the United States, both by consumers and by the federal government. At least for American consumers, this is changing and it will force a rethinking of the policies of the last decade in both the United States and in many of the largest emerging market countries. At the federal government level, both in the U.S. and elsewhere, the current deficits resulting from the stimulus packages, the support measures for the financial sector, and other policies are, in general, the appropriate response to the current crisis. However, those deficits cannot be sustained without threatening the credit worthiness of the country or forcing tax and spending adjustments that will be politically unacceptable. So change will come. It will either be forced in a disorderly manner, or it can be managed through policy adjustment. The latter would obviously be a better process!

But there are other reasons for change. Some emerging market countries, China in particular, have persisted with polices that one can argue may not have been in their own best interest. They have accumulated far larger reserves than can be justified by almost any logic and done so at the cost of more rapid improvement in the living standards of their people. [10] Also, they have accumulated assets—dollar denominated, and sometimes yielding negative returns—that suggest that this has been a very costly trade off for these countries. [11] In the case of China, there are different views regarding what can be done to increase spending by Chinese consumers, a sine qua non for an orderly correction of the imbalances. Some argue that the creation of social safety nets already underway by the Chinese authorities, will decrease the felt need to save. Others argue that the high savings rates are, at least in part, the result of (relatively) declining rural incomes in the country and that greater infrastructure and other investments and an expansion of banking in those areas will help bring about the needed change. Whatever the remedy, most observers believe that it is possible through changed policies to generate much larger internal demand in China. The outcome of China's current stimulus package may hold important lessons in regard to the capacity to spur domestic demand through public policy.

Such a fundamental restructuring of the Chinese economy and some other large emerging market economies will cause these countries to become somewhat less coupled to the industrial world, and to the U.S., in particular. This is probably to the good for the performance of the global economy. However, this will occur in an orderly manner only if this systemic issue is addressed through internationally coordinated policies. The IMF has a role to play here both in the conduct of its surveillance responsibilities and in its role as a forum for the engagement of senior policy makers on the economic and financial issues that confront individual countries and the global economy. However, it will have the authority and capacity to play that role only if fundamental changes are made to the governance structure and some of the operations of the institution. [12]

Stimulus Packages

The third question raised above can be answered only as more experience is gained with the policies that emerging market countries have designed and implemented to help counter the current recession. While the initial impressions are generally positive, it will take more time to see their results and judge their effectiveness. There has been debate on the potential costs and benefits of such measures since the crisis turned for the worse in the fall of 2008 and countries began to introduce stimulative packages. At the meeting of The Group of Twenty in Washington, D.C. in November, 2008 a Declaration was issued by the Leaders pledging to "Use fiscal measures to stimulate domestic demand to rapid effect, as appropriate, while maintaining a policy framework conducive to fiscal sustainability". [13] Commitments were also made, with fiscal implications, to "Continue our vigorous efforts and take whatever further actions are necessary to stabilize the financial system".

Even as the measures were being prepared and announced, many of the familiar critiques of fiscal policy were voiced:

- Fiscal policy–especially spending measures-inevitably acts with sometimes long and unpredictable lags. This runs the risk that the impact on the economy may well be felt only after the economy has already begun to recover.
- The effectiveness of spending measures is likely to be adversely affected if those measures are rushed and not subjected to the scrutiny possible in calmer times.
- The possibility of withdrawal of the stimulus is limited when large projects are involved and which must be brought to completion to produce intended results.
- Such spending can be counterproductive in terms of its

impact on the economy if it is not accompanied by a credible plan to restore fiscal rectitude so as to avoid adverse or negative effects in the financial markets.

These and other arguments must be taken seriously if fiscal stimulus measures are to have their intended effects. Needless to say, it is not possible to generalize across the many countries that have adopted such policies, nor has there been sufficient time to assess the impact of most of the packages that have been announced and are being implemented. But there are some negative signs already emerging that must be taken seriously and, to the extent possible, used to adapt policies already announced or even in place to counter the potential negative effects. Many of the stimulus packages have focused on infrastructure. There can be no doubt that almost all countries are in need of sometimes substantial investment in infrastructure to improve the growth prospects of their economies. However, those projects with long planning horizons and long gestation periods must be kept under review to avoid a situation in which such projects inappropriately crowd out private spending as a recovery begins to take hold. To the extent such projects are judged to be worth pursuing, consideration should be given to raising taxes to pay for them.

Even more important, plans must be elaborated for the withdrawal of stimulus: tentative plans to cancel or phase out projects, plans to increase taxes to better marry the size of the stimulus to the needs of the economy as recovery takes hold. Credible plans to wind down and reverse the stimulus and to restore long term, sustainable fiscal positions should be elaborated. This last point is worth emphasizing in light of the enormous financing demands that are going to emerge from the measures already announced by so many countries. The financial tensions emerging in the debt markets cannot be permitted to intensify to the point where they begin to crowd out emerging private activity that will be needed to sustain any recovery. As noted earlier in the paper, this is already becoming an issue. In the recent downgrades and lowered outlooks announced by the credit rating agencies, the "...fiscal deterioration associated with providing support for their respective economies ..." has been highlighted. The impact on interest rates and on the receptivity of markets to debt auctions is already becoming evident.

None of this argues for premature withdrawal of the stimulus that is needed to help foster a sustainable recovery in many countries and in the global system. The lessons from the reversal of policies in the United States in 1937 and in the similar experience of other countries need to be remembered. However, the markets will need to be continuously reassured that these policies are temporary and that they will be adjusted to the needs of the economy as their impact begins to be felt. This is also an argument for better global coordination of these policies. The markets that fund sovereign debt are global and the policies that affect the behavior of participants in those markets must be globally coordinated and consistent.

Conclusion

Some of the causes of the current crisis are clear. These include the failure to correct the global imbalances that ballooned in the years leading up to the crisis; the absence of the needed degree of transparency in financial markets; the failures of national regulatory and supervisory systems and the absence of sufficient mechanisms for international regulatory coordination; the failures to prevent the emergence of perverse incentives in the financial system, especially in mortgage markets in the United States; the willingness of senior people in the banks and other financial institutions to accept financial innovations and instruments that even they now admit they did not understand. And there are many others.

In general terms, the lessons to be learned are implicit in the causes. But there is a great deal more that needs to be done to translate the lessons into specific measures that will have the power to correct the practices that got the world into this mess–and that has been so costly both to societies and to so many individuals. The measures needed will affect both domestic agencies and international organizations.

Discussion in this Forum can make an important contribution to the ongoing debate about preventing another crisis of the nature and magnitude now confronting the entire world. In addition to the three questions elaborated above, other questions that would be worth discussing include the following:

1. Have the emerging market countries decoupled from the industrial world to any significant degree 1. or have the two groups, on the contrary, become even more mutually dependent on each other? Is "decoupling" - framed as a proposition about the linkages between the major industrial countries and the emerging market countries - even a useful concept any longer? Are not the inter-linkages between the larger emerging market countries – China, Brazil, India and others – becoming analytically and empirically just as relevant?
2. What are the prospects that the macroeconomic structures in key countries that led to the global imbalances of the last decade – and helped bring about the current crisis, will change with a recovery in those countries, avoiding a return to another unsustainable pattern of growth?
3. Related to this, can the emerging market countries succeed in stimulating their domestic economies, i.e., by structurally increasing domestic demand, if growth in the industrial countries remain as weak, or even weaker, than projected?
4. What are the prospects for access by the emerging market countries to global credit and capital markets given the continued deleveraging that is likely to occur in major financial institutions and the possibility that they will be crowded out of the debt markets by sovereign borrowers facing the need to finance unprecedented fiscal deficits and to roll over existing debt?
5. Is protectionism a serious threat? Is it possible that the

authorities in countries adopting such measures are carefully responding to the inevitable political demands for protection in a recessionary environment while not doing much that could threaten a recovery of trade?

Source: www.emergingmarketsforum.org.
©Emerging Markets Forum. Reprinted with Permission.

The Emerging Markets Forum is a not-for-profit venture of the Centennial Group, a Washington based strategic advisory firm specializing in emerging market economies. The Forum was created to allow senior political and corporate leaders and public servants to reach actionable conclusions on economic, political and social issues facing emerging market economies. The agenda for the Forum is driven by the priorities of the emerging market countries

Jack Boorman is Member of the Advisory Board of the Emerging Markets Forum; Former Director of the Policy Development and Review Department, and Former Counselor and Special Advisor to the Managing Director, International Monetary Fund.

Notes

1. That pattern has now been reversed with emerging stock markets significantly outperforming advanced county markets since the beginning of this year.
2. In Asia, remittances are expected to fall by almost 30 percent this year to US$ 95 billion from the peak of over US$ 130 billion reached in 2008, but to rebound to about US$ 115 billion in 2010. The countries in the region that are the largest recipients of remittances (India, China, the Philippines, Vietnam, Bangladesh and Pakistan) will see flows decline from over US$ 123 billion in 2008 to less than US$ 90 billion in 2009. A recovery to about US$ 107 billion is forecast for 2010.
3. The recent actions taken by Latvia to reduce its budget deficit, in large part through sharp cuts in spending, constitute one of the most dramatic examples of such policies.
4. The OECD estimates that its member governments will issue almost US$ 12 trillion in debt (gross) in 2009, about one-third more than the US$ 9 trillion issued two years ago. The U.S. alone is expected to sell almost US$ 8 trillion in government securities. There have already been some troubling signs in

government debt markets in the industrial countries: a failed issue by Germany earlier in the year; a recent sharp uptick in the 10 year bond rate in the United States and a generally poor reception to the government's 10-year bond auction which saw an unusual yield markup on issue. In the market for U.S. debt in particular, there is an additional threat of "roll-over risk" as the average maturity of government debt is only about 4.7 years – unusually short by industrial country standards. In the emerging market countries, there are troubling signs as well. There was a failed auction by Latvia of US$ 100 million in short term treasury bills in early June; and warnings have been issued by some of the rating agencies over the creditworthiness of some Asian countries, including the lowering of outlooks for India and Taiwan from stable to negative by Standard and Poor's and a cut in Malaysia's long term local currency rating from A-plus to A by Fitch.

5. These measures do not include "automatic" increases in agricultural protection, contingent protection (e.g., anti-dumping), WTO-sanctioned measures to retaliate against trading partners that have not complied with findings of a WTO dispute settlement pancl, or financial sector subsidies. Antidumping cases surged in 2008, with initiations rising by 15 percent and findings with imposition duties growing by 22 percent. India is the most active, accounting for 29 percent of total initiations. See Trade Protection: Incipient but Worrisome Trends, Elisa Gamberoni and Richard New farmer, in Trade Notes, Number 37, The World Bank, March, 2009.
6. Some of the original arguments about decoupling rested on the ever-increasing trade among the emerging market economies themselves. But much of this trade reflected the fundamental shift that was occurring in the locus of manufacturing – the supply chain – in the global economy. Much of that trade between the emerging market economies–and, indeed, even between the industrial and emerging market economies–reflected the specialization of manufacturing in different countries on inputs and components that were then shipped elsewhere for further processing and assembly before shipment to the final user. In many ways, this led to an increase in the inter-linkages between economies rather than a reduction. Interestingly, this increased interdependence through supply

chains may have helped limit the protectionist response of some countries to the downturn in the global economy as export interests are relatively much more powerful than before in many countries.

7. That outcome would appear quite likely – at least for a number of years, as a structural shift appears to be taking place in the saving habits of individuals in response to the significant decline in asset values that has occurred. The assumption that saving out of current income was unnecessary as wealth could more painlessly be accumulated through ownership of houses and other real assets has been severely tested and found wanting. It is no coincidence that the highest net debt to GDP ratios in the U.S. were registered just before the depression of the 1930's and just before the current crisis. In the earlier episode, the saving rate increased, and debt levels fell, for a long period after the depression.
8. There is an interesting contrast between the U.S. and Canada as regards the regulation of the mortgage market. In the U.S., interest payments (within generous limits) are deductable from federal income taxes; minimum required down payments all but disappeared during the housing boom that began in the mid 1980's; mortgage originators were not required to hold on their own books any part of the mortgages they created. The vast majority of mortgages ended up being bundled into securitized instruments, further distancing the debtor from the ultimate creditor; and most mortgages were written with variable interest rates, many with "teaser" initial rates. Many of these policies and practices were introduced or endorsed as a means of encouraging home ownership in the United States. By contrast, in Canada, none of these policies or practices was permitted. But the results in the two countries are remarkable. In recent years, the home ownership rate in the U.S. reached a peak of 68.4 percent of the population. In Canada, the rate has been around 68 percent! Canadian banks, now amongst the largest in the world, have suffered virtually no mortgage related losses in the current crisis. There is surely a lesson here!
9. "Lessons of the Financial Crisis for Future Regulation of Financial Institutions and Markets and for Liquidity Management", International Monetary Fund, February 4, 2009.
10. An important question regarding the IMF needs to be addressed

in this connection: was one of the motivations for the large reserve accumulation that took place in so many emerging market countries motivated, at least in part, by a lack of trust in the institution? The IMF is, among its other functions, intended to be the global reserve-pooling organization. Why have the emerging market countries felt the need to insure themselves through the accumulation of their own excessively large holdings of reserves? Some of this has to do with the experiences of those countries that fell into crises over the past two decades in dealing with the IMF; some of it had to do with the increasing stigma that became attached to borrowing from the institution; some of it may have come from the perception – and reality! – that the resources available to the IMF were not nearly sufficient to the needs of 21st century global financial markets; and some of it may have been the result of a growing disparity in the IMF between the economic and financial place of these countries in the global system and their place in the governance structure of the IMF. Hopefully, the reforms recently made in the IMF and those that are now under discussion will fundamentally change the institution in a way that will permit all countries to see it as a trusted partner in the event of a need for financial support.

11. It is also likely that the existence of these claims—in the form of obligations to foreign holders of US treasury bills and agency securities—led to second best policy choices by the U.S. government in deciding on actions to deal with certain aspects of the recent financial crisis.
12. See Jack Boorman, "Global Governance and Reform of the International Monetary Fund: An Update", Emerging Markets Forum, Mumbai, India, June 24, 2009.
13. Declaration: Summit on Financial Markets and the World Economy, November 15, 2008.

5

The Multilateral Response to the Global Crisis: Rationale, Modalities and Feasibility

Eduardo Fernández-Arias, Andrew Powell and Alessandro Rebucci

1. Introduction

To respond successfully to the ongoing global economic crisis, emerging economies require significant multilateral assistance. Several countries in emerging Europe are already in "crisis resolution" mode, and assistance is now focused on containing the fallout, but for much of Latin America and the Caribbean (LAC) there is still time for "active prevention" to pay significant dividends. But the challenges remain large; the total public sector borrowing requirements of the seven largest economies of LAC are estimated at some US$ 640 billion for 2009-2010, while these countries' international gross reserves stood at about US$ 450 billion at end June 2008 (IDB, 2009a). Given strong trade linkages with the epicenter of the crisis (the United States and Europe), emerging Asia's position is arguably at least as fragile as that of LAC, but confidence is underpinned in Asia by Japan's and China's reserve position.

Moreover, as widely discussed after the Asian crisis, emerging economies are more constrained in terms of their monetary, fiscal and lender of last resort responses than their industrialized country counterparts. [1] It is almost a definition of being emerging that domestic government bonds are not seen as a riskless asset, especially in these circumstances. As the probability of a crisis at home rises, money tends to flow out of the economy to foreign assets as investors, particularly larger and more sophisticated ones, seek a perceived safe haven. This implies countercyclical monetary policy, especially through the direct use of the central bank balance sheet. Such a policy, however, as currently being undertaken in advanced economies, may well de-anchor inflation expectations. [2] It also implies a sharper trade-off between financial stability and monetary stability, as injections of liquidity to the financial system may simply fuel capital flight, causing exchange rate depreciation and monetary instability. This in turn implies that financing a countercyclical fiscal policy will become increasingly expensive and risky as domestic interest rates rise, maturities shorten and more debt is issued in foreign currency - assuming such markets even remain open. International reserves could be used instead, but only at the cost of exercising the insurance option they represent, and hence at the risk of higher probability of a sudden stop or a currency crisis run down the road. At the limit, sole reliance on domestic policy tools at the individual country level may well result in a worsening of the situation rather than ameliorating it.

Discussion continues as to the true source of the current crisis. However, whether it is considered microeconomic in nature and related to a sequence of regulatory failures in the world's financial system, or fundamentally a macroeconomic phenomenon related to global imbalances feeding a housing boom and financial bubbles, it is clear that this crisis did not start in emerging economies. Moreover, the crisis is global and may well be prolonged. If there is a sharp V-shape recovery, the pain will most certainly be less. However, in the midst of wide uncertainty among analysts, it looks increasingly plausible that the recovery may be slower: at least a "U" if not the extremely worrisome "L". To the extent that core financial markets are not performing well, emerging economies may find it increasingly difficult to roll over both public and private sector liabilities. While financing a fiscal deficit or investment is a flow issue, rolling over outstanding liabilities is a problem of stocks. The more prolonged the crisis in financial markets, the greater the concern that emerging economies will have to deal with their stocks of liabilities, and the greater the adjustment that will be required if that cannot be achieved. In somewhat similar vein to the Asian crisis, such a problem would be the counterpart of a quintessential Sudden Stop. [3]

Nonetheless, there remains the conviction that individual countries are able (and ought to be able) to weather the storm alone, and this conviction is held both among certain quarters of the international policy community and, above all, among emerging economy officials themselves. On the one hand, it is often argued that countries should have done more to prepare themselves for a rainy day, and on the other hand there is extreme reluctance to seek early assistance from the IMF on the part of national authorities in many countries. These views are both contradictory and shortsighted. It is difficult to argue that in good times individual countries should have accumulated reserves sufficient to self-insure against the possibility of a systemic event like the crisis that has materialized—and if they had done so, they surely would surely have been accused of pursuing mercantilist exchange rate policies. Moreover, self-insurance is a second-best option relative to insurance through international cooperation. Similarly, the reluctance to enter into a precautionary arrangement with the IMF under the current circumstances is akin to a troupe of trapeze artists deciding not to have a safety net for fear that the circus manager will assume they do not have the requisite skill. [4]

However, it is also the case that emerging economies are highly heterogeneous. We suggest below a broad working categorization. Based on this scheme, we suggest the types of multilateral support that should be made available. We argue below that there should be two overarching objectives for multilateral support. The first is to reduce the likelihood of a country suffering a Sudden Stop in capital flows and hence a deep crisis as a reaction to the stock adjustment problem. The second is to maximize the number of countries that might safely pursue some type of countercyclical fiscal policy as called for by the G20. The greater the number of countries that pursue such a policy, the more effective such policies become, as at the limit the "leakage" from a global package is zero. Moreover, we suggest a division of labor between the International Monetary Fund and Multilateral Development Banks in providing multilateral support.

The paper is organized as follows. In Section 2, we review the case for a strong multilateral response to the global crisis in emerging markets (EMs), and in Section 3 we discuss modalities of intervention and associated risks. The specific role of Multilateral Development Banks is discussed in Section 4. The question of the financial feasibility of such a multilateral response is dealt with in Section 5. The paper concludes with a discussion of the international financial architecture issues raised by the global crisis that cannot be addressed immediately but will need to be dealt with once the current crisis has been tamed.

2. Why Should Multilaterals Intervene?

The rationale for multilateral intervention in response to the global crisis in emerging markets is now fairly well understood. Nonetheless, opposition to a forceful and assertive response is still strong, both in certain quarters of the international policy community and in some individual countries. This is evidenced by the relatively late and limited financial resources with which potential creditor countries have come forth in supporting multilateral financial institutions, as well as the reluctance with which emerging countries have requested access to those resources. It is therefore worthwhile to review the case before discussing the modalities and risks of such intervention.

2.1 Limits of Traditional Policy Instruments: As private sector financial institutions hoard liquidity and investors seek the perceived safety of US government liabilities, there are severe financing constraints on emerging economies' policy responses to the crisis. The optimal response to the crisis in an emerging economy is similar in nature to the one of more advanced economies. However, while the United States faces its most severe financial crisis since the Great Depression, funding costs for the US Government have actually fallen. Other advanced countries enjoy a similar position, albeit to a lesser extent. But this is not the case in EMs. In general, EMs are facing higher interest rates on domestic government debt and higher spreads over risk-free rates than before the crisis, and both are significantly higher than in industrialized economies.

An interesting apparent exception is Chile. At least initially, after the collapse of Lehmann Brothers, when the crisis truly became global there appeared to be a flight to quality within Chile towards domestic Government bonds in local currency and in local currency indexed to inflation. Rates on domestic bonds actually fell. Of course Chile is an outlier in Latin America in several respects, most notably for its low level of public sector debt and the large magnitude of Central Bank and fiscal reserves constituted in foreign assets. Indeed it might be argued that this flight to domestic public sector assets is the antithesis of being an emerging economy, and it is tempting to suggest a new answer to the old question of the optimal level of reserves: namely, the level that leads to a response to crisis such as seen in Chile. As we argue above, however, it would be grossly inefficient for all countries to maintain such a level of reserves. Nonetheless, while not optimal for all, Chile's case does illustrate the potential power of unconditional access to a large stock of reserves under the current circumstances.

2.1.1 Fiscal Policy: In most cases it is not feasible to respond to the crisis with fiscal stimulus, let alone with quasi-fiscal credit support policies, without multilateral support. Even countries with sustainable fiscal policies might still face a relevant trade-off between expansionary policies and liquidity considerations. As we noted above, only a handful of emerging economies may be strong enough both from a fiscal sustainability and international liquidity perspective to pursue expansionary fiscal policies without risk. In fact, in some countries, fiscal adjustment as opposed to fiscal stimulus may be the "optimal" policy response to the crisis—particularly in the absence of a multilateral backstop because, under certain conditions, a fiscal contraction can be expansionary (Giavazzi and Pagano, 1989).

To fix ideas, consider the potential impact of two alternative fiscal policies in a country with no fiscal sustainability problems: one neutral towards the business cycle (i.e., no changes in either government expenditures or tax rates in response to recessionary pressures), and the other countercyclical (i.e., a rise in government expenditures and/or a reduction in tax rates). Since active fiscal policy will in principle imply a larger deterioration of the fiscal deficit, this deficit will add to the gross financing needs of the country, possibly affecting negatively the maturity and cost of this financing, i.e., shorter terms and higher rates. Therefore, a countercyclical fiscal policy implies deterioration in liquidity ratios relative to the neutral fiscal policy stance (IDB, 2009a), and even countries with sizable international reserves to back these policies would find it risky to use a sizable portion of their self-insurance policy.

Other countries in the region, may not even have the luxury of considering these tradeoffs, or can only do so at substantially higher downside risks. In fact, given the pro-cyclical fiscal policies pursued in many countries during the expansionary phase of the 2000s (on average LAC-7 countries increased public expenditures by 80 cents out of every additional dollar of revenue between 2003 and 2007, as discussed in IDB, 2008), pursuing a countercyclical policy during the downturn, which implies raising expenditures even further, may imply exponential debt dynamics, creating fiscal sustainability problems. In these cases countercyclical fiscal policies should simply not be an option (or may well be an option that becomes very costly ex post), unless there is a credible commitment to tighter fiscal discipline in the future. [5]

Of course, other forms of shoring up future fiscal discipline would also serve the same purpose of relaxing the fiscal sustainability constraint. For example, there is evidence in G7 countries that discretionary counter-cyclical policy is asymmetric and generates debt bias, while automatic stabilizers such as unemployment insurance do not (IMF, 2008). The reason is that automatic stabilizers are temporary but discretionary policy tends not be rolled over after the downturn. It is important to introduce automat city in fiscal policy (contingent rules) so that discipline becomes more credible. More generally, addressing some of the long-term imbalances such as a deficit in social security would also help to shore up sustainability and open more space for fiscal action in the downturn.

2.1.2 Monetary Policy: Most emerging market countries are today better positioned than in the past to allow the exchange rate to absorb the initial impact of the global crisis. For instance, the "fear-of-floating" coefficient in the monetary policy rule of many emerging markets has decreased significantly in most countries (Ortiz, Ottonello and Sturzenegger, 2009). This is partly related to smaller foreign exchange exposures, but also to the monetary policy credibility acquired through the implementation of flexible inflation targeting regimes for more than a decade. Indeed, in the same sample of countries, the speed with which central banks react to shocks (which is inversely related to measures of commitment to a given monetary policy stance) decreased significantly in most of the countries that recently adopted an inflation targeting regime.

The greater policy flexibility at the onset of the crisis is important. Past experience suggests that initial conditions are crucial in terms of the policy flexibility necessary to minimize the likelihood of, or mitigate the impact of, sudden stops on economic activity (Cavallo and Izquierdo, 2009). Both theory (e.g., Benigno et al., 2009; and Braggion, Christiano, and Roldos, 2005) and new evidence (Ortiz, Ottonello and Sturzenegger, 2009) show that the ability to pursue expansionary monetary policies in periods of financial turmoil can reduce the size of output contractions. A flexible exchange rate response would have several additional benefits in addition to leaving more room for other uses of scarce international reserves. First, it would prevent the loss of market share in the context in which downward pressure on the nominal exchange rate is global. Second, it may help contain the deflationary impact of commodity price decline in those cases in which deflation pressure were to emerge (Catão and Chang, 2009).

Nevertheless, exchange rate flexibility is not a silver bullet. Unlike in previous episodes of country-specific Sudden Stops, this is a global event. Not all countries can depreciate, and the global nature of the present shock means that devaluations may not have significant expansionary effects even in the absence of adverse balance sheet effects. For most EMs, even if a flexible exchange rate response could be effected the economy would need an additional policy instrument to help contain the output gap opened up by the external shock.

Indeed, the nature of the shock imposes an important constraint. First, the global nature of the Sudden Stop faced by emerging capital markets and the concern regarding financial systems across the globe limits the use of the financial system as a vehicle for countercyclical monetary policy. Banks in many emerging countries are currently holding large amounts of liquidity and are unlikely to respond to a reduction in interest rates to expand credit as in normal times. Similarly, a reduction in liquidity or reserve requirements is also likely to be met by even higher levels of liquidity rather than increases in credit. [6] Moreover, to the extent to which the shock faced by emerging markets has a permanent component (i.e., deleveraging is not temporary), a monetary policy response that aims at preserving the pre-shock equilibrium would not be desirable either. In some countries, however, lowering benchmark interest rates might support valuations of riskier assets and also lower the total cost of borrowing for households and firms, and hence ultimately contain the likelihood of generalized insolvency. Through this channel, monetary policy can contribute effectively toward containing the negative spillovers from the real sector to the financial sector of the economy (Mishkin, 2009). However, this potential benefit must be weighed against the potential risk of the effect of lower interest rates on capital flows.

A second limit is imposed by the risk of losing credibility by attempting to use directly the central bank balance sheet in domestic currency to respond to the shock. A powerful additional instrument through which central banks in advanced economies are responding to the crisis is the direct use of their balance sheet to substitute for markets and intermediaries that are impaired, so-called quantitative easing. This means lending directly in domestic currency, and in a potentially unlimited manner, to the private sector, as opposed to loosening the funding conditions of the core domestic financial system through price signals to implement a more accommodative monetary stance. A key challenge to implementing such a policy is how to prevent inflation expectations from running out of control; and the risk of de-anchoring inflation expectations is much higher in emerging markets because of weaker policy institutions and their past histories of monetary instability. In emerging markets, therefore, aggressive quantitative easing in domestic currency would inevitably set off inflationary expectations, thus squandering their recently hard-won inflation-fighting credibility, and thereby fuelling a flight to safer currencies. In emerging markets, quantitative easing (or more conventionally called, lending of last resort) must therefore be conducted in hard currency, using either own or borrowed reserves (Calvo, 2009). [7]

Most inflation-targeting central banks outside emerging Europe have lowered their reference rate in line with inflation, which is declining globally. Unlike in the more advanced economies, as inflation subsides, there may be room for emerging central banks to seek additional interest rate reductions within inflation-targeting frameworks. Indeed, recent analyses of optimal policy in the presence of financial frictions suggest that a tightening of domestic financial market conditions should be met by responding more than normally to the output gap (e.g., Cúrdia and Woodford, 2008). Naturally, a central bank must weigh the case for such a reduction against the potential for capital flight and exchange rate instability when this is a constraint on the monetary policy framework.

2.2 Benefits of Multilateral Intervention: Having reviewed the limits to individual countries' ability to respond to the global crisis, we now move on to discuss the possible global benefits of a multilaterally supported response. Countercyclical multilateral lending is needed to sustain access to external finance after excessive market retrenchment. In so doing, multilateral intervention bridges short-term financing needs and covers liquidity risks while the temporary market disruption lasts. This kind of intervention contains the damage to fundamentals that a full-blown liquidity crisis would provoke and relaxes the constraints on national policies facing the downturn. For example, multilateral intervention may back up international reserves, freeing them for policy uses or directly financing countercyclical fiscal policy.

Apart from partially offsetting the external shock suffered by each country and empowering domestic policies, multilateral intervention addresses systemic dimensions that are crucial in a global crisis. First, providing abundant multilateral financing to respond to the crisis is desirable from both the individual country viewpoint and, especially, the global perspective. As long as the international trade regime remains open, there are positive externalities from sustaining aggregate demand. Moreover, the growth payoff from fiscal stimulus rises with the number of countries adopting it as, at the limit, there is no loss of effectiveness due to international spillover from a global package. While the total demand from emerging countries may be small, emerging countries tend to have larger marginal propensities to consume out of income and hence fiscal stimulus packages may be more effective. Emerging countries also have higher propensities to import, and hence leakages may be higher, but if many countries pursue such packages this problem is reduced. In fact, such leakages imply that in particular the advanced countries will be helped. It is therefore better to err on the side of too much financing rather than too much adjustment under the current circumstances. Interestingly, unlike the traditional case for unilateral free trade, protectionist fiscal packages, at the limit the failure to enact fiscal stimulus policies on account of import leakages, may be in the interest of individual countries. This reinforces the need for multilateral institutions to guard against protectionism even in the best-run economies.

Second, even if positive spillovers from financial stimulus were negligible, the threat of large negative spillovers as a result of the global economic crisis is credible and imminent, as the Great Depression experience teaches and as recent country initiatives highlight. Pressures to raise trade protectionism and competitive devaluations in a deflated world economy are rising and may lead to a global trade war that spirals out of control (World Bank, 2009). Protectionism rises as a countercyclical domestic policy response to the crisis as an attempt to increase domestic demand and production. In a global recession, such a policy response is globally disastrous but may be individually beneficial. Multilaterals can fight this on two fronts. First, they can offer financing to support individual economies as well as the global trade system. Second, they can make financing in situations of outright crisis conditional on avoiding such disruptive policy responses. There is a strong argument for action through multilateral institutions able to internalize international spillovers.

Multilaterals have an opportunity to oppose protectionism in fiscal policy in this global recession and at the same time encourage, and finance, stimulus packages that would be otherwise discarded or scaled back by national authorities because boosted demand "leaks out" of the domestic economy. This is also an opportunity for multilaterals to coordinate global stimulus action. From the point of view of an individual country, a stimulus package that restricts spending to products with high domestic value added (in other words, impedes spending on imports) has a higher GDP-multiplier and can be presumed to be more beneficial in terms of GDP reactivation (despite its inefficiency, like that of any other trade barrier). This would be appropriate for a national recession but not in the case of a global recession like the present one, because the reactivation of depressed GDP in the rest of the world is equally valuable from a global perspective.

Multilaterals should also be mindful of the potential for policy reform backsliding due to instability and defend against that possibility. The international community should be mindful of rewarding the good policies implemented in the past by now helping to avoid unwarranted external adjustments at a time of global recession that may erode the economic or political basis for supporting reforms. Nonetheless, in many countries macroeconomic policies have been insufficiently countercyclical during the boom years to create the necessary space to respond quickly and effectively to the global economic downturn. Similarly, multilateral conditionality in these cases can help assure that policy interventions that may be beneficial in the short term do not become important obstacles to the resumption of income and productivity growth in the medium to long term, as illustrated by IDB (2009b).

3. How Should Multilaterals Intervene?

In the current phase of the downturn, there is a premium on fast and decisive action. A consensus has emerged that a lack of confidence and heightened uncertainty about systemic risk is leading to a collapse of global economic activity and international trade. It is therefore paramount to move aggressively and quickly to short-circuit the negative feedback loop from tighter global financial conditions to a deeper world recession. Moreover, acting sooner rather than later is desirable also in light of the fact that traditional lending countries in the multilateral lending institutions are facing daunting challenges in managing their own fiscal responses to the crisis, as well as in light of the political backlash against financial sector support programs. The situation has already reached a point at which the domestic fiscal needs of advanced economies may soon start to crowd out possibilities for supporting emerging countries.

A first important role of multilateral intervention is to provide a backstop for liquidity or lender of last resort; see Calvo (2009) for a recent note on the issue. A traditional counterargument is that this may provoke moral hazard. Several papers, however, argue that this is not necessarily the case. Morris and Shin (2003) and Corsetti, Guimarães and Roubini (2006) suggest that, in the presence of appropriate fiscal policy, a lender of last resort providing sufficient liquidity can prevent a bad "run-equilibrium" and therefore increase rather than reduce the incentives for that "appropriate" fiscal policy. [8] Arozemena and Powell (2003) develop a repeated game, and show that assuming a lender of last resort can punish countries by removing its backstop, an equilibrium is supported with no moral hazard but with liquidity protection that prevents "runs" from occurring. [9] An interesting feature of all these theoretical models is that the lender of last resort does not actually have to disburse. The access to the backstop allows countries to roll over debt in private markets, eradicating the necessity for actual disbursements.

A second counterargument is that risky debt appears for a reason, hence multilateral involvement must attempt to replace the discipline of shortening maturities for something else (Jeanne, 2008). In the context of the current crisis, the higher probability of a run (that is discipline) does not reflect a country's poor behavior so much as the global context, hence it shows the limits of discipline when the shock is systemic. In a similar vein, D'Amato, Grubisic and Powell (1997) and Levy-Yeyati, Peria and Schmukler (2009) both suggest market discipline has a limit in banking when shocks are systemic.

A second role for multilaterals is to help provide global fiscal stimulus while at the same time preventing an increased risk of liquidity problems or preventing the liquidity difficulties experienced over the past several months from turning into solvency issues, which would be much harder to resolve.

At the same time, the fundamentals of the current global slowdown may themselves raise solvency questions. The possible permanence of some of the changes observed, such as a drop in unsustainably high world growth and the anticipated deleveraging in global financial markets, has structural, non-cyclical implications that call for adjustment to a lower-growth, medium-term equilibrium. The provision of financing without regard for needed adjustment would increase required adjustment down the road and backfire.

International financial institutions then have multiple roles in the current circumstances, and the particular role to be played will depend on the situation in a specific country. These roles include (a) backstopping liquidity; (b) providing long-term finance, particularly for financing countercyclical fiscal policies and/or protecting particular fiscal expenditures (thereby altering the composition of fiscal expenditure); and (c) facilitating fiscal adjustment. In what follows we suggest a categorization of countries to describe the potential roles of multilaterals in each. The two over-arching objectives of support are first to reduce the likelihood of a crisis and second to attempt to maximize the number of countries that might contribute to the global efforts towards fiscal stimulus. A third objective we consider important is ensuring that fiscal and expenditure policies are appropriately designed.

A. A country with no liquidity problems (high reserves and/or assured normal access to credit): In a case of financial self-sufficiency, the country may implement appropriate domestic policies without multilateral support. In practice, the absence of liquidity problems in this crisis is in all likelihood accompanied by a fiscal situation with enough space to consider countercyclical fiscal and quasi-fiscal policies, as opposed to the need for fiscal retrenchment or adjustment to maintain fiscal sustainability. In such cases multilaterals should insist on non-protectionist stimulus packages but not actually intervene in order to preserve resources for the other cases listed below.

B. A country with fiscal space but potential liquidity problems: Some countries may be considered to have fiscal space to enact a countercyclical fiscal policy from a solvency perspective but face a high cost of borrowing and have liquidity concerns (potentially insufficient reserves and a debt structure that does not eliminate liquidity risks). In these cases multilaterals may play at least two important roles. First, they may provide long-term financing (or guarantees such that countries can finance long-term) to improve countries' debt maturity structure and reduce liquidity risks. This is particularly important to finance any fiscal stimulus in such a way that the country's liquidity position does not deteriorate. Second, multilaterals may provide a back stop to reserves essentially augmenting access to international liquidity. In relation to the Guidotti-Greenspan rule, all else equal, this would serve to reduce the denominator (the amount of liabilities coming due in one year) and increase the numerator (the stock of international reserves) respectively, while enabling the country to produce a strong countercyclical response (Fernandez-Arias and Montiel, 2009). Multilateral development banks (MDBs) currently provide longer-term financing, and so their comparative advantage is in relation to the first role. The second role is a natural one for the IMF to play, and for a country with fiscal space it is likely that there would be access to the new Flexible Credit Line (FCL) or a high access precautionary program. [10] In this case, multilateral intervention would have no strings attached to the fiscal policy package being financed other than ensuring that the package is not protectionist and is aligned with the multilateral effort being coordinated.

C. A country with no fiscal space and potential liquidity problems: Unfortunately, many emerging countries simply do not have the fiscal space to effect a countercyclical fiscal policy, and indeed they should be deterred from doing so. In fact, several countries may need to adjust fiscal policy to reduce deficits given the negative impact of the global crisis on the prices of key exports and the resulting decline in fiscal revenues. In these cases multilaterals may again provide a backstop to reserves and longer-term financing, but this should be offered on the basis of the typical "no-new-debt rule." In other words, multilateral financing should replace rather than add to market debt. In the case of countries where adjustment is required, multilateral financing may help with the fulfillment of public sector borrowing requirements in order to avoid the costs of abrupt adjustment, but within a framework designed to reduce fragility and regain fiscal sustainability. This implies agreed-upon budget envelopes that permit gradual adjustment to a new medium-term budget equilibrium. Indeed, support should be non-precautionary, with ex post conditionality under this modality.

Again providing a back stop to reserves is a natural role for the IMF. Countries in this category would not qualify for the FCL, but most would be advised to seek a traditional Stand By facility. The IMF is also the agency charged with assessing the fiscal situation and advising on the macroeconomic adjustment effort that may be required. MDBs again have a comparative advantage in supplying long-term development financing and should work with countries to ensure that resources are employed as efficiently and effectively as possible. For example, they focus on the development effectiveness of public investment and development policy as well as structural reforms fostering growth and fiscal discipline. Furthermore, expenditures that protect vulnerable groups should be maintained as far as is feasible.

D. A country with more serious sustainability problems: A smaller set of emerging countries have more serious issues in relation to the sustainability of policies given debt levels. The current crisis is putting countries in this category in an extremely difficult position. At some point the question may become whether to adjust fiercely or combine a smaller adjustment with a debt restructuring. This places multilaterals in a difficult position. Should they lend to countries that may face a debt restructuring, or should they hold off—which would most likely force the restructuring to occur? The lack of a framework in the current international financial architecture for countries to restructure debts akin to corporate debt restructurings (such as Chapter 11 in the United States) tends to make multilaterals very reluctant to cease financing. However, at some point the restructuring may become inevitable, and in general it is optimal to restructure early rather than delay. Moreover, if core financial markets are closed in any event, restructuring may not imply severe short-term costs. In any event, it is clear that multilateral intervention in a country with solvency problems needs to provide for both an agreed framework for fiscal adjustment and potential debt restructuring.

In summary, in a phase of impending downturn, heavy ex-post conditionality is not warranted except for insolvency cases in which there are few incentives to use additional liquidity productively. In these cases, traditional ex post conditionality is still justified to ensure the effectiveness of the financial support to countries. Other than that, financing should be made available on the basis of ex-ante conditionality under the liberal concepts of "good performer" and "sustainable framework." The gain from advancing the reform agenda through conditionality (extracting a conditionality concession in exchange of support) pales in comparison with the risk of impeding the success of swift crisis support through delay or lack of cooperation.

Implicit ex ante conditionality is appropriate. To reward past good policies, multilaterals should lend more and more freely than in the past, provided that such support should be accompanied by appropriate monitoring to ensure that policies remain on track and support is productive (Jeanne, Ostry, and Zettelmeyer, 2008). Countries with sizable debts that are able to commit to policies of fiscal discipline in the future and save in the subsequent boom phase of the cycle should receive higher levels of financing on account of their enhanced fiscal sustainability. In that case, additional financing could be attached to conditions that preserve and enhance medium term sustainability.

One exception, however, is the condition that all types of multilateral financial support must go exclusively to countries that refrain from protectionist measures. This blanket condition is justified because, in the context of a global crisis, protectionism to safeguard local demand may be in each country's individual interest, but at the expense of the collective good. So the effort would be geared toward preventing the adoption of measures disruptive of the international prosperity.

Indeed, the recent change in the IMF's lending toolkit goes precisely in this direction. And perhaps even too much in this direction, as in practice it will be difficult to differentiate conditionality across member countries, while some cases would still benefit from the commitment device provided by traditional ex post conditionality.

4. What is the Specific Role of Multilateral Development Banks?

By virtue of their countercyclical lending at medium and long-term maturities, MDBs play a supporting role to the

IMF's pivotal role of backstopping liquidity. In fact, in small countries, MDBs can also aim at covering balance of payments and general budget support, including funding domestic financial intermediation, at a systemic level. Besides this supporting role, however, MDBs have specific roles concerning the development effectiveness of multilateral financing.

A strategic objective of MDBs is helping to design appropriate expenditure composition policies and, when warranted, expenditure-increasing policies in order to protect social programs and enhance medium-term productivity growth. [11] For example, a specific objective of MDBs is to protect the tremendous social progress of the past several years by providing targeted financial support for the most effective social protection programs. Such an effort is crucial in helping to make prudent economic policies politically sustainable until the world economy becomes more stable and resumes growing. MDB activity in these areas can also help to avoid perverse incentives, particularly in the labor market, that may increase informality, with negative implications for medium-term growth. Another priority area is infrastructure investment, as protecting large national investment programs may provide additional automatic stabilization to the economy during the downturn and can also set the stage for a smooth recovery once demand resumes growing globally. These objectives apply not only to the national government but also to sub-national governments.

MDBs should also focus on development-oriented structural reforms through policy based loans. These include policy and institutional reform aimed at fostering productivity and growth in the private sector as well as the reform of the State to better fulfill its development role, including fiscal discipline. For example, MDBs can help ensure that "transitory" measures, such as quasi-fiscal credit policies, are credibly transitory. More generally, MDBs would focus on the reform of fiscal institutions to ensure fiscal discipline and soundness in support of development objectives. While the IMF is the agency in charge of monitoring the budget envelope in the short run, MDBs should focus on reforms that would generate better frameworks for fiscal policy. Finally, MDBs may also be effective partners of bilateral donors who want to help achieve critical mass coordinating around an overall plan to address cyclical financial needs or other sector-specific objectives, including serving as a financial conduit on their behalf without any balance sheet burden.

5. Is it Feasible to Gear up Multilateral Lending Substantially?

Preventing or supporting external adjustment in the developing world with targeted multilaterally financed programs may remain feasible, even at the current level of capitalization, provided the temporary exceptional financing promised at the recent G20 meeting materializes in full. For instance, lending to finance fiscal stimulus and backstopping liquidity to the tune of, say 2-3 percentage points of GDP pale in comparison with the gap that would be produced if a financial collapse were to occur in the near future, with historical average stabilization packages of 5-10 points of GDP. Nonetheless, financing is endogenous to the severity of the crisis. So it is useful to think about other ways to expand demand and contain supply of resources for multilateral intervention regardless of the envelop size at any point in time.

To expand the supply of multilateral financing, multilateral financial institutions should therefore use their balance sheets creatively to the extent possible. In a process of global deleveraging and global credit deterioration, they could use their preferred creditor status, combined with their ability to affect the international regulatory standards at the global level, to leverage their balance sheet above normal criteria on a temporary basis. The alternative is that countries do that individually, lending directly to potentially insolvent households and firms, and hence increasing the probability of bigger country busts in the future.

Second, the existing system of bilateral insurance agreements between systematically important EMs and all of the G3 central banks should be strengthened. Brazil and Mexico in LAC, for instance, should seek to establish arrangements with the European Central Bank and the Bank of Japan similar to those established with the Federal Reserve Board. Similarly, there is scope for strengthening sub-regional arrangements such as the Fondo Latinoamericano de Reservas (FLAR) and the Corporacón Andina de Fomento (CAF) as a complement rather than a substitute to multilateral assistance. Nonetheless, as shown by the experience of Asian countries, barring individual countries' accumulating cushions of global dimensions, regional arrangements cannot effectively insulate against global shocks.

Third, and more generally, there are two distinct sources of foreign liquidity that should be recycled to global capital markets through institutional arrangements. The first is the traditional recycling of hard currency from countries underrepresented in the multilateral system but with large stocks of foreign reserves. The second is recycling of G3 funds attracted by the flight to quality. Both types of recycling, as with petrodollars in the 1970s, could simply be channeled through the IMF, as Japan, the United States, the Euro zone and a few other countries are doing. However, there are also alternative proposals on the table, such as setting floors on emerging market assets prices similar to those being implemented for toxic assets in the United States. Both recycling mechanisms can provide arrangements serving the objectives of both borrowers and lenders in a global crisis.

As discussed above, a way to contain demand of multilateral financing is to use the crisis as an opportunity to engage in institutional reform by establishing a credible commitment to strengthen future fiscal balances along the lines of a structural fiscal framework. The key would be to establish an independent and reputable agency to produce and disclose the structural position of the fiscal accounts in such a way that national debate on fiscal aggregates revolves around these structural estimations. The benefits are clear. First, it is efficient because it allows the stabilization of tax rates and public spending. Second, it would enlarge the sustainability space and allow a larger scope for a countercyclical response in the current downturn, be it a stimulus package or a shallower adjustment. Third, and related, such an approach would attract more financing from the market. Not only are the benefits clear, but the time is also right from a political economy viewpoint. The implementation of a structural fiscal framework in this downturn would not come accompanied by an adjustment to the current fiscal balance, as would happen in boom times, but rather with a friendly expansion.

Several other actions may help contain the cost of multilateral intervention. First, it is important to persuade individual countries to go to multilaterals sooner rather than later. Specifically, there is a nced for peer pressure: leading emerging economies in the G20 should be encouraged to go to the IMF early, while the large bilateral donors should make it a condition for support, especially now that the arsenal of lending facilities of the IMF has been modified in the right direction. MDBs could be an intermediary to facilitate this process rather than being used as an alternative to avoid going to the IMF. Moreover, the so-called stigma problem is misleading in the current circumstances. As the recent examples of Mexico and Poland illustrate, the world economy is in a state in which markets would likely cheer similar initiatives and would take a benign view of countries that try to move proactively.

It is also important to prioritize countries and activities, recognizing systemic relevance and matching country size with appropriate source of support. There are applicable operational notions of country vulnerability, but the current circumstances require a notion of "systemic relevance." In other words, there is a need to distinguish systemically important countries or systematically important activities in certain countries. Moreover, we need to differentiate large from small countries to treat them differently because magnitudes are too great in systematically important countries.

Under either modality of fiscal support discussed above, reserves or budget support, there are risks that intervention remains inadequate if it is limited to fiscal concerns. As there are competing demands on limited stocks of foreign reserves or lines of credit in hard currency, the issue arises of how to prioritize them. Obviously, official reserves are needed to lean against the wind and smooth changes in the equilibrium real exchange rate. They must also be used to roll over public sector debt coming due in foreign currency (and possibly domestic currency, when monetizing the debt poses significant inflationary risks). Foreign currency liquidity may be needed to provide credit to the private sector previously provided by private foreign and domestic residents, or to facilitate the rollover of private sector liabilities in case the shock were to be very protracted. In past episodes of Sudden Stops, for instance, it has proven to be crucial to support trade credits (such as in the case of Brazil in 2002). [12] In the current environment, protecting domestic credit growth to small and medium enterprises likely to be rationed out of the market may be equally important. Finally, additional potential claims on reserves include the provision of foreign currency liquidity to the banking sector if it is under stress from the deposit side of the balance sheet (as in Uruguay in 2002) or from the pulling back of foreign lines of credit.

In practice, with scarce hard currency resources, support must be prioritized. In fact, in addition to fiscal stimulus and backstopping liquidity, there is a need to preserve the flow of private credit. As part of this attempt, multilaterals may be backing active financial policies of directed lending, either through public or private banks. A multilaterally financed initiative is more likely to be successful, as country-led initiatives risk running out of money before the crisis is over.

Given that countries are directing lending into economies with increasing insolvency, there is a risk that once they were to run out of own resources, they would face a much worse situation.

To be sure, it is important to avoid the institutional arrangement that emerged for the international trade regime whereby progress (or lack thereof) with multilateral liberalization has been crowded out by a proliferation of bilateral trade agreements. Also, tied bilateral financial aid in this context may serve as a cloak for protectionism on the part of the donor. Multilateral institutions ought to remain central and guarantee a level playing field by requiring bilateral arrangements to abide by common principles.

6. Looking Ahead

Full reform and recapitalization of the multilateral financial institutions cannot be put in place in time to avert the spreading of the current crisis, but it should be an objective for the post crisis era. The current situation does not provide time to change the international financial architecture, but we should not lose sight of the shortcomings of the system for post-crisis reform.

The secular increase in international financial integration requires a recapitalization of the system regardless of the need to intervene in response to the current crisis. The current crisis, however, has vividly exposed the risks associated with the notion that an increased role of private capital markets justifies moving toward elimination of public sector intervention in the form of multilateral surveillance and lending. The global nature of the current crisis that is affecting all countries in all regions at the same time, albeit in slightly different manners across countries, strengthens this case and calls for an urgent response. [13]

The governance structure of the multilateral system is also inadequate. The international monetary system is one in which countries that have embraced globalization and are now in large and persistent international creditor positions hold such small stakes in the system that they have no incentive to participate fully, or assurance that will be able to do so—including by means such as putting significant resources at the system's disposal. Vice versa, countries that are progressively less integrated into the world economy continue to be overrepresented in the system by virtue of arcane and outdated representation formulas. The G20 represents an interesting development in this regard and is a natural forum for discussions between creditor and borrower nations.

There is also an urgent need to revisit multilateral policies on crisis prevention and crisis resolution. First, it is important to foster the emergence of country insurance products for crisis prevention. The most effective way of securing countercyclical financing to countries in need is not through ex-post multilateral lending, but instead through ex-ante establishment of contingent contracts that deliver countercyclical private financing. Contingent contracts transferring resources to countries in the event of low export prices or generalized credit rationing in international financial markets, to mention two examples of relevant exogenous shocks, would amount to automatic financial stabilizers. Multilateral financial institutions have a role to play in helping to develop these instruments, which would entail a contingent increase in their balance sheet exposure in exchange for a reduction in the capital needed to provide countercyclical financing. If the private sector is successfully engaged in participating in these country insurance schemes, the multilateral capital required to address countercyclical needs would be minimized. [14] Of course, countercyclical lending is premised on the assumption of pro-cyclical repayments. This implies adequate terms of lending to match the required cyclical flows and clarity about the countercyclical purpose of these facilities.

Second, discussions on institutional arrangements for crisis resolution should resume in earnest. Unfortunately there remains a gaping hole in the international financial architecture in relation to debt restructuring, and the international community's heralded "solution" of Collective Action Clauses still appears inadequate to deal with these cases. This implies that countries forced by the current crisis to restructure debt obligations will likely see "punishment" far out of proportion to their "crime" and far more suffering than if a comprehensive resolution technique such as an efficient bankruptcy resolution procedure had been put in place. There is still much work to be done here, as unfortunately may become evident if the world economy does not improve relatively soon and debt restructuring become necessary in critical cases.

Source: www.iadb.org
© 2009 Inter-American Development Bank Washington, DC. Reprinted with Permission.

Paper prepared for the IDB XXVIII Meeting of the Latin American Network of Central Banks and Finance Ministries. The views expressed in this paper are of the authors and may not represent those of the Inter-American Development Bank or its Executive Board.

Notes

1. See G20 (1998) on crisis prevention.
2. See Calvo (2006) on monetary policy in EMs.
3. See Cavallo and Izquierdo (2009).
4. Note that with no safety net in place the audience might also be in danger as other countries may be affected by a crisis in a neighbor that might have had a precautionary facility in place.
5. As we argue below, a key reform in this direction would be the establishment of an independent fiscal council in charge of estimating the structural fiscal balances actually run by governments and a budget rule setting prudent targets for these balances. A credible reform in this direction with a real bite in the future would allow countries and multilateral institutions to go further in any active policy in the present.
6. Monetary policy lags may be shorter in emerging markets than in advanced economies, hence making it more effective (Catão, Pagán and Laxton, 2008). The shorter duration of financial contracts, possibly underpinning this stylized fact, however, makes these economies more vulnerable to sudden increases in

risk premia, thus suggesting that financial frictions may result in tougher constraints in these economies.

7. Calvo (2009) points out that a global financial regulator should be established alongside a global lender of last resort to be effective, in analogy with the institutional arrangement prevailing at the national level.
8. In these models a "global game," with particular assumptions regarding what lenders know about fundamentals and what lenders know about other lenders, supports a unique equilibrium.
9. The one period version of this game is one where the trade-off for the lender of last resort is to provide liquidity protection but at the cost of moral hazard. The interesting feature is that the only equilibrium is in mixed strategies representing the tension between (say) the IMF wishing to provide support and a country's being tempted to pursue riskier strategies in the presence of unconditional support. A "minimum punishment strategy" supports a unique equilibrium in the repeated game.
10. Note however that as long as the country is free to use international reserves for budget support, both roles are formally equivalent from a financial viewpoint. Under those conditions, the role of the MDBs in this equation is to ensure whatever fiscal space there is, is used appropriately in sound operations. In order for the opinions of these institutions to be heard it is surely the case that they should have resources committed.
11. See García (2009) for a more technical discussion of the modalities of fiscal stimulus in LAC.
12. Protecting trade credits was vital during Sudden Stops as their disappearance constraints further the availability of foreign currency in the domestic market.
13. Recent theoretical analysis of multilateral and commercial lending confirms the social optimality of the former, given the pro-cyclicality of the latter (Boz, 2009).
14. The argument has been made that contingent private loans would have the effect of private creditors lowering their country credit ceilings anticipating future over indebtedness, without changing the fundamental problem. Derivatives that do not create debt but simply transfer resources ex-post, such as insurance or swaps, may be more attractive in this regard.

References

Arozamena, L., and A. Powell. 2003. "Liquidity Protection versus Moral Hazard: The Role of the IMF." *Journal of International Money and Finance* 22(7): 1041-1063.

Benigno, G., H. Chen, C. Otrok, A. Rebucci, and E. R. Young. 2009. "Optimal Stabilization Policy with Occasionally Binding Financial Frictions." Washington, DC, United States: Inter-American Development Bank. Unpublished manuscript.

Boz, E. 2009. "Sovereign Default, Private Sector Creditors and the IFIs." IMF Working Paper 09/46. Washington, DC, United States: International Monetary Fund.

Braggion, F., L. Christiano and J. Roldos. 2005. "Optimal Monetary Policy in a 'Sudden Stop.'" NBER Working Paper 13254. Cambridge, United States: National Bureau of Economic Research.

Calvo, G. 2009. "Lender of Last Resort: Put It on the Agenda." *Vox*, 23 March. Available at: http://www.voxeu.org/index.php?q=node/3327

Catão, L., and A. Chang. 2009. "Food Prices and Monetary Policy." Washington, DC, United States: Inter-American Development Bank. Unpublished manuscript.

Catão, L., A. Pagán and D. Laxton. 2008. "Monetary Transmission in an Emerging Targeter: The Case of Brazil." IMF Working Paper 08/191. Washington, DC, United States: International Monetary Fund.

Cavallo, E., and A. Izquierdo, editors. 2009. *Dealing with an International Credit Crunch: Policy Responses to Sudden Stops in Latin America*. Washington, DC, United States: Inter-American Development Bank.

Corsetti, G., B. Guimarães and N. Roubini. 2006. "International Lending of Last Resort and Moral Hazard: A Model of IMF's Catalytic Finance." *Journal of Monetary Economics* 53(3): 441-471.

Cúrdia, V., and M. Woodford. 2009. "Credit Frictions and Optimal monetary policy," BIS Working Paper 278. Basel, Switzerland: Bank for International Settlements.

D'Amato, L., E. Grubisic and A. Powell. 1997. "Contagion, Banks Fundamentals or Macroeconomic Shock? An Empirical Analysis of the Argentine 1995 Banking Problems." Working Paper 2. Available at www.bcra.gov.ar/pdfs/invest/trabajo2.pdf.

G20. 1998. "Report on the Working Group on International Financial Crises." Available at http://www.bis.org/publ/othp01.htm

Gamberoni E., and R. Newfarmer. 2009. "Trade Protection: Incipient but Worrisome Trends." *Trade Note* 37. Washington, DC, United States: World Bank: International Trade Department. http://siteresources.worldbank.org/NEWS/Resources/Trade_Note_37.pdf

García, G. 2009. "Qué hacer y qué no hacer en política fiscal durante la actual crisis internacional?" Washington, DC, United States: Inter-American Development Bank. Unpublished manuscript.

Fernández-Arias, E., and P. Montiel. 2009. "Crisis Response in Latin America: Is the 'Rainy Day' at Hand?" Research Department Working Paper 686.

Inter-American Development Bank (IDB). 2008. "All that Glitters May Not be Gold: Assessing Latin America's Recent Macroeconomic Performance." Washington, DC, United States: IDB.

——2009a. "Policy Trade-offs for Unprecedented Times: Confronting the Global Crisis in Latin America and the Caribbean." Washington, DC, United States: Inter-American Development Bank (IDB).

——2009b. "Social and Labor Market Policies for Tumultuous Times: Confronting the Global Crisis in Latin America and the Caribbean." Washington, DC, United States: Inter-American Development Bank (IDB).

Jeanne, O. 2008. "Debt Maturity and the International Financial Architecture." Forthcoming in *American Economic Review.*

Jeanne, O., J. Ostry and J. Zettelmeyer. 2008. "A Theory of International Crisis Lending and IMF Conditionality." IMF Working Paper 08/236.Washington, DC, United States: International Monetary Fund.

Miskin, F. 2009. "Is Monetary Policy Effective During Financial Crises?" NBER Working Paper 14678. Cambridge, United States: National Bureau of Economic Research.

Morris S., and H.S. Shin. 2003. "Catalytic Finance: When Does it Work?" Cowles Foundation Discussion Paper 1400. New Haven, United States: Yale Cowles Foundation for Research in Economics.

Ortiz, A., P. Ottonello, F. Sturzenegger. 2009. "Monetary and Fiscal Policies in a Sudden Stop: Is Tighter Brighter?" In: E. Cavallo and A. Izquierdo, editors. *Dealing with an International Credit Crunch: Policy Responses to Sudden Stops in Latin America*. Washington, DC, United States: Inter-American Development Bank.

Schmukler, S.L., E. Levy-Yeyati and M.S. Martínez Peria. 2004. "Market Discipline under Systemic Risk: Evidence from Bank Runs in Emerging Economies." Econometric Society 2004 Latin American Meetings 318. http://www.bis.org/bcbs/events/rtf04schmukler.pdf

6

Learning from the Financial Crisis

Sir John Gieve

The years after sterling left the ERM were the most successful and stable in my lifetime. In early 2007, for example, inflation had not moved by more than a single percentage point away from target in the previous 10 years, the output of the economy had grown in every quarter since 1992 Q3 (Chart 1) unemployment had fallen by 5 percentage points from its peak in the early 1990s and living standards had steadily increased. Interest rates had been low and stable.

Chart 1: GDP and employment

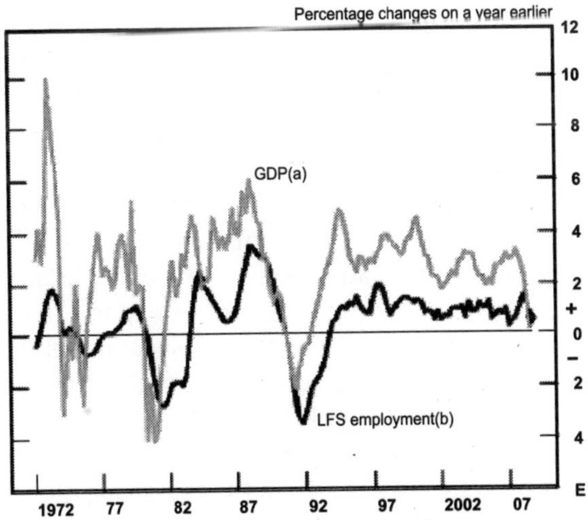

Source: ONS (including Labour Force Survey)

However as we know now, that was the end of "the Great Stability". The summer ushered in a period of extraordinary turmoil in Western financial markets which we are still trying to calm. And this year has seen the onset of recession not just in Europe but throughout the advanced economies. Despite the dramatic policy measures of the last months, the outlook for 2009 is bleak and the prospects beyond are uncertain.

That move—in the space of only 12 months—from the policy maker's dream of steady non-inflationary growth to the biggest banking crisis since the outbreak of World War I and the onset of recession sets the questions for this evening.

First, how did we get into this position?

Second, what are the immediate challenges for policy?

And finally, what lessons should we draw for the future?

How Did We Get Here?

The path that led from losses in the US sub prime housing market to a collapse of confidence in the Western banking system and a savage credit squeeze has been described many times, most recently in the Bank's *Financial Stability* and *Inflation Reports*. I don't need to repeat that here but I would highlight two features: first this is a global story; second, the nature of the crisis has changed over the past 15 months and has called for a changing policy response.

A Global Crisis

You cannot explain recent developments on a national basis, even in the US. The roots of the crisis lay in global imbalances in trade and capital flows between advanced and emerging economies. The rapid growth of exports from Asia, and latterly the Gulf, was reflected in a substantial build up of savings. In China the national saving rate peaked in exceeded 50 percent of GDP. Those funds flowed back to the developed world and to the US in particular. That kept interest rates low and allowed a rapid growth of credit. Following the dotcom bubble, there was a particular appetite for fixed income investments which led to an increasingly risky search for yield. That was the platform for the excesses of lending to the sub-prime housing market in the US and a sharp rise in house prices more generally.

The impact was not confined to the US. The flow of funds into the US was re-exported to the advanced economies, especially through the growing securitization markets, and helped finance the rapid increases in house prices in the UK (Chart 2) and many other countries. And that internationalisation of markets was reflected also in the build up in our banks of portfolios of AAA-rated securities which offered a slightly better yield than traditional bonds and many of which were based on sub-prime assets.

Chart 2: House prices and earnings

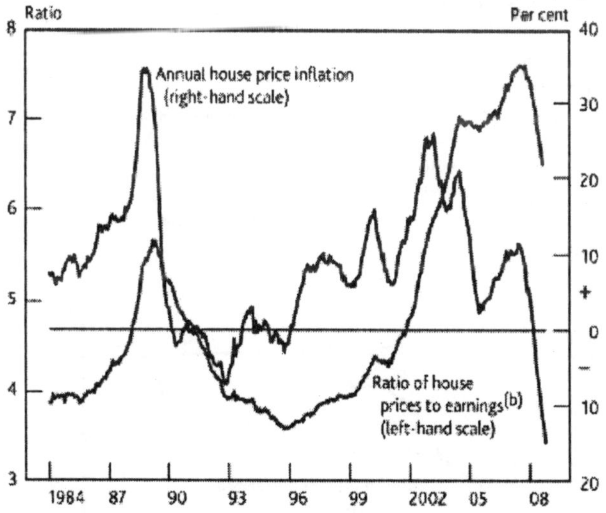

Source: Halifax, Nationwide, ONS and Bank calculations

So when losses emerged in sub-prime market, they not only hit US banks but ricocheted through the international financial system. Much of the commentary has focused on the structured credit losses in banks' trading books and treasuries and they have certainly been large.

But equally as important was the impact on the liability side of balance sheets. Banks had not only expanded their balance sheets too far, they had in the process become reliant on wholesale funding markets which had not been tested in a downturn. In the UK, the gap between customer lending and deposits moved from zero at the turn of the century to over £700 billion in 2008 H1 (Chart 3). That proved a structural weakness when investors realised that the AAA label concealed substantial and uncertain risks and withdrew from the securitisation markets.

Chart 3: Major UK banks' customer funding gap, household saving ratio and foreign interbank deposits

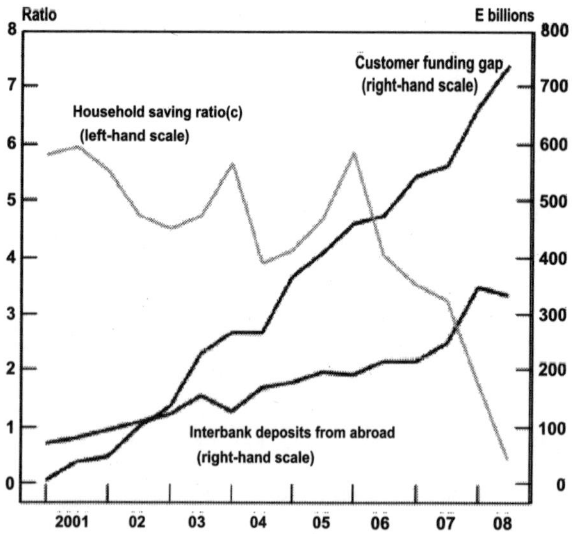

Source: Bank of England, Dealogic, ONS, published accounts and Bank calculations.

Just as the origins of the crisis lay in global imbalances its effects are also global. Initially, the impact of the crisis seemed to be concentrated in the US and a handful of European banks in Germany, the UK and Switzerland which had pursued particularly risky strategies. The euro area as a whole did not see a marked reduction in credit growth. Meanwhile the emerging economies of Asia continued to boom. With wages and prices rising, many of the people I met in India and China at the start of the year rather welcomed the prospect of a fall in Western demand as a means of taking a little of the heat out of their own economies.

But despite different starting points and policies, we have now seen bank failures in many countries in Europe and acute pressures develop everywhere. And the US, Japan, the euro area and the UK have all entered recession. This summer has also brought a slowdown in growth in the Far East and other emerging economies which is likely to test political as well as economic regimes.

The Challenge for Policy

It was clear last autumn that the financial crisis was leading to a squeeze on credit and lowering the prospects for growth and inflation in the UK. That was why the MPC, which had been raising rates as late as July, cut Bank Rate in December last year and followed with two more reductions in February and April. While the euro area started with lower rates and initially seemed less affected than the UK by a credit crunch, expected increases in rates were delayed.

However, these downside pressures were not the only challenge to policy. Oil prices which had been pushed up by the rapid growth in emerging markets took another dramatic jump and food prices began rising more quickly too. Between 2007 and mid-2008 oil more than doubled in price, while food prices rose by around 80 percent. At the same time sterling which had climbed to US$ 2.10 in November 2007, fell back. The result was that consumer price inflation in the UK rose well above target to 3 percent in April and over 5 percent in September, its highest rate since 1992 (while RPI inflation has been over 4 percent for all but 4 months out of the past two years).

Not surprisingly expectations of inflation also rose sharply (Chart 4), raising the risk that higher inflation would become embedded in decisions on the prices for other goods and services and on pay. Of course commodity prices and inflation more generally have now begun to come down but I believe the risk of dislodging expectations was a real one, not a mirage. Certainly I felt that to reduce rates during months when inflation was not only rising rapidly, but was rising faster than we had forecast, would be confusing and might weaken confidence in our resolution and the credibility of the inflation target . On similar grounds, despite the appreciation of the euro, the ECB raised rates in July this year.

Chart 4: CPI and households' inflation expectations for the year ahead (scaled to match CPI on average)

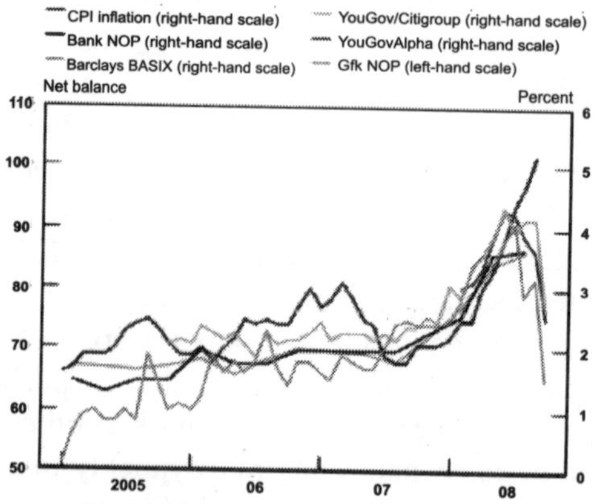

Sources: The AlphaMonitor: consumer, YouGovAlpha, Bank of England, Barclays Capital, Citigroup, GfK NOP, research carried out by GfK NOP on behalf of the European Commission and YouGov.

In the spring and early summer, the financial crisis also was showing some signs of stabilising in the US and in Europe, particularly after the takeover of Bear Stearns in March signalled that the "state safety net" in the US had been extended to cover investment as well as commercial banks. The introduction of the Special Liquidity Scheme in April here and extensive liquidity measures in the US led to a period in which funding pressures eased and Libor spreads and CDS premia softened. Our August forecast was for a pronounced but limited deterioration in growth. The threat of a strengthening feedback loop from a contracting banking sector to a severe downturn in the real economy had not disappeared but did not seem the central case.

But the risks and the challenges changed dramatically in the autumn.

First, the losses incurred by investors in the rescues of Fannie and Freddie combined with the decision to allow Lehman Brothers to go into administration, led to a dramatic loss of confidence in financial markets (Chart 5) threatening a savage further twist in the squeeze on credit for households and companies.

Second, we saw a sharp weakening in oil prices (Chart 6), with the odds implied by options of such a fall less than 1 percent. Other commodity prices also fell. And, even before that was reflected in consumer prices, the public's inflation expectations turned down decisively.

In short, the balance of risks between inflation being above or below target in the medium term shifted decisively to the downside.

That was the background to the internationally coordinated reductions in interest rates in early October and the aggressive cut of 150 basis points in Bank Rate in November, the largest reduction in official interest rates since 1992 (indeed I believe it was only the third time Bank rate had been cut by 150bp since the Bank was founded over 300 years ago).

Chart 5: Sterling three-month interbank rates relative to future expected policy rates

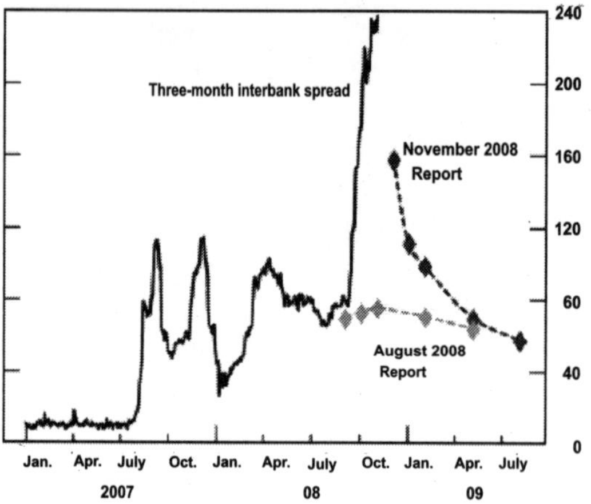

Sources: Bloomberg and Bank Calculations

Chart 6: Oil prices

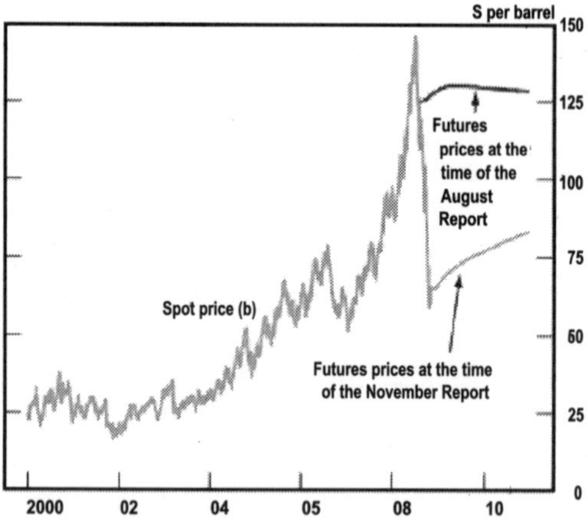

Sources: Bloomberg and Thomson Datastream

Even so, our latest medium term projections for inflation show inflation remaining below target in the medium term and suggest further reductions may be necessary (Chart 7). Of course, there are large uncertainties around that projection; more so than usual. In particular, they take no account of any fiscal measures that the Government may announce next week.

Chart 7: CPI inflation projection based on market interest rate expectations

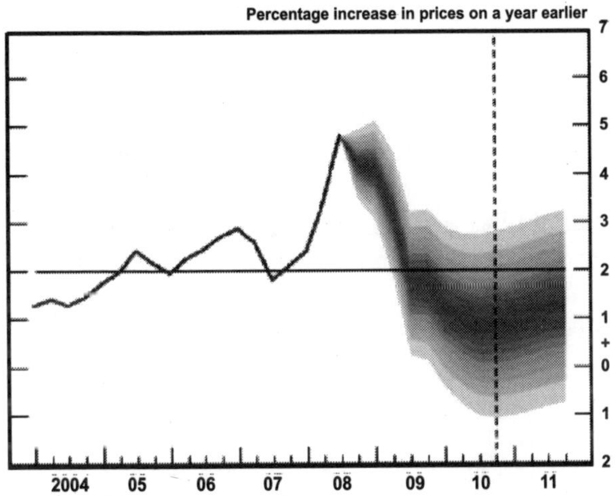

Just as we had to change gears on monetary policy, so we needed to change our approach to the banking sector. The tripartite authorities—the Bank, FSA and Treasury—were criticised for the handling of Northern Rock and for being slow off the mark when the crisis started in 2007. But we learned from that experience. We have established new ways of providing the market with the liquidity that it needs. And, as the crisis has widened, we have dealt with vulnerable and failing banks, such as Bradford and Bingley, more speedily and cleanly.

But as the crisis deepened in late September, it became clear that we needed more than a case by case approach here to tackle the continuing loss of confidence in the banking system in the UK, in euro area and in the US. On October 8, therefore we announced a comprehensive package of measures including support for recapitalisation, guaranteed funding and enhanced liquidity. That very quickly became the template for action in other advanced and some emerging countries.

The central plank of the package was the offer to underwrite capital issuance of at least £50 billion and it is important to be clear what that was intended to do. It was not to establish new regulatory minimum ratios. It was intended to underpin confidence in the banks and to ensure that each institution would have a sufficient capital buffer both to absorb losses that are likely to arise during a recession and to continue lending on normal commercial criteria. Under the new Basel II rules the ratio of capital to risk weighted assets is almost bound to fall as arrears and losses mount. The aim of the package was to create the headroom for that to happen and to remove the capital pressure on banks to deleverage quickly by refusing even good credit requests.

The capital raising is not complete of course but the process is underway. Banks and building societies have already secured around £50 billion of guaranteed funding in the market and has facilitated new bank debt issuance without the need of a guarantee. Overall there has been some easing in the money markets and some repair in confidence. The complete seizure that was looming has been averted.

However, we are clearly not out of the woods yet. Financial markets across the world are still badly impaired; sprcads have not yet returned to their summer levels; and, while banks look more secure, many hedge funds for example are under increased pressure. In the wider economy, we are only in the early stages of a recession in the advanced economies and of the slowdown in emerging markets. So we must be ready to take further action if required whether monetary, fiscal, or directly in the financial sector.

Lessons for the Medium-Term

That is the immediate prospect. I want to finish by drawing out some lessons for the medium term.

1. Closer International Co-ordination of Macroeconomic Policy: The first lesson is the vital importance of international cooperation in a global economy.

For several years we worried about the growing imbalances between the US in particular and emerging Asia. We can now see how painful the rebalancing is proving. No doubt we could do better in national policy making but we also need to recognise that the sum of policies which make sense at the national level may well not be optimal at the global level. To give one example, for most economies individually a change in the oil price is an external event – something beyond the reach of policy. But clearly that is not true of the global economy as whole.

Of course we have a great deal of experience in the EU of establishing common rules and policies. We know it is a painstaking process among 27 countries. But on finance and the economy we need to go wider than the EU and wider than the G7 to engage the new economies which account for so much of world growth. That is why it was so important and welcome that the recent meeting in Washington was of the G20 rather than the G7. Alongside the IMF it is going to play a key role in global macroeconomic coordination.

2. Better Ground Rules for Cross-Border Financial Crises: The failure of Lehman Brothers has confirmed that cross-border failures of large and complex firms are just as damaging and difficult to manage as we had feared. We need to ensure that proper contingency plans are prepared between the authorities most concerned for failures not just within the EU, where a lot of work is in hand, but on a global basis.

As a start I hope we can establish a robust and predictable framework of rules and conventions that ensure that home authorities will co-ordinate a cross-border response better. The Financial Stability Forum is working on these urgently.

This is not easy. In particular emergencies there are often different national interests at stake and the sheer pressure of events can limit cross-border consultation.

However, if we do not tackle this we will see the growth of national restrictions on the terms on which cross-border operations are permitted—in terms of capital, liquidity and legal structure—and that could have great economic costs.

3. Strengthening Banks' Resilience: The financial crisis has revealed a number of gaps and flaws in the regulatory and accounting conventions especially for banks. We need to put those right quickly and on an international basis. The G20 Summit has asked the Financial Stability Forum to take that forward.

For example the events have shown up the lack of any agreement on liquidity requirements on banks. The FSA is developing proposals for UK which will deliver tougher standards. But we are pressing also for international agreement in the Basel Committee. Events also brought home the need for a fundamental review of both the amount and the definition of capital requirements.

4. Developing Macro-Prudential Tools: The last lesson I have drawn is that we need to bridge the gap between macroeconomic policy and the regulation of individual firms. We need a third club in our bag which can directly dampen the financial cycle. This is needed both for financial stability and for wider economic management.

As we have been reminded over the past 15 months, it is primarily in the 'bad times' that banks need to demonstrate that they have adequate financial resources. We need to ensure that banks build up resources in good times to a greater extent, which can then cushion the shock in bad times. I think of this as 'protecting banks from the economic cycle'.

But we have seen also how the financial sector can drive the wider business cycle, by becoming over-confident in the upswing and over-constrained (by lack of financial resources–capital and liquidity) in the downswing. It seems to me that mechanisms which oblige banks to build up resources in good times can serve a second useful purpose of dampening the economic cycle. I think of this as 'protecting the cycle from banks'.

We need two-way protection and I would like to describe three ways you might go about providing it.

The first is the Spanish system of dynamic provisions, which requires banks to build a general reserve that can be drawn on in downturns. Each period, banks are required to make general provisions equal to the difference between the 'inherent' losses (based on the growth of loans and a long-term average of incurred losses) and the specific provisions on impaired assets for the period. The difference, if positive, is treated as an expense in the profit and loss account. If negative, it is treated as income–provided that the general reserve has been previously built up to the required level.

The specific provisions made by Spanish banks fluctuate substantially through the business cycle, as one would expect, falling during upswings and increasing in downturns. But the flow of general provisions moves in the opposite direction, acting as a countercyclical mechanism. In the last boom, the accumulated stock of total provisions grew steadily between 2005 and 2008, to a level which at the start of this year was twice as large as their non-performing loans. That figure has fallen sharply in recent quarters, in the face of fast-growing credit losses, but it did ensure that Spanish banks were better placed than their counterparts in other countries to absorb such losses without immediately eating into their core capital. The Bank of Spain estimates the current level of general provisions could absorb losses associated with a doubtful assets ratio of 9 percent (the current level is 1.5 percent). The general reserve is also substantial in comparison with the tier 1 capital ratios, representing 1.3 percent of the risk-weighted assets.

I know that general provisions fall foul of modern accounting practice and can be unpopular with tax authorities. But the Spanish example demonstrates that – despite all the technical arguments there might be about the details – a mechanism with broadly the right features is practicable and can generate worthwhile additional reserves against the losses which crystallise in cyclical downturns. It does not require precise estimates of the length of the cycle, or predictions of when the cycle will turn; and it can be capped, so that the reserve does not continue to grow inexorably in an extended upswing. I think it merits serious consideration for more widespread adoption, irrespective of the accounting and tax treatment such reserves might attract.

One key feature of such reserves is that they should be useable. That is, the markets and analysts need to accept that using such reserves to absorb write-offs when losses are high is the natural counterpart of building them up when losses are cyclically low. It is not a sign of weakness or of inadequate capitalisation, but of prudent management of the cyclical pattern of losses. From the point of view of market acceptability, separating cyclical reserves from more structural capital requirements seems a valuable idea.

The second scheme I want to promote is growth-related capital requirements.

Losses tend to be lower in the early stages of a loan's life than when it is fully seasoned because borrowers are more certain of their own and the economy's near term prospects. A loan book which is growing more rapidly than average will be weighted towards such unseasoned loans, and so will appear to be performing better than a balanced portfolio of loans of different vintages. In addition, rapid growth of lending tends itself to be associated with taking on poor business – even if that is not obvious at the time it is written. Typically, rapid growth can only be achieved by drawing in marginal borrowers to the market. That is true of the banking sector as a whole. And when such growth is achieved by an individual bank, over and above that achieved by its peers, adverse selection – attracting weaker borrowers, who are unable to raise funds from other lenders – is an additional factor depressing the quality of the loan book. The simple fact is that rapid absolute and relative growth is strongly associated with poorer average loan quality and, sooner or later, sharply higher nonperforming loans.

The proposal is that, the risk weighting (and so, the capital requirement) of bank loans should include a growth-based component. This could be linked either to the economy-wide growth rate of a particular type of business, or to the growth rate of an individual bank's lending relative to the market as a whole; or some combination of the two. This would make it more expensive for banks to expand their balance sheets faster that normal when confidence is high and could be a useful means of dampening banks' contribution to the business cycle.

The third, less direct, mechanism to discourage over-rapid expansion would be on the liabilities side. Rapid balance sheet expansion tends to be fuelled by access to less stable sources of funding, attracted perhaps by higher interest rates as the bank seeks to meet its balance sheet aspirations (and feels able to pay, because—as already explained—loan loss experience is good). Such funding could be treated as an added risk factor in assessing a bank's liquidity needs and those needs should be reflected in a requirement to hold high quality liquid assets. So banks which are funding their expansion in this way will need to match that expansion with an increasing stock of safer and lower-yielding assets. This will tend to reduce their profit margins and so discourage rapid growth which is funded from less stable sources.

Of course these outline proposals need a lot more work. Striking an appropriate balance between the prudential objective of protecting the banks against the cycle and the macroeconomic objective of dampening lending in the upswing will not be easy. And they are never going to be the whole answer. The more we raise the cost of cost of increasing lending by banks, the greater the incentive we will create for the growth of intermediation outside the regulated banking sector or to foreign banks not subject to such counter-cyclical requirements. Even if such unregulated competition had no consequences for banks themselves, it could certainly undermine the desired countercyclical effects. And the secondary banking crisis of the early 1970s is a reminder that we cannot anyway be relaxed about changes in the scale of lending taking place outside the regulated sector.

Conclusion

To sum up, the last 15 months have brought home the costs of unbalanced growth in the world economy. Although the correction started with a bursting property bubble in the US, it has expanded into a global financial crisis and brought on recession throughout the advanced economies and a sharp deceleration of growth elsewhere. The immediate priority is to deal with this downswing. The extraordinary measures we have taken in this country and others are having a positive impact but we may need to do more. We must also learn some lessons for policy in the medium term including the need for far better coordination of policy internationally and the need for some new policy instruments alongside interest rates to dampen the financial cycle.

Source: www.bankofengland.co.uk
© Bank of England 2008. Reprinted with Permission.

This was a speech given by SIR JOHN GIEVE, DEPUTY GOVERNOR, BANK OF ENGLAND, at European Business School London on 19th, November 2008 during 2008 Europe in the World Lecture Panel discussion.

7

The Global Crisis and Latin America: Financial Impact and Policy Responses

Alejandro Jara, Ramon Moreno and Camilo E Tovar

The financial effects on Latin America of the global crisis which began in summer 2007 were initially limited but intensified after the bankruptcy of Lehman Brothers in mid-September 2008. Global deleveraging in the international banking system and diminished investor risk appetite resulted in falling demand for emerging market assets and a sharp depreciation in the currencies of emerging market economies (EMEs). Gross capital inflows reversed and financing conditions tightened, reducing liquidity in foreign exchange and domestic money markets, and raising bond yields in both international and local currencies.

Episodes of financial stress are not unknown in Latin America. [1] However, some features distinguish the current episode from the crises of the late 1990s (e.g. the Asian crisis) or the Argentine and Brazilian episodes in the early 2000s. First, the shock originated in the financial sector of advanced economies rather than in Latin America or another emerging market region. Second, the significant reduction of Latin American *public* external debt gave governments more leeway to play a stabilising role for *private* markets, where external debt had remained high. Finally, new kinds of vulnerabilities have surfaced, mainly associated with financial innovation and integration rather than with macroeconomic imbalances or banking sector weaknesses.

Policy responses have also differed this time around, as they sought to smooth the flow of both external and domestic financing. Central banks took steps to provide liquidity in foreign exchange and domestic money markets and facilitate the extension of credit. To supplement their foreign reserves, Brazil and Mexico agreed to open a currency swap line with the US Federal Reserve. More recently, Colombia and Mexico have sought access to the IMF's newly established Flexible Credit Line (FCL). Finally, central banks have been able to adopt a countercyclical monetary policy stance, thanks to flexible exchange rate regimes, a limited exchange rate pass-through to inflation and the greater credibility built up by policymakers.

The rest of the article is structured as follows. In the next section we analyse the impact of global financial shocks on Latin American financial markets, comparing the current crisis with previous shocks and paying particular attention to capital flows, international bank and securities financing, exchange rate adjustment and the cost of foreign and domestic currency financing. [2] In the subsequent section, we focus on the policy responses, examining in particular the provision of foreign currency liquidity as well as measures taken to stabilize domestic money and capital markets. The conclusion summarises the key policy lessons to be drawn.

Financial Impact of the Crisis in Latin America

External Financing Dries up: Up to the onset of the financial turmoil in August 2007, Latin America had experienced an unusually benign external environment. A combination of net capital inflows and current account surpluses had contributed to significant foreign reserve accumulation (Graph 1, left-hand panel). Gross inflows and outflows were at record highs, with foreign direct investment (FDI) as the main source of external financing [BIS (2009), Jara and Tovar (2008)].

However, gross capital inflows to Latin America began to contract significantly in the third quarter of 2008. Over the year as a whole, gross portfolio inflows declined by US$ 76 billion (Graph 1, centre panel). [3] FDI was more stable, but is expected to fall in 2009. Current account surpluses have also declined or turned to moderate deficits. Several factors have contributed to the abrupt reversal in gross capital inflows: the increase in international risk aversion, efforts by financial institutions in developed countries to boost liquidity or shore up their balance sheets, high currency volatility, the terms-off-trade collapse and the derivatives exposure of some large corporations in Brazil and Mexico (see Box 1).

One difference in the current situation is that in this decade the region has accumulated large gross (non-reserve) assets invested abroad (US$ 180 billion by end-2007); such assets were almost non-existent in previous crises (Graph 1). [4] The partial repatriation of those assets during 2008 helped stabilize the external financial position of the region during the current crisis. In 2008, gross outflows decreased by almost US$ 42 billion and net flows amounted to US$ 53 billion (Graph 1). [5]

Graph 1

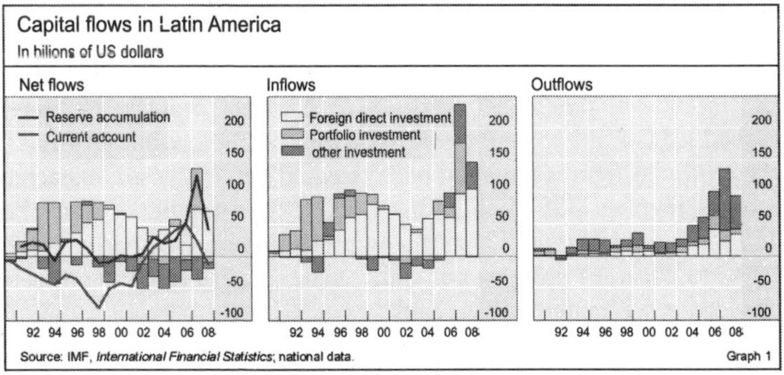

Cross-border Bank Financing and Bond Issuance: Cross-border bank financing fell after mid-September 2008 as international banks reduced new credit and refused to roll over existing loans. This was reflected in a sharp decline of signings of syndicated loans and cross-border financing in the region (Graph 2).

Box 1: Derivatives-related Exposures in the Corporate Sector: The Case of Mexico and Brazil

In Latin America, on-balance sheet foreign currency mismatches have decreased substantially since the implementation of flexible exchange rate regimes during the 1990s (IMF (2008)). However, the low currency volatility and the nominal appreciation trend observed in several countries before August 2008 led some corporations to increase their off-balance sheet foreign exchange exposure through derivative positions. As a consequence, a number of companies in Brazil and Mexico started betting against the depreciation of their currencies by selling foreign exchange options in the offshore market. These contracts allow corporates to sell US dollars at a favourable rate when the exchange rate rises above a "knock-out" price (i.e. the domestic currency appreciates), but force them to sell dollars at an unfavourable rate if the exchange rate falls below a "knock-in" price (the domestic currency depreciates), offering financing and currency trades at favourable rates, but with the drawback of having to deliver dollars at a loss if the domestic currency depreciates past a certain threshold.

The sharp currency depreciation observed in Latin America after mid-September 2008 resulted in large losses for some of the top companies in Brazil and Mexico when the exchange rate triggered the "knock-in" provision, forcing them to sell double the amount of US currency at the higher price. [a] In Mexico, derivatives losses reached US$ 4 billion in the fourth quarter of 2008, while in Brazil, where official figures have not been released yet, losses are expected to be as high as US$ 25 billion. A major food retailer (Comercial Mexicana), which sought bankruptcy protection on October 9, 2008, lost up to US$1.1 billion on non-deliverable forward (NDF) contracts it had made with international banks. [b]

The complexity of such deals and the fact that they were done privately highlights the lack of transparency in these markets, as many of these companies did not disclose any information on their derivative positions. [c] One result was a review of derivatives exposures across the region as policymakers realised that these exposures could pose systemic risk. Looking forward, policymakers will need to balance financial stability against market development in considering possible regulation of corporate derivatives risk. [d] [e]

Contd..

(a) One month after the Lehman Brothers default, in Mexico and Brazil the currency depreciated by more than 30%. (b) Gruma SA, the world's largest maker of corn flour, and Alfa SAB, the world's largest maker of aluminium engine heads and blocks, also suffered from considerable mark to market losses on derivative instruments during this period. On 10 October glass maker Vitro SAB announced that a large part of its $227 million of derivatives losses had come from natural gas forwards. (c) Comercial Mexicana was rated AAA on a local scale when it first filed for bankruptcy. (d) In Colombia, for example, the central bank established in May 2007 a maximum leverage position on forwards over the financial entities' net worth, a measure that was widely criticised but later proved to reduce the impact of the crisis. (e) In some cases corporate derivatives have contributed to reducing financial vulnerabilities, as shown by the use of oil price hedge and currency swaps by the Mexican state-owned petroleum company (Pemex), which helped it to stabilise its 2009 budget.

Cross-border claims on Latin America declined by US$46 billion in the fourth quarter, compared to US$ 56 billion for emerging Europe and US$ 160 billion for Asia and the Pacific. In percentage terms, cross-border bank claims on Latin America dropped by 40 percent on an annualised basis during the fourth quarter, comparable to contractions experienced during previous crises in the region.

Graph 2

Debit flows in Latin America

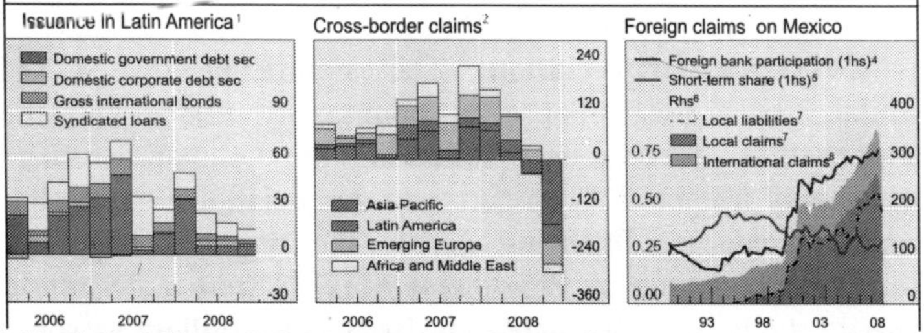

[1] Argentina, Brazil, Chile, Colombia, Mexico and Peru; in billions of US dollars. [2] Change in BIS reporting banks' cross-border claims in all currencies, by location of borrower; in billions of US dollars. [3] The sum of international claims and locally extended claims in local currency. [4] See footnote 3 in McGuire and Tarashev (2008) for a description of how this rate is calculated. [5] Ratio of short-term claims to total international claims. [6] In billions of US dollars. [7] In local currency. [8] Cross-border claims in all currencies and foreign currency claims extended by banks' foreign offices on residents of the host country.

Sources: IMF, *IFS*; Dealogic; BIS debt securities and consolidated and locational banking statistics. Graph 2

A noteworthy development is that a large proportion of foreign banks' operations are now local rather than international. For example, in Mexico there is a large foreign bank presence and most foreign bank credit takes the form of local claims (Graph 2). By contrast, earlier in this decade Latin America had a relatively large share of international claims. Locally booked claims in the region tend to be funded locally (i.e. in the borrowing country), and could therefore be more stable than (external) crossborder financing (Moreno and von Kleist (2007), Jara and Tovar (2008), McGuire and Tarashev (2008)). [6] Indeed, recent experience suggests that the shift may have stabilised financing in the region: as noted in the Highlights section in this issue, exchange rate adjusted local claims in local currency have remained relatively stable in many EMEs, including Chile and Mexico, even as international claims have declined sharply.

As for international bond financing, issuance plummeted (Graph 2), particularly for borrowers in the corporate sector, which have the greatest external refinancing needs. [7] However, in some countries, such as Chile and Colombia, there was some continued issuancc of local bonds. This is consistent with the view that local capital markets may have to some extent acted as a "spare tyre" during the crisis, reducing vulnerabilities to declines in international bond finance (see Box 2 for further discussion).

Currency Depreciation: The significant reversal in capital flows, the collapse in commodity prices and the deterioration of confidence following the Lehman Brothers bankruptcy triggered sharp currency depreciations and higher costs of external financing across the region (Graph 3). Currency dynamics in Brazil and Mexico were particularly volatile, fuelled by the increased demand for dollars as some large corporations sought to close unhedged foreign currency positions, often incurring large losses as they did so (see Box 1). Depreciation was not quite as steep in countries such as Chile, where firms were not exposed to such losses, or Colombia, where firms were constrained by law in the risks they could take in the foreign exchange derivatives market.

The size of the exchange rate adjustment was very large. However, four features may have dampened any disruptive effects: (i) the widespread use of flexible exchange rate regimes, which reduced incentives for speculative attacks; (ii) the limited exchange rate pass-through to inflation; (iii) lower currency mismatches, as well as the lower levels of dollarisation across the region; and (iv) the greater credibility of central banks, which may also have contributed to curbing destabilising speculation and limiting the exchange rate pass-through to inflation. These factors facilitated the policy responses discussed below:

Box 2: Performance of Domestic Bond Markets during the Current Crisis

It has been argued that domestic bond markets could provide a "spare tyre" to offset the withdrawal of external financing during periods of financial stress. However, the performance of these markets during the current crisis has been mixed. On the one hand, domestic government bond markets have provided a financing alternative and have exhibited as much resilience as international bond markets. On the other hand, foreign investors have tended to reduce their bond holdings and there has been a shift towards shorter-maturity instruments. [(a)]

Financing Alternative for Governments: Although domestic bond issuance in most of the region fell during autumn 2008, it later resumed at lower levels. Most governments have been able to roll over short-term debt, swap maturing for longer-maturity debt, or sell new debt.

Resilience of Domestic Government Bond Markets: While domestic bond returns became more volatile during the episode of stress that followed the Lehman episode, their volatility was lower than that for international bonds, and is now at levels comparable to those before the episode. To be sure, recent policy efforts to supply liquidity and to stabilise domestic bond markets may have played a role in the decline in volatility. Such performance suggests that, from the point of view of a Latin American resident whose revenues and

Contd...

expenditures are to a large extent in local currency (e.g. a government), there are advantages to relying on domestic markets for financing. (b)

Lower Foreign Investor Holdings: This is illustrated by the experience of Mexico, which has one of the most developed and open domestic bond markets in Latin America. The share of foreign holdings of government bonds declined abruptly after the Lehman bankruptcy. The market was disrupted, and there was a sharp increase in bond yields, particularly at longer maturities. To satisfy the demand for short-term instruments and counter the rapidly falling demand for long-term bonds, the Mexican Treasury reduced long-term bond issuance during the fourth quarter of 2008 (both for fixed rate and inflation-indexed instruments) and increased the issuance of shorter-term instruments.

(Graph A)

Features of domestic government and corporate debt securities in Mexico

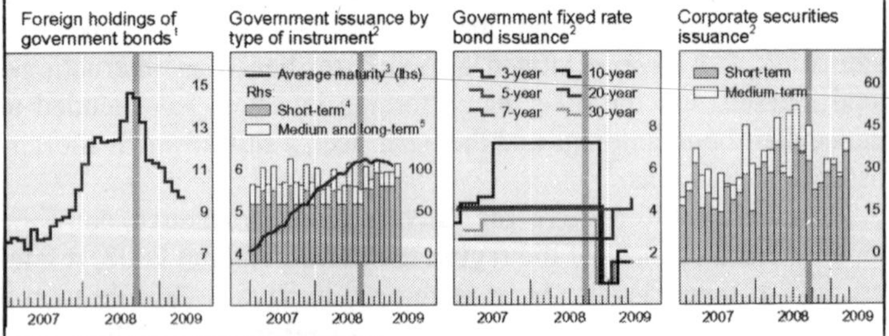

The shaded area indicates the month of September 2008.

[1] As a percentage of total government bonds outstanding. [2] In billions of pesos. [3] Of outstanding government securities, in years. [4] Cetes. [5] Bondes-D (variable rate), UDI bonds (inflation-linked) and fixed rate bonds.

Source: Bank of Mexico.

Graph A

Shift towards Shorter Maturity Instruments: In Mexico, private domestic issuance (financial and non-financial) was disrupted. No medium-term bond issues were made during October and November. The issuance of short-term securities also declined, but remained at levels comparable to those seen during 2007. Across the region there have been some exceptions in which highly rated corporates placed new debt at relatively long maturities. For instance,

Contd..

this is the case of private banks in Colombia (e.g. Bancolombia and Davivienda).

Overall, the performance of local currency bond markets as an alternative to international bond financing during this crisis has been mixed. This may reflect a less advanced stage of development and the severity of the global shock. An important issue for policy is that local currency funding for the government appears to have been more stale than funding for corporations.

(a) Over the past decade bond markets in the region have deepened, becoming the main source of debt financing. In 2008, outstanding domestic debt securities reached an average of 37% of GDP, compared to 9.6% for international debt securities. For an overview of the development of these markets, see Tovar and Quispe-Agnoli (2008), Jeanneau and Tovar (2006, 2008), BIS (2007) and Scatigna and Tovar (2007). (b) The comparison may not be entirely fair because efforts to supply liquidity and to stabilise domestic bond markets may have helped reduce volatility in domestic bond markets.

Higher Costs of Foreign Currency Financing: The increase in the cost of external financing—usually denominated in US dollars—took several forms. For example, in Peru, the 90-day prime rate in foreign currency rose relative to the interbank average interest rate in foreign currency (Graph 3). In Chile, the spread between the US dollar rates implied by the foreign exchange swap market rose sharply, reaching over 500 basis points above Libor. This reflected disruptions in the FX swap markets. Furthermore, dollar-denominated liquidity lines that small banks used to lend to exporter clients dried up or became too expensive.

Spreads on Latin American sovereign external debt widened to a peak of 914 basis points after the Lehman bankruptcy, an increase of 135 percent, and have remained at decade-high levels since (Graph 4). The widening in spreads was highly synchronised across emerging markets and appeared to be correlated with fluctuations in the VIX index, a widely used proxy for risk aversion. However, country-specific factors also played a role. Spreads widened the most in Argentina and Venezuela, two economies which followed heterodox economic policies during the boom years (Graph 4). Furthermore, as might be expected, countries with lower sovereign ratings experienced larger increases in spreads.

Graph 3

Exchange rates and the cost of financing

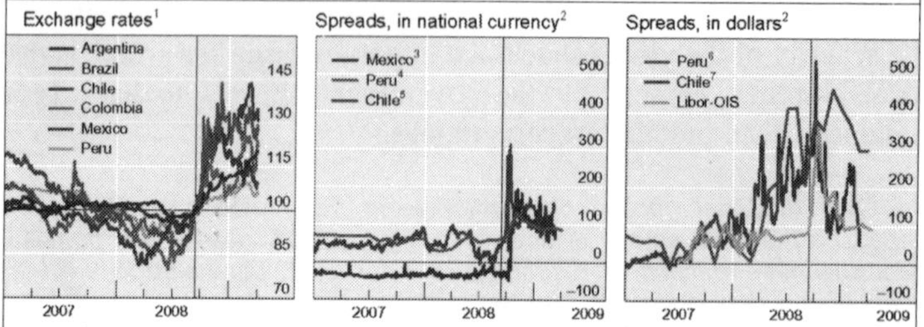

[1] Against the US dollar; a rise indicates a depreciation. The vertical line marks the date of the Lehman Brothers bankruptcy on 15 September 2008 (= 100). [2] In basis points. [3] Of the 30-day commercial paper rate to the overnight rate. [4] Of the 90-day prime rate in national currency to the interbank average interest rate in national currency. [5] Of 180-day prime deposit rates to peso swap contracts. [6] Of the 90-day prime rate in foreign currency to the interbank average interest rate in foreign currency. [7] Of 90-day onshore US dollar rates to Libor.

Sources: Central Bank of Chile; Central Reserve Bank of Peru; Bloomberg; Datastream; JPMorgan Chase. Graph 3

Tightening in Domestic Funding Markets: Domestic funding markets were greatly affected by the crisis as well. In Argentina, the three month interbank-overnight spread widened. In Mexico, there were sharp increases in commercial paper rates, reflecting a drying-up of financing in that market segment. In Chile, local peso money markets were subject to significant pressure, as seen in the widening spread between prime deposit rates and the implicit interbank term rate in swap contracts (Graph 3). [8] In Brazil, domestic interest rates for small and medium-sized banks increased as local asset managers moved their deposits to larger banks in search of higher-quality deposits. More recently, funding markets have remained strained, notwithstanding some reductions in rates at short maturities.

Longer-term government bond yields also increased for all maturities (Chile being the main exception). In Brazil, Colombia and Mexico yields rose sharply, particularly at the long end of the curve, reflecting the fact that investors felt more secure in shorter-dated securities. However, bond yields then fell across the region starting in late 2008, largely in response to expectations of monetary easing, which were driving the short end of the curve. Thus, domestic market interest rates are currently well below the levels they reached ahead of the Lehman failure (Graph 5). In spite of these declines, the spreads between long-term and short-term bond yields have risen (Graph 5).

Graph 4

Sovereign and corporate spreads for international bonds

In basis points

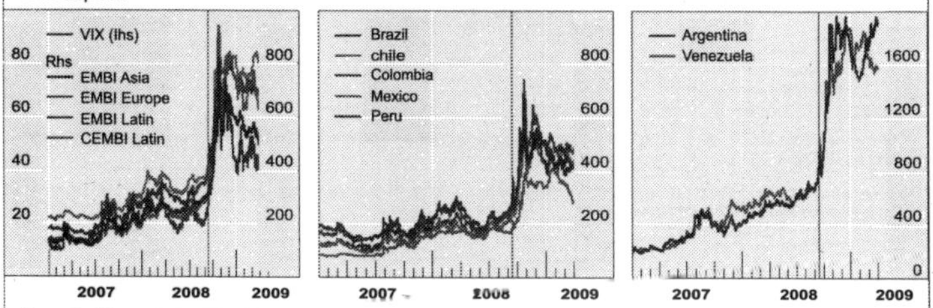

The vertical line marks the date of the Lehman Brothers bankruptcy on 15 September 2008.

Source: JPMorgan Chase.

Graph 4

Policy Responses and Issues

As they entered the current crisis, many Latin American sovereigns had reduced or stabilised their external debt, but private external borrowing had either increased or remained high. Central banks thus sought to provide foreign currency liquidity to the private sector, to ensure both the continued operation of foreign exchange markets and the continued availability of external financing, including trade finance. Central banks also intervened to counteract tighter financial conditions in domestic funding and credit markets.

Foreign Currency Liquidity and External Financing: Most central banks in the region supplied foreign currency liquidity through intervention or operations in the foreign exchange market, including foreign exchange spot, repo and swap transactions. In some cases, reserve requirements on foreign currency deposits were lowered. [9] The Central Bank of Brazil set up facilities to provide trade finance and also to help companies roll over their foreign debt. [10]

Graph 5

Government bond yields in local currency[1]

In per cent

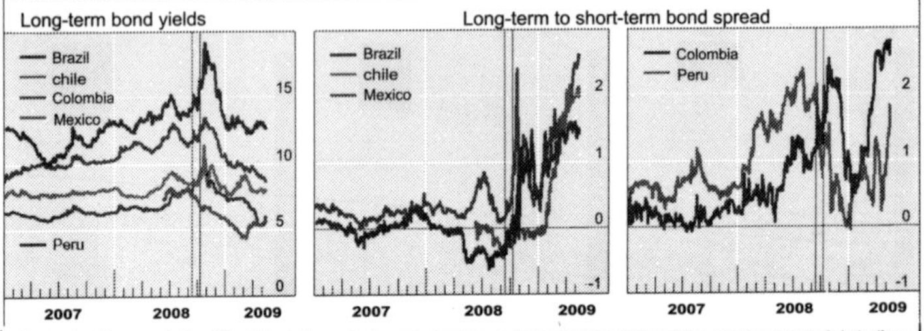

The vertical lines mark the date of the Lehman Brothers bankruptcy on 15 September 2008 and the announcement of derivatives losses by Mexican corporates on 9 October 2008.

[1] Long-term bonds: for Brazil, eight-year; for Chile, nine-year; for Colombia, 11-year; for Mexico, 15-year; for Peru, 10-year. Short-term bonds: for Brazil and Chile, three-year; for Colombia, Mexico and Peru, one-year.

Source: Bloomberg. Graph 5

Foreign exchange market intervention has been an important way of providing foreign currency liquidity, although it has generally been scaled back in 2009 as foreign exchange markets stabilised (Graph 6). There was some variation in intervention tactics. For example, some countries focused on operations in the spot market, while Brazil and Chile implemented a large number of operations in the swap market. One explanation for the latter is that foreign exchange swap markets are active in Brazil and Chile. Another explanation is that in contrast to spot transactions, swaps do not deplete foreign reserves as they involve the reversal of the foreign currency sale by the central bank at some future date.
Some of the foreign exchange market intervention was non-discretionary, to underscore that central banks were not targeting an exchange rate level, which past experience has shown can trigger speculative attacks. For example, in October 2008, Mexico adopted a rule according to which the central bank would auction US$ 400 million (lowered in March 2009 to US$ 300 million) on any day after the exchange rate depreciated by 2 percent or more.

Graph 6

Central bank intervention in the foreign exchange market[1]

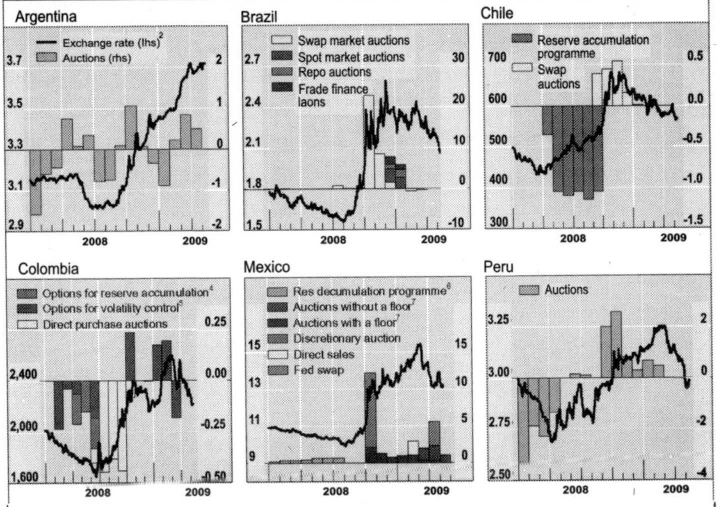

[1] The figures correspond to the sum of assigned auctions in the month, expressed in US dollars. Positive values indicate a sale of US dollars. [2] Against the US dollar; an increase indicates a depreciation. [3] Net of issuance and redemption of foreign exchange swap contracts. [4] Long positions of put options. [5] Net of long put and short call options. [6] Interventions to slow the pace of reserve accumulation. [7] An auction with a floor is a procedure in which the Bank of Mexico auctions a specified amount of dollars on any day after the currency depreciates by 2% or more. A minimum price (floor) is set at 1.02 times the currency value of the previous day. On 9 March 2009, the Bank of Mexico started to auction a specified amount of dollars without a minimum price (floor).

Sources: Datastream; national data. Graph 6

A minimum price or floor was set at 1.02 times the average currency value of the previous day. Colombia also followed a rule in which large exchange rate movements triggered auctions of so-called volatility "call" options (giving market participants the option to buy foreign currency from the central bank). This mechanism was triggered in October 2008, and in the first two months of 2009. [11] More recently, the Central Bank of Mexico implemented two important changes to its intervention procedures. The first was to conduct daily auctions with no price floor (in recent weeks these have accounted for a large part of the daily auctions), and the second was direct sales in its foreign exchange market operations.

Though intervention in foreign exchange markets was in

some cases associated with depletions of foreign exchange reserves–as much as 15 percent compared to mid-2008 levels in Peru and 7 percent in Brazil–conventional indicators suggest that reserve holdings are still ample (Table 1). Foreign reserves in Latin American economies on balance increased in 2008, and were much larger than in 1996, prior to the Asian crisis. Indicators of foreign reserve adequacy are generally well above conventional thresholds of 100 percent (i.e. one year's cover) relative to short-term external debt or 25-50 percent (three to six months' foreign exchange cover) relative to imports.

Table 1

Foreign reserve adequacy[1]

Outstanding year-end reserves position

	In billions of US dollars				As a percentage of: GDP	Short-term external debt[2]				Imports			
	96	07	08	09	08	96	07	08	09	96	07	08	09
Argentina	18	44	44	44	14	60	200	279	274	75	99	77	84
Brazil	58	179	193	186	12	111	292	342	329	109	149	111	115
Chile	16	17	23	24	14	201	86	113	114	89	38	40	47
Colombia	9	20	23	23	9	142	201	390	352	69	61	58	57
Mexico	19	86	94	84	9	60	256	241	218	21	31	30	29
Peru	11	27	30	30	24	166	284	248	243	135	137	106	111
Venezuela	11	24	33	19	10	273	347	972	569	125	57	72	42
Memo:													
Latin America[3]	*142*	*397*	*440*	*410*	*13*	*145*	*238*	*369*	*300*	*89*	*82*	*71*	*69*
Asia[4]	*246*	*2,327*	*2,685*	*2,712*	*40*	*284*	*624*	*889*	*908*	*60*	*120*	*106*	*120*
Southeast Asia[5] 91		*270*	*283*	*289*	*27*	*119*	*431*	*500*	*498*	*39*	*64*	*54*	*60*
Central Europe[6] 40		*124*	*133*	*138*	*17*	*383*	*177*	*169*	*175*	*49*	*31*	*29*	*33*
Other[7]	*29*	*569*	*513*	*465*	*15*	*59*	*260*	*279*	*254*	*19*	*96*	*70*	*70*
Total EME's[8]	*548*	*3,688*	*4,054*	*4,015*	*22*	*188*	*343*	*452*	*429*	*58*	*80*	*68*	*72*

1 For the outstanding year-end position, regional aggregates are the sum of the economies listed; for percentages, simple averages. For 2009, latest available data. [2] Consolidated cross-border claims to all BIS reporting banks on countries outside the reporting area with a maturity up to one year plus international debt securities outstanding with a maturity of up to one year. [3] Argentina, Brazil, Chile, Colombia, Mexico, Peru and Venezuela. 4 China, Chinese Taipei, India and Korea. [5] Indonesia, Malaysia, the Philippines and Thailand. 6 The Czech Republic, Hungary and Poland. 7 Russia, South Africa and Turkey. [8] Sum of the regions listed.

Sources: IMF; Thomson Reuters; national data.

At the same time, foreign reserve adequacy depends in part on other characteristics of the economy not captured by conventional indicators. For example, despite comparatively low reserves and falling export revenues, Chile's foreign reserves have been remarkably stable. One explanation is that both the government (through its sovereign wealth fund) and households (through pension funds) have very large holdings of foreign assets, which has contributed to reassuring markets. Reserves have also been stable in Colombia; in this case, government regulations limiting domestic US dollar interbank loans and foreign exchange counterparty risk appear to have played a role. More generally, it has been argued that the commitment of international reserves in response to the crisis has been lower in Latin America than in some other EMEs (e.g. Korea and Russia). This could reflect lower perceived exposures to external refinancing risk or to currency mismatches in Latin America. [12]

External resources have provided significant additional support to Latin American EMEs during the current crisis. In October 2008 large reciprocal currency arrangements were established by the central banks of Brazil and Mexico with the US Federal Reserve, totalling US$ 30 billion each (these arrangements will expire on October 30, 2009). [13] More recently, G20 initiatives have increased resources for international financial institutions. In particular, at its 2 April 2009 summit the G20 called for a tripling of IMF resources to US$750 billion, a new SDR allocation (which would increase the availability of foreign reserves) of US$ 250 billion, US$ 100 billion of additional lending by multilateral development banks and the allocation of US$ 250 billion for trade financing. In the meantime, as part of its efforts to enhance the scope and effectiveness of its crisis-related operations, the IMF has created the FCL aimed at countries with sound fundamentals. Two Latin American economies, Colombia and Mexico, have obtained access to the FCL. The financing is for one year, and amounts to US$ 47 billion for Mexico and US$ 10.5 billion for Colombia.

Stabilising Domestic Markets: As discussed above, the crisis was also associated with tighter financial conditions in domestic markets, and authorities responded with a variety of policy measures. There was no immediate systematic effort to offset tighter financing conditions by lowering policy rates. Central banks delayed lowering rates until late 2008 or early 2009, after much of the initial market turbulence following the Lehman bankruptcy had subsided. This reflected continuing concerns about inflationary pressures and the potential impact of any additional exchange rate depreciation that might accompany lower rates. Since late 2008, however, rates have fallen sharply in Brazil, Chile and Colombia as the focus shifted to the impact of slowing growth. In contrast, in Mexico and Peru policy rates have declined much more gradually.

Central banks also modified their operating procedures. Apart from implementing open market operations to dampen volatility in short-term interest rates, some central banks also increased the range of assets accepted as collateral to improve access to short-term funding (e.g. Argentina, Brazil, Mexico and Peru).

Many central banks also relied heavily on lower domestic currency reserve requirements: in Peru, for example, marginal reserve requirements were lowered from 25 percent in September 2008 to 7.5 percent in December 2008 and to 6 percent by March 2009. Brazil's reserve requirements were also lowered significantly from much higher levels, and in Colombia reserve requirements were lowered and marginal reserve requirements removed.

Steps were also taken to maintain the flow of credit to offset the possible impairment of the transmission mechanism of monetary policy. For example, to improve funding conditions in the commercial paper market, the Mexican government extended guarantees to issuance by some corporations. In October 2008, state-owned development banks in Mexico offered partial guarantees to facilitate the rollover of short-term domestic debt. Measures were also taken to support the operation of banks. For example, in Brazil, state-owned financial institutions were authorised to buy shares in banks facing difficulties. Government institutions were also authorised to purchase the assets of local banks (particularly small and mid-sized banks).

The effectiveness of measures to support domestic interbank and credit markets may be assessed in two ways. One is the extent to which interbank rates at longer maturities have stabilised. As noted above, spreads of rates at longer maturities to overnight rates have fallen from their peaks, suggesting a certain degree of normalisation. Another is the growth in domestic credit to the private sector. Here there appear to be wide variations in performance across countries. Credit has broadly remained on a rising trend in Brazil, Peru and Venezuela but has flattened in Argentina and Colombia (Graph 7). In contrast, in Chile and Mexico credit dropped in September 2008 but recovered thereafter, with particularly sharp swings in Chile. Nevertheless, while a collapse in bank credit of the kind observed in previous crises has so far been avoided, the risk remains high that credit will fall sharply due to the ongoing economic downturn.

Graph 7

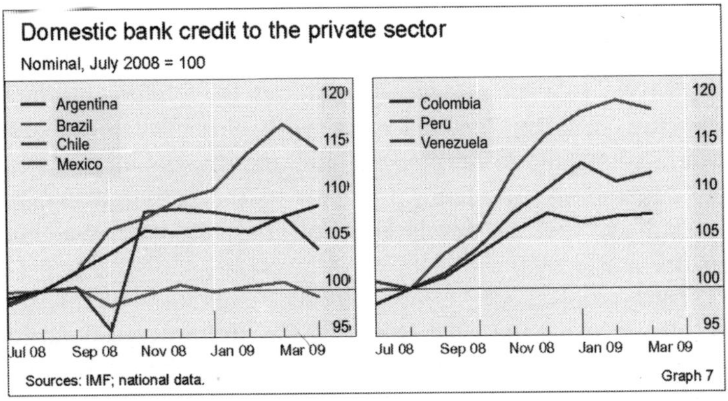

Conclusions

The world economy is experiencing a severe economic

and financial crisis. Despite initial signs of decoupling, Latin America was strongly affected after the Lehman Brothers bankruptcy, as were other EME regions. Nevertheless, compared to previous crises, the disruption to the functioning of domestic financial markets has so far been less severe. The unprecedented (non-reserve) foreign asset accumulation by residents in some countries and the progress made in developing domestic debt markets (particularly in government securities) appear to have played important roles. Furthermore, policy responses across the region were significant, and in many cases preemptive. Nevertheless, new vulnerabilities became apparent, such as the corporate foreign currency exposures from derivatives transactions that led to bankruptcies of leading firms, and which contributed to foreign exchange or domestic market instability in Brazil and Mexico.

The recent experience with the crisis offers a number of policy lessons. First, there is a need to ensure that risks assumed in financial markets are well understood by market participants and policymakers. This could help prevent bankruptcies of large and otherwise economically viable firms and disruptions to local funding markets of the kind observed in the region during the current crisis.

Second, while local currency bond markets could play a "spare tyre" role and effectively substitute for foreign currency financing, in Latin America more work is needed to deepen these markets and to develop a liquid and diversified investor and issuer base. Financing problems in the corporate sector also indicate that the development of corporate bond markets remains a priority.

Third, public sector efforts to reduce external vulnerability over the past decade have enhanced the ability to respond to crises. In particular, the recent crisis illustrates the importance of having large foreign currency resources available to cope with external shocks. Central banks have drawn on international reserves to stabilise foreign exchange markets and to support the flow of foreign currency financing. Greater credibility has also given them some scope to inject domestic liquidity and lower interest rates counter cyclically. However, the crisis has revealed that a stronger public sector could not completely offset private sector vulnerabilities.

Finally, recent initiatives have significantly increased the amount of external foreign currency resources available to EMEs and broken new ground in how such resources are provided (e.g. through the Federal Reserve's reciprocal currency arrangements or the IMF's FCL). An important question is whether these arrangements will be seen as sufficiently large and durable as to provide an alternative to costly self-insurance via reserve accumulation in EMEs.

Source: BIS Quarterly Review, June 2009 www.bis.org
© Bank for International Settlements, BIS. Reprinted with Permission.

The views expressed in this article are those of the authors and do not necessarily reflect those of the BIS. We thank Claudio Borio, Már Gudmundsson, Patrick McGuire, Frank Packer and Agustín Villar for useful comments and Sergio Vargas for excellent research assistance.

Notes

1. The analysis that follows focuses mostly on Brazil, Chile, Colombia, Mexico and Peru. There is some discussion of Argentina and Venezuela, but certain characteristics make their financial systems less comparable with the other five countries.
2. For a related discussion, see Caruana (2009). For an overview of the impact of the crisis on the real sector in Latin America, see IADB (2009) and IMF (2009b).
3. Other gross inflows (mainly banking flows) also decreased sharply, especially in Brazil, where they fell by more than US$ 18 billion. As discussed below, however, special factors accounted for much of the decline in Brazil.
4. See Jara and Tovar (2008) for a detailed discussion.
5. This largely reflected the repatriation of banking flows into the region. Portfolio decisions of institutional investors may also have played a role. However, some data suggest that repatriation might not have continued in some countries in 2009.

6. Peek and Rosengren (2000) document great volatility of cross-border flows in the Latin American case before 2000.
7. External refinancing needs for the corporate sector in Latin America are estimated at 8 percent of GDP. This compares favourably with Asia (9 percent) and emerging Europe (23 percent). See IMF (2009a).
8. See García (2009) for a detailed account of this episode.
9. For example, the Central Reserve Bank of Peru lowered the marginal reserve requirement on foreign currency from 49 percent in October to 30 percent in December 2008. In December, the legal reserve requirement on foreign currency was lowered from 9.0 percent to 7.5 percent and in March 2009 from 6.5 percent to 6.0 percent.
10. Foreign currency trade finance in the region has also been supported by international organisations. For example, between July 2008 and March 2009 the International Finance Corporation increased trade finance guarantees in Latin America and the Caribbean by 86 percent over a year earlier, to US$ 520 million.
11. The Colombian central bank sold US$ 235 million in October 2008 and US$ 369 million in the first two months of 2009.
12. See Aizenman (2009).
13. The provision of Federal Reserve swap lines for Brazil and Mexico is unprecedented. Whether this signals a new approach to interacting with emerging market central banks or is a temporary response to the global crisis remains uncertain. The drawdown of these resources has been relatively recent and comparatively limited. On April 21, 2009 the Bank of Mexico auctioned US$ 4 billion out of this swap line to support the rollover of maturing debt in the Mexican corporate sector. However, only US$ 3.2 billion was placed.

References

Aizenman, J (2009): "Reserves and the crisis: a re-assessment", *Central Banking*, vol 19, no 3.

Bank for International Settlements (2007): "Financial stability and local currency bond markets", *CGFS Papers*, no 28, June.

——(2009): "Capital flows and emerging market economies", *CGFS Papers*, no 33, January.

Caruana, Jaime (2009): "Financial globalisation, the crisis and Latin America", speech at the XLVI Meeting of Central Bank

Governors of the American Continent and LXXXVII Meeting of Central Bank Governors of Latin America and Spain, Punta Cana, Dominican Republic, 14 May.

García, P (2009): "Financial turmoil, illiquidity and the policy responses. The case of Chile", *Economic Policy Papers*, no 29, Central Bank of Chile.

Inter-American Development Bank (2009): *Policy tradeoffs for unprecedented times: confronting the global crisis in Latin America and the Caribbean.*

International Monetary Fund (2009a): *Global Financial Stability Report: responding to the financial crisis and measuring systemic risk*, Washington, DC, April.

——(2009b): *Regional Economic Outlook, Western Hemisphere: stronger fundamentals pay off*, Washington, DC, May.

Jara, A and C E Tovar (2008): "Monetary and financial stability implications of capital flows in Latin America and the Caribbean", *BIS Papers*, no 43, November.

Jeanneau, S and C E Tovar (2006): "Domestic bond markets in Latin America: achievements and challenges", *BIS Quarterly Review*, June, pp 51–64.

——(2008): "Financial stability implications of local currency bond markets: an overview of the risks", *BIS Papers*, no 36, February, pp 65–87.

McGuire, P and N Tarashev (2008): "Bank health and lending to emerging markets", *BIS Quarterly Review*, December.

Moreno, R and K von Kleist (2007): "What can BIS statistics tell us about the risks of crises in emerging markets?", in "Research on global financial stability: the use of BIS international financial statistics", *CGFS Papers*, no 29, December.

Peek, J and E Rosengren (2000): "Implications of the globalization of the banking sector: the Latin American experience", *New England Economic Review*, September/October.

Scatigna, M and C E Tovar (2007): "Securitisation in Latin America", *BIS Quarterly Review*, September, pp 71–82.

Tovar, C E and M Quispe-Agnoli (2008): "New financing trends in Latin America: an overview of selected issues and policy challenges", *Economic Review*, no 3, pp 1-14.

8

Crisis Management in the European Union

Sylvester C.W. Eijffinger

---

1. Crisis Management in the European Union: An Introduction

The ECB is doing crisis prevention in many ways, in particularly through promoting co-ordination and co-operation between national supervisors, mainly through the ESCB Banking Supervision Committee, and providing liquidity management on the inter-bank markets. The ECB has reduced the rate for its main refinancing operations within the past month from 4.25 percent to 3.25 percent. A non-binding Memorandum of Understanding (MoU) on Cross-Border Financial Stability was also signed last summer between the Financial Supervision Authorities, Central Banks and the Finance Ministries of the European Union. Stress test and crises management simulations have also taken place. This MoU is designed to facilitate the management and resolution of crossborder systemic financial crises and will seek to facilitate private sector solutions, to minimise the economic and social costs, while promoting market discipline and limiting moral hazard. Those parties that have specific common financial stability concerns are encouraged to develop Voluntary Specific Cooperation Agreements with a view to provide for more specific and detailed, procedures and arrangements of crisis management and resolution for their respective countries and in relevant contexts. However, in practice it looks like Member States have taken very different approaches in face of banking problems and crisis management, for example in the Benelux countries, in Ireland, in Germany, in Denmark and in the UK to mention some. Even if in most cases the direct effects have been national, major spillover effects may arise both for foreign banks operating in the region and/or policy measures to be taken in another Member State. In a statistic prepared for the ECON Committee of the EP, financial institutions were ranked according to their size and diversification of ownership among EU Member States in order to do a 'pre-selection' of financial institutions potentially vulnerable to systemic risk and important for cross-border stability in the EU.

Section 2 will describe the development of the crisis with the denial phase, the discovery phase and disposal phase of the crisis. Then we analyse in Section 3 the nationalisation of banks and the three conditions that need to be fulfilled to make a bailout as unattractive as possible. In Section 4 four important lessons for the credit crisis are drawn for the future. Finally, in Section 5 the benchmarks for the new financial system are analysed: sustainability, integrity and transparency.

2. Development of the Crisis: The Denial, Discovery and Disposal Phase

This credit crisis, as we all know, has its roots in the sub-prime crisis of summer 2007. However, at that point it was not acknowledged that this sub-prime crisis could grow out to be a larger crisis; even more so, this was denied. The development of the crisis is quite aptly put in The Economist of April 3, 2008: .First there was disbelief and denial. Then fear. Now comes anger. The anger is of course caused by the failure of financial supervision, which will become clear in a later part of this paper.

The denial phase is exemplified by several points, especially by Chairman Bernanke of the Federal Reserve, who said that .the Fed does not see the tightening of credit conditions in the market as severe enough to have macro-economic implications. [1] He did note that the subprime crisis was not completely played out yet, so conditions could still worsen. However, the Fed also noted that the Bear Stearns case was reassuring as its losses could be absorbed by the financial system without much adverse effects for credit supply; the Fed did not see an immediate threat of a broad credit crunch. Even in 2008, just before the collapse of Lehman Brothers, its CEO Richard Fuld seemed to deny that there was something wrong. He blamed short sellers for the .symptoms of a sickness rooted in denial, just to shield himself from the 'pain of reality' [2] that was imminent. In October 2008 some finance directors of non-financial companies still denied that there was a liquidity problem, even if interbank rates had shot up through the roof. [3]

Note: this graph represents the total return on the MSCI World Market index, which can be used as a proxy for the cost of capital. We can see that the marginal cost of capital has increased tremendously, as the value of equity capital has declined during the last half of 2008.

Then, during the course of 2008, the discovery phase started. Banks started to write off bad loans and securitization products, a process that also uncovered many hidden linkages among financial institutions. Asset holdings by banks and other financial institutions had been very opaque, hiding the linkages to (among others) subprime mortgages in the United States. Because of the losses on their loans and other assets, many banks were in serious trouble. In the end contagion of the subprime crisis became reality when several banks started to collapse, the most notable example being Lehman Brothers. [4] Because of the lack of confidence in the markets, marginal costs of capital and interbank lending rose tremendously as risk premiums went up (see also the graphs below). A good illustration is also the fact that banks in the euro area deposited record amounts of euros at the ECB, i.e. they did not want to lend that money to others, a clear sign of lack of confidence. In the first graph, the value of existing equity capital has declined greatly and thus the costs to attract new capital have risen. In the second graph, we see that the risk premia for interbank lending have risen during the course of the crisis. Therefore, banks could not attract enough buffer capital or renew their short term financing.

This led to the disposal phase of the crisis: national governments stepped in to rescue banks that were important for the financial system, to prevent a systemic crisis from happening. These actions were aimed at restoring the confidence and thus liquidity in the markets. As we can see below, the costs of capital (a measure for solvency) and interbank money market rates (a measure for liquidity) have indeed surged but declined during the last half of 2008 by the emergency measures by governments and central banks. This can be best seen in the development of the three-month Euribor interbank interest rate.

3. Bailouts and Nationalisation of Banks: Three Conditions that Need to be Fulfilled

Several banks and insurers in Europe have been nationalized or bailed-out, i.e. assisted with emergency (tier 1) core capital. Examples of this include the government takeover of ABN AMRO and Fortis in the Netherlands, the emergency assistance to ING, AEGON and SNS Reaal, the bailout of Dexia in Belgium and the bailout of UBS in Switzerland.

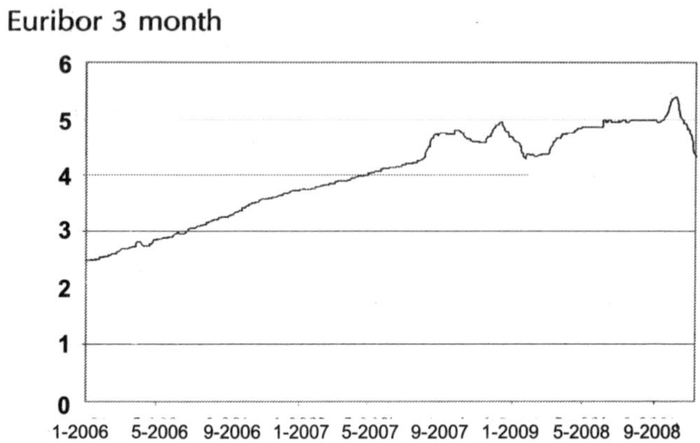

Note: this graph represents the three-month Euribor interbank interest rate. We have zoomed in to better show the increase during 2008, followed by a spike in September and a decline after government injections.

Bailouts or nationalisations by the government need to satisfy three criteria. First, the nationalisation needs to be temporary to keep intact the level playing field on the financial markets. This holds for both banks and insurers. Second, the government and thus the taxpayers need to face an upward risk, which arises when the bank is privatised after the nationalisation period. Although it is not the intention for the government and taxpayers to make a profit of the bailout or nationalisation, they are entitled to this upward risk because they are providing risk-bearing (tier 1) core capital. Additionally, the government should profit from the transaction in the form of high interest rates that financial institutions have to pay for the emergency assistance. Third, there should be a downward risk for the financial institution involved and its executives and shareholders. They have caused the problems that the bank or insurer is faced with, so they also have felt the pain by respectively giving up bonuses and options and lower stock prices.

These three conditions need to be fulfilled to make a bailout as unattractive as possible by making the costs as high as possible, so that the management of the institution has an incentive to revert to the normal course of business as soon as possible. Since public money is involved, the government should be accountable both at the national level and the EU level to make sure that these conditions are fulfilled and to avoid competition in conditions between the EU countries. [5] This should also hold ex ante: the circumstances in which this assistance takes place are very rare, and the conditions will be very painful. [6]

4. Four Important Lessons from the Credit Crisis

This credit crisis has provided us with four important lessons: (1) the top management reward and remuneration structure has been excessive, (2) the risk management models based on Basel II have proven to be inadequate, (3) the financial supervisors in the US and Europe have not been involved thoroughly enough and (4) the US framework of financial supervision has proven to be too much fragmented and totally ineffective.

First, top executives reward and remuneration packages have been asymmetric in the sense that there is no downward risk or limited liability for top managers. The reward structure should be more aimed at the long term, and both the upward and downward risks should be symmetric and stretch beyond their term in office.

These executives have chosen an Anglo-Saxon reward structure. This means that they cannot have Rheinland protection as well. Managers should take their responsibilities when things take a turn for the worse. We can think of negative bonuses and conditional options (in case of large risks that only manifest after the manager's term in office is over), or the manager may resign when staying in office is no longer credible. The compensation structure should hold .In good times and in bad times. This also means that the Boards of Directors (Trustees) should no longer only consist of top managers, but also of independent experts who hold themselves far enough from the Executive Board. This may lead to difficult discussions in the short term for executives, but it creates broader support for a financial institution's long-term strategy.

Secondly, the risk management models based on Basel II have not passed the stress test of the credit crisis. This was to be expected, as ex postrisk (certainly in times of crisis) is not a good proxy for ex ante uncertainty. Furthermore, during this the fat tails and the skewness of the return distribution have proven to be more important than the mean and the variance. [7] The devil was in the tail! Hopefully this failure of the financial econometricians and risk managers in mapping the uncertainties results in a revaluation for the intuition of 'old-fashioned' bankers, insurers and financial economists. We should acknowledge that monitoring the return distributions give a false and incomplete picture of the fundamental uncertainty in an environment of innovation and long-term risks.

The Basel Committee itself has already indicated, through its Chairman Nout Wellink, that a thorough revision of the risk management and capital adequacy regulations is needed. [8] The Basel committee already proposed raising capital requirements for complex structured credit products, liquidity facilities to support asset-backed commercial paper conduits and credit exposures held due to trading. Additionally, the committee said that standards for liquidity management needed to be strengthened. Another problem is the pro-cyclicality of the capital requirements, which has to be addressed by the Basel Committee. It is evident that the capital requirements should become more anti-cyclical.

Several researchers have additionally proposed improvements for risk management and capital planning to make banks more resilient to crises. Alexander and Sheedy

(2008), among others, propose a new method for stress testing to incorporate heavy tails and thus to take into account extreme events, something which the current methods did not do. Their method also incorporates abnormal market characteristics during crises, such as an increased probability of further large movements (besides the initial crisis), increased correlation between markets, a greater implied volatility and reduced liquidity (in interbank markets). Blum (2008) additionally proposes a restriction on the leverage ratio of banks to induce truthful reporting of risks. This makes it also easier for supervisors to sanction dishonest banks.

These measures should make banks more prepared for crises with the scale and nature of this one by creating strong capital cushions, robust liquidity buffers, strong risk management and supervision and better market discipline.

Thirdly, it has become clear that national central banks and financial supervisors have to be much more involved with risk management in financial institutions. We have seen that CEOs do not understand the risk management models and aim for higher yields and the risks connected to those yields. Regulators have to provide incentives for banks to take into account risks better when searching for higher yields. This does not necessarily have to come from more strict supervision. Because of their strategic interaction with financial institutions, supervisors should use modern game-theoretic concepts like constructive ambiguity and incentive compatibility to realise smarter and more efficient supervision.

However, clear-cut rules also need to be set. Following Freixas (2003), we can set some conditions for (cross-border) financial supervision. It has to be made clear to banks that the probability of a bailout is lower than they currently expect. As a consequence, banks face tighter capital regulation, and more collateral has to be held in transactions. This guards the system against contagion of bank failures. Additionally, the discipline on honesty in disclosure of risk in loans should be tougher, as it already is in New Zealand.

Moreover, some ambiguity about bailouts may be necessary, but not too much: it should become clear to financial institutions under what conditions they can get emergency funding and what the availability of this funding will be (Fellgett, 2003). When this is clear, governments should not teem too long with regulatory forbearance and (unconstructive) liquidity support in the hope insolvent institutions will recover [9]. This only increases the strain on the system and increases the probability of a crisis. However, policymakers should also take into account the trade-off between helping banks at the taxpayer's expense, creating moral hazard, and rescuing the financial system.

It is also important to note that these methods of regulation may alleviate the problem that bankers and traders are always one step ahead of regulators. By creating the proper incentives, activist regulation may not be as necessary anymore and liberalisation can do its much needed work. [10]

Finally, the credit crisis has showed us that the American system of financial supervision has failed and that the European supervision of banks and insurers also needs significant improvement. The economists of the Bank for International Settlements (BIS) blame lax monetary policy mainly in the US and the supervisory practices of the Federal Reserve. [11] US policymakers have learned their tough and expensive lessons, and will have to streamline their supervisory practices drastically. This will certainly involve a larger role for the Federal Reserve as supervisor and/or the creation of a new overall supervisor.

European politicians will have to agree on a European federal supervisor, either a European Financial Services Authority (EFSA) or a European System of Financial Supervisors (ESFS). This European supervisor has to serve as an umbrella organisation for the national central banks and supervisors and should be responsible for the complete financial supervision in the European Union, mainly dealing with the cross-border effects of individual supervisor's actions (see: my Briefing Paper of June 2007 and Schoenmaker and Oosterloo, 2007). It should be independent from the ECB to guarantee monetary stability, but the two bodies must cooperate and inform each other. National supervisors remain to exist, as they have insights in local financial institutions and markets. For cross-border banking and finance, however, uniform EU-wide rules should be adhered to. While the reform of US supervision will imply a larger role for the Federal Reserve, the Maastricht Treaty does not provide for the ECB to have a responsibility for prudential supervision in Europe. The ECB is only responsible for financial stability in the EU.

Before this can be realised, it is not a good idea to set up a European emergency fund. Without uniform supervision, such a fund can provide the wrong incentives (moral hazard), and induce free-riding behaviour and regulatory competition between member states that may lead to a 'race to the bottom' (Garcia and Nieto, 2007). Moral hazard is caused by the asymmetric risk that bankers have in joining the fund: they can take new risks without having to worry about adverse developments, since government pays for cleaning up the mess that may occur. The free-riding behaviour stems from some countries having more strict regulation than others. Countries with weak banking systems and regulation profit from countries with strong banking systems, as the former are more prone to financial crises. Additionally, countries that do not sign up for the fund profit from it anyway, as financial stability is a public good. This also leads to regulatory competition between member states, to lure big banks and financial institutions to their country. Goodhart and Schoenmaker (2008) come up with a mechanism for the European Union to be able to coordinate crisis management. Member states have to agree ex ante on a specific burden sharing mechanism. In this system, member states contribute to the fund according to the geographical spread of bank business. This guarantees long-term coordination better than ex post, improvised coordination.

We see that we cannot yet set up a European emergency fund without having European-wide supervision and policy coordination in guarding financial stability. A complete European safety net and regulation mechanism that goes beyond the current Memoranda of Understanding must be guided by the principles of constructive ambiguity and incentive compatibility (Freixas, 2003). Supervisors have to be able to agree ex ante upon the payments they make to the safety net, as to alleviate the problems with improvised cooperation that stem from its public good nature. Such a coordination mechanism also allows for more efficient information collection by national supervisors, better information provision to the central supervisory authority and lower social costs for using public money to rescue banks. Europe has also needed a crisis to make a leap forward. If this credit crisis is the 'wake-up call' for Europe, then it has had its use after all. A quote by Freixas and Parigi (2008) sketches how the new supervisory practice should look like: ..the issue is less to understand what rules the LOLR [Lender of Last Resort] should follow but what architecture of prudential regulation, risk supervision, monetary policy, deposit insurance and ELA is best to guarantee financial stability by providing liquidity to banks..

5. Benchmarks for a New Financial System: Sustainability, Integrity and Transparency

As an analogy to a country after a major war, we can state that the bigger the financial crisis, the bigger the reorganisation. This holds for the whole financial system, and especially for big financial institutions that have always been deemed 'too big to fail'. As Joseph Stiglitz puts it: [While they] may be too big to fail, they're not too big to be reorganised. [12] The benchmarks for the new financial system that will emerge must be: (1) sustainability, (2) integrity and (3) transparency.

Sustainability consists of a long-term view on the

architecture of the financial system. This includes the trade-off that banks face, between holding collateral and increasing the risk of systemic crisis (Freixas 2003). This can be obtained by giving the proper incentives to banks, among others by agreeing on European-wide regulation and coordination of crisis management. Executive compensation structures, for instance, have to be revised to give managers a long-term view and avoid excessive risk-taking without incurring any losses.

Integrity deals with incomplete information about complicated investment products, both for consumers and for corporate investors. An example of this is the Lehman notes, despite the high leveraging considered by consumers as 'safe bonds', and the 'Woekerpolisaffaire' in the Netherlands, indicating the problems around investment insurance products for consumers. These have led to media attention and even law suits. A similar issue played in 2001, when consumers that had leased stocks (i.e. bought them with borrowed money) incurred a huge amount of interest. These problems are examples dealing with financial institutions that provide too little information about complicated products. Additionally, rating agencies need stricter regulation to be able to properly assess the risk of (complicated) financial products. [13] This can for instance be achieved by making the regulator select the appropriate agency to rate a certain issuer. Rating agencies also have to provide more information about the models they use to rate several types of products, including complicated securitisation products. [14] Together with standardized reporting and originator principles in the US and Europe this has to restore the confidence in derivative markets.

Transparency, which is the cornerstone of any system that relies on confidence. As Freixas and Parigi (2008) have put it, the lack of transparency is what has lead to significant adverse selection in the interbank market and prohibitively high interest rates. An intervention by government can only be a partial substitute for well-functioning interbank markets. Therefore, transparency of complicated products should increase so that appropriate risk premia can be assigned. Regulators have already identified transparency and standardisation as two key areas to improve upon in 2007 [15], but the crisis has prompted them even more to do this. However, risk distribution should not be wiped out completely, as it is important to protect the banking system and financial stability, given that it is transparent enough. Additionally, note that financial regulators and supervisors cannot foresee and counteract every step that the market takes. As stated in The Economist (April 3, 2008): .The experience of the past year is an object lesson in the limited power of regulators. Financial engineering and innovation has a price, which is that financial crises do occur every now and then. Regulators and supervisors have to let markets develop in order to achieve economic growth. They should learn the lessons of the past crises, but they can never prevent the next financial crisis, which will show itself in a different shape.

Source: www.cepr.org
© Center for Economic Policy Research, CEPR. This article first appeared as CEPR Policy Insight No. 27, www.cepr.org. Reproduced with Permission.

Sylvester Eijffinger is Professor of Financial Economics at Tilburg University and Board Member of the European Banking Center in Tilburg, as well as Visiting Professor of Economics at Harvard University in Cambridge, MA during the Spring semester of 2008.

Notes

1. The Economist, .Bernanke sees little threat of credit crunch., July 19, 2007.
2. Financial Times, .Denial disguises reality of Lehman crisis, September 14, 2008
3. Financial Times, .Finance directors should plan early, October 28, 2008
4. The Economist, .Cross-border contagion, September 18, 2008.
5. Recently, AEGON also applied for US$1 billion from the US Troubled Asset Relief Program because the more favourable

conditions compared with the Dutch bailout. This is bailout arbitrage or competition.

6. Fellgett, Robin (2003), Comments on Freixas, Xavier (2003), "Crisis Management in Europe", Chapter 4 in J. Kremers, D. Schoenmaker and P. Wierts (Eds.), Financial Supervision in Europe, Edward Elgar, Cheltenham.
7. De Grauwe, Paul (2008), .Return to narrow banking., in What G20 leaders must do to stabilise the economy and fix the financial system, Barry Eichengreen and Richard Baldwin (Eds.), VoxEU.org, CEPR
8. Business Insurance, .Subprime crisis triggers effort to strengthen banking system, June 9, 2008.
9. Laeven, Luc, .The cost of resolving a financial crisis., October 31, 2008, VoxEU.org.
10. The Economist, .Link by link: a short history of modern finance, October 18, 2008.
11. The Economist, .A monetary malaise., October 11, 2008.
12. Stiglitz, Joseph E., Reversal of Fortune, November 1, 2008.
13. Buiter, Willem H. (2008), .Some suggestions for the G20 on November 15th., in What G20 leaders must do to stabilise the economy and fix the financial system, Barry Eichengreen and Richard Baldwin (Eds.), VoxEU.org, CEPR.
14. Kiff, John, Paul Mills and Carolyne Spackman, .European securitization and the possible revival of financial innovation,. October 28, 2008, VoxEU.org, CEPR.
15. Financial Times, .Watchdogs look for more transparency on securitizations, October 10, 2007.

References

Alexander, Carol, Elizabeth Sheedy (2008), Developing a stress testing framework based on market risk models, Journal of Banking & Finance 32 (10), pp. 2220- 2236.

Blum, Jurg M. (2008), Why `Basel II' may need a leverage ratio restriction, Journal of Banking & Finance32 (8), pp. 1699-1707.

Buiter, Willem H. (2008), .Some suggestions for the G20 on November 15th., in What G20 leaders must do to stabilise the economy and fix the financial system, Barry Eichengreen and Richard Baldwin (Eds.), VoxEU.org.

De Grauwe, Paul (2008), .Return to narrow banking, in What G20 leaders must do to stabilise the economy and fix the financial system, Barry Eichengreen and Richard Baldwin (Eds.), VoxEU.org.

Fellgett, Robin (2003), Comments on Freixas, Xavier (2003), .Crisis Management in Europe, Chapter 4 in J. Kremers, D. Schoenmaker and P. Wierts (Eds.), Financial Supervision in Europe, Edward Elgar, Cheltenham.

Financial Times, .Bernanke sees little threat of credit crunch, July 19, 2007 Financial Times, .Watchdogs look for more transparency on securitisations, October 10, 2007.

Financial Times, .Finance directors should plan early, October 28, 2008

Financial Times, Denial disguises reality of Lehman crisis, September 14, 2008

Freixas, Xavier (2003), .Crisis Management in Europe, Chapter 4 in J. Kremers, D. Schoenmaker and P. Wierts (Eds.), Financial Supervision in Europe, Edward Elgar, Cheltenham

Freixas, Xavier and Parigi, Bruno Maria (2008), .Lender of Last Resort and Bank Closure Policy., CESifo Working Paper Series No. 2286.

Garcia, Gillian G. H. & Maria J. Nieto (2007), .Preserving Financial Stability: A Dilemma For The European Union., Contemporary Economic Policy 25(3), pp. 444-458, Western Economic Association International.

Goodhart, Charles A.E. and Schoenmaker, Dirk (2008), .Fiscal Burden Sharing in Cross-Border Banking Crises. International, Journal of Central Banking, Forthcoming.

Kiff, John, Paul Mills and Carolyne Spackman, European securitisation and the possible revival of financial innovation, 28 October 2008, VoxEU.org.

Laeven, Luc, .The cost of resolving a financial crisis, October 31, 2008, VoxEU.org.

Schoenmaker, Dirk and Sander Oosterloo (2007), Crossborder Issues in European Financial Supervision, in: David Mayes and Geoffrey Wood (eds), The Structure of Financial Regulation, Routledge, London, 264-291.

Stiglitz, Joseph E., .Reversal of Fortune, November 1, 2008, http://wyww.truthout.org/103108R.

The Economist, .A monetary malaise, October 11, 2008

The Economist, .Link by link: a short history of modern finance., October 18, 2008

The Economist, .Cross-border contagion, September 18, 2008

9

UK Poverty and the Economic Downturn

Moussa Haddad and Antonia Bance

Summary

Introduction: Challenges and Opportunities

The major social policy challenge of the current economic recession is how to prevent a precipitous rise in poverty in the UK. In addition to limiting the numbers of people plunged into poverty because of the recession, government must also mitigate the impact on people already living below the poverty line. But, this paper will argue, responses to the recession present an opportunity to make a step-change, ensuring that actions taken also help build a fairer, more sustainable society in which poverty is ended in the long-term.

Analysis: The Recession and Poverty

The UK is now in recession, which is likely to continue at least into 2010. Unemployment is already at the highest level for 11 years, and may reach three million or more in the next two years. House repossessions are rising. People in poverty have been hit particularly hard by recent cost of living rises, with incomes—both benefits and wages for the low paid—failing to keep pace. We are seeing recent reductions in some forms of poverty reverse.

Recession leads to a number of risks to the livelihoods of those in and vulnerable to poverty. It is clear that redundancies and low benefit levels will lead to hardship. We also fear an increase in exploitation and vulnerable employment. There is also a particular risk that, as in previous recessions, the immediate damage caused to people's lives can lead to the scarring of lives and communities and to long-term unemployment. This makes it especially important that government does not give in to the temptation to balance budgets by cutting back on essential public services and protection just as they are most needed.

Recommendations

Government action should be based upon a long-term vision of moving to a society based on sustainability, with good quality jobs that allow people to have a more secure livelihood, but also backed up by a welfare state safety net which neither traps people nor leaves them living in poverty. We need a people's bail out that provides not just immediate relief, but builds towards this long-term vision.

- Make the tax system more progressive, including by increasing the threshold at which income tax is paid and lowering tax and benefit tapers.
- Invest in infrastructure, including a comprehensive energy efficiency programme, an expansion of free, high quality childcare and social care and a social house building programme.
- Introduce an emergency increase in out-of-work benefits and tax credits.
- Put further welfare reform on hold, and renew the welfare state so it becomes a genuine safety net for all.
- Effectively enforce existing employment rights.
- Set a maximum level of interest and widen eligibility for social fund hardship loans
- Give more help to struggling homeowners and private tenants.
- Redouble government's commitment to equality, anti-discrimination and community cohesion.

Introduction

The UK is the sixth richest country in the world. [1] In a society with such great resources, poverty is not inevitable.

Yet it still exists, and in a recession it could increase.

This paper sets out initial thinking from Oxfam about how to prevent the deepening recession causing a major rise in poverty here in the UK. Previous recessions have led to larger numbers of people experiencing poverty for a limited time, but they have also entrenched long-term poverty and exclusion for some people and some communities. Bold action now can mitigate the short-term impacts and prevent the slow-burn effects of recession on people's life chances, aspirations, and opportunities.

The challenge is to minimise the impact of recession on people already living below or near the poverty line, and ensure that those who previously had an adequate income are not plunged into poverty. Oxfam believes that the UK government must set out a broad approach to meeting both challenges. This must include action to raise the incomes of the poorest, alongside protecting the incomes of those who are vulnerable to poverty, reforming the tax and benefits system for the long term, and transforming attitudes towards poverty. Economic and pro-poor arguments converge: money spent on mitigating recession is best directed towards those on low and moderate incomes who will put that money back into the economy.

Background: the nature of poverty in the UK

In the United Kingdom, many of the conditions for poverty eradication are met: democracy and good governance, a relatively independent media and judiciary, well-resourced provision of basic services, and laws enshrining rights and prohibiting anti-discriminatory practice. Yet millions of women and men live in relative poverty and are systematically excluded from the benefits of this rich society, as a result of systemic structural discrimination, powerful institutions, vested interests, and negative public attitudes such as racism.

While basic material needs are generally met, close to a quarter of the UK population still survives on the margins. The

UK government defines poverty as having an income of 60 percent or less of the median: using this measure, 13.2 million people in the UK live in poverty—that is 22 percent of the population. [2] Over the last fifteen years, steady economic growth and government action to tackle poverty have made a difference; but insufficient and stealthy redistribution of income and unequal access to services and opportunity mean that inequality remains a defining characteristic of UK society.

Already, before the inevitability of recession was evident, progress on poverty reduction was slowing. Despite more than 15 consecutive years of economic growth, in which average earnings have gone up by 80 percent, the numbers living in poverty dropped by only 7 percent, and have begun to rise again. [3] While there had been significant, though mixed, achievements in the period 1998–2003, progress on a range of anti-poverty indicators stalled in the five years 2004–2008. [4] Levels of child poverty have begun to rise again in the past two years, having been in decline since 1998/99. [5] And while poverty among all other age groups has decreased overall since 1997, the number of childless working-age adults living in poverty has risen by 500,000. [6] Meanwhile, those remaining in poverty despite being in work— the working poor - form a larger proportion of the total numbers in poverty. [7]

In addition, a number of factors had already worsened the position of people living in poverty prior to the onset of recession.

The cost of living has risen sharply in recent years, which has hit those living in or close to poverty particularly hard, especially as incomes have not kept pace. Though inflation has now eased, food prices are still more than 10 percent higher than a year ago, and the cost of fuel and light has risen by 36.3 percent in the same period. [8] As poor people spend more of their incomes on these essential items, the pressure on their budgets has been greatest. Though the figure is not officially collected, it has been estimated that this effect has more than doubled the most recent inflation rate for the poorest 10 percent of people, compared with the average, [9] with a particularly pronounced effect on pensioners. [10] A range of international factors, including rising demand in India and China and the expanding use of bio-fuels replacing food production, mean that prices for both food and fuel are likely to rise in the long term, even if they have eased slightly in the immediate term.

In addition, even before the recession, the income of poor people had not risen in line with costs or with the average incomes of the rest of society. Benefit levels are set below the poverty line and have lagged further and further behind earnings. The gap between unemployment benefits and earnings has grown by 20 percent since 1997. Within the last year, inflation has been volatile, reaching both highs and lows, yet benefits have failed to compensate for the fluctuating cost of living. With increases in the national minimum wage also lagging, the incomes of poor people have actually decreased in real terms over the past year. The latest increase in the minimum wage of 3.8 percent was easily outstripped by the then inflation rate of 4.7 percent, while benefit levels rose by only 2.3 percent in April 2008.

Implications of recession for people living in poverty

The UK is now officially in recession: GDP fell in each of the last two quarters of 2008, and the Bank of England has accepted that this period of stagnation is likely to continue until 2010. This recession is likely to have a severe impact on both the rate of poverty and the nature and depth of poverty. It will also widen the pool of people vulnerable to poverty.

It is difficult to estimate the precise number of people who will experience poverty as a result of the recession; this may not become clear for some years, and statistics may not take full account of the numbers of people living in poverty due to factors such as under-reporting of intra-household poverty, for example.

Unemployment and the welfare state

The unemployment rate has been increasing, and the latest figures—2.03 million for the three months to January 2009—were the highest for 11 years. [11] The number of unemployed people is expected to rise substantially, with some forecasting that 3 million or more will be unemployed in the next two years. [12]

The number of people claiming benefits will rise substantially; in the most recent previous recession in 1993, almost one-sixth of the entire British population was receiving income support. So, as thousands of people become newly unemployed, the welfare state will be a crucial safety net. But the cash value of Jobseekers' Allowance is just £60.50 per week for those aged over 25, and even less for younger people, and so unemployment will be an enormous financial shock for which many are unprepared. This will have an impact on their ability to take up opportunities and to manage their commitments, not least given the high levels of debt and low levels of savings in the UK. [13] Many of these claimants may move into informal work to make ends meet, which may expose them to the risk of exploitation and criminal prosecution.

The damage caused by unemployment can lead to longer-term blight on lives and communities, as well as immediate difficulties. Redundancies in previous downturns have, for many, led to sustained unemployment; those who were better educated and without dependent children quickly returned to employment, leaving the most disadvantaged behind. Spells of unemployment when young can be particularly damaging; more than a third of the estimated three million who will become unemployed in this recession are likely to be aged 18-24, which may leave a legacy of long-term unemployment and a 'lost generation'. [14]

Insecurity at work

During a recession, the risk of being exploited at work is

greater, as workers are scared of losing their jobs or may be desperate for any paid employment, and so are prepared to put up with worse pay, conditions, and treatment. Since the last recession, the UK labour market has changed and become more flexible, with more people employed on temporary contracts, with many fewer rights on dismissal and little job security. Particularly at risk are women, ethnic minorities, migrants, and young people, all of whom are more likely to be in low-paid or temporary employment. [15] Incomes are projected either to remain static until 2010, or, in a deeper recession, to fall by 1 percent in 2009 and 2010 before recovering. [16]

Vulnerability to poverty

One of the effects of the recession will be to increase the number of people who are vulnerable to poverty. Already reeling from the rising costs of feeding their families and heating their homes, people living in or on the edge of poverty are desperately vulnerable to the effects of recession. They tend to have few savings, and an external shock such as an illness, the loss of a job, or a broken boiler can represent a devastating blow.

This vulnerability is already shared by a high proportion of the UK population, with just under half the population living in poverty for at least one of the ten years between 1991 and 2000. [17] While people do move out of poverty, many do not move far up the income scale, and many more experience poverty intermittently. Middle-income people may still find themselves vulnerable in the current economic climate, risking poverty through the loss of a home or a job. Some groups may have more personal resources (both financial and human resources, and also social capital) on which to draw than others, but this recession is nonetheless broadening the extent to which people feel vulnerable to poverty and financial hardship.

This has a particular impact on women, who, in the UK as

elsewhere, tend to find themselves in the front line when external shocks affect a household's livelihood. Acting as 'shock absorbers', women tend to deprive themselves in order to help their families to cope, or they take on the extra burden and stress of debt. In these circumstances, unscrupulous lending at punitive interest rates, such as those charged by doorstep lenders and pay-day loan services, have the potential to turn a shock into a long-term crisis for poor people.

Housing insecurity

The effect of the recession is also to increase housing insecurity. Repossessions rose by 55 percent in 2008 to a twelve-year high of 40,000. [18] A significant proportion of these involved landlords with buy-to-let mortgages, repossessions of whose properties doubled from the first half of 2007 to the first half of 2008; [19] in some cases, tenants, unaware that the owner was in difficulties, may lose their home at a few days' notice. In addition, in areas of high-cost privately rented housing, the income available from work may not cover the cost of renting, which may make people who are dependent on Housing Benefit unable to afford to work. It is also likely that the numbers of people in temporary accommodation will rise, as social housing is scarce and difficult to access. Declining levels of social housing (down by 117,000 in the last year alone) [20] mean that the social housing that does remain is often in estates where there are high levels of deprivation and few employment prospects.

Economic and moral case for helping the poorest first

In a time of recession, more than ever, government has an active role to play. This includes promoting economic stability and curbing market excesses, redistributing wealth and tackling inequality, ensuring the security of welfare systems and public services, and encouraging employment. Recession will place strains on the budgets of governments around the world, with tax revenues dropping as the financial costs of unemployment, homelessness, and business failure rise, and tax revenues decline. This presents the danger that short-term budgetary constraints will be allowed to hamper the long-term fight against poverty. Yet if there was any doubt that the UK government has the resources and the will to act when it needs to, the vast sums of money spent on propping up the banking system have dispelled it. Hundreds of billions of pounds have been made available to banks in an effort to avert financial meltdown—throwing into sharp relief, for example, the £4.2 billion needed to meet the interim child-poverty target. [21]

Decisions that determine who loses most in a downturn must be made in the light of who benefited from the preceding period of growth. The neo-liberal consensus, on which economic growth was built, largely benefited the already affluent; moreover, the cheap credit and housing-market bubble which led to this recession were not created by people living on low incomes, so they should not bear the brunt of an economic crisis to which their actions did not contribute.

In an economic downturn, policy makers may seek spending cuts to balance the books. Aside from the economic arguments against cutting spending, it should be noted that people experiencing poverty are much more dependent on public services than those who are better off. At a time when recession means that the resources of people in poverty are shrinking, and when broader vulnerability and insecurity cause the number of people reliant on public services to increase, public services become even more important. Most vulnerable to cuts are likely to be investments in social protection - the very programmes that people in poverty need in times of crisis. The burden of reductions in social spending will fall most heavily on the poorest, likely to be disproportionately women, families with disabled members, and ethnic minorities. There can be no justification for cutting social-protection spending just when it is needed most.

The current UK government has declared itself committed to spending money to prevent recession turning into depression. Invoking the spirit of Keynes, the government has argued for fiscal pump-priming, putting money into the hands of people who might then spend it, and bringing forward public-works projects. The measures in the November 2008 Pre-Budget Report increased government borrowing in order to put money into the economy immediately. While there are risks in raising levels of national debt, this counter-cyclical spending, if used judiciously, offers great opportunities for poverty reduction and for social investment which will help to create the conditions in which poverty can be ended. However, to do so, new investment must be made, in addition to already-planned investment being brought forward; and secondly, 'investment' must be considered broadly in terms of the future challenges for the UK, which include the needs of our ageing society and the threat of climate change.

Up until now, the UK government's willingness to play an active role in combating the crisis has been most evident in the financial sector, which it sees to be at the heart of the economic downturn. Yet the effects of this crisis are increasingly being felt by ordinary people, and most acutely by those already in or near poverty, who are most vulnerable and have the fewest resources to fall back upon. Government action has started to take account of the effects on the so-called 'real' economy, with measures such as its recent support for the motor industry, [22] but it needs to go further.

There is a cold economic logic behind the targeting of spending increases and tax cuts at poor people: these people will spend rather than save. Poor people have a higher propensity to spend any increases in their income—especially given the costs of food and fuel—so that any increase in income will be used to pay for these and other essentials, for which current incomes are inadequate—and so the money will be re-circulated into the wider economy.

What needs to be done?

As the reality of the vulnerability of broad sections of society becomes apparent, there is an opportunity for government action to provide the security that is lacking in people's lives, and to help prevent the crisis that many people are facing right now from becoming a long-term catastrophe that entrenches millions in poverty and will take decades to solve.

The UK needs a broad-based 'people's bail-out', focusing on human and social capital as well as financial assets. In order to mitigate the impact of the recession on people living in poverty, prevent poverty rising, and reduce poverty overall, government needs to take a number of actions. The focus should be on creating a society based on sustainability, with good-quality jobs that enable people to have a more secure livelihood, supported by a safety net which neither traps people nor leaves them subsisting in poverty.

Introduce a fairer tax policy

The political will to use fiscal levers to combat the downturn provides an opportunity for tackling poverty. The existing tax system takes a substantially larger proportion of the income of the poorest tenth than it does from the richest tenth. [23] The government should make the tax system more progressive–for example, shifting from indirect taxes to income taxes at higher earnings levels, building on the small changes in this direction that were included in the November 2008 Pre-Budget Report. This will also have a long-term benefit, by preventing the economy from overheating when it begins to grow again. Where the government takes the opportunity to reframe the tax system in favour of environmental taxation, any regressive effects should be tempered by increasing the progressiveness of other aspects of the tax system.

For sound economic reasons, tax cuts should be aimed at low-paid people, as they are more likely to put the money straight back into circulation. The November 2008 reduction in VAT—a particularly regressive form of taxation—was welcome, but its redistributive effect should not be overstated, because VAT is not currently charged at the full rate on most basic items. Tax thresholds should be increased, so that the burden of taxation is removed or diminished for people on low incomes.

In order to reduce the poverty trap, tax and benefit tapers—marginal tax rates—should be lowered, so that work is strengthened as a route out of poverty and people do not become trapped in low-paid work. As well as increasing tax thresholds, this will include measures such as reducing the taper at which housing and council tax benefits are withdrawn, and making tax credits more flexible and responsive to changes in income, so that they are not abruptly withdrawn as incomes rise, thereby causing hardship.

And it is also important that tax that is levied is collected. Building an effective global financial system will require increasing levels of regulation and transparency internationally, and part of this will involve tackling tax havens across the world. If this can be achieved in a spirit of international co-operation, then the old arguments about competing for global talent by turning a blind eye to tax loopholes can be broken.

A more effective international financial system can then emerge, giving the UK and other governments more resources to meet their priorities.

Box 1: The Tax System

- The poorest fifth of households pay more of their income in tax than the richest fifth of households—38.6 percent and 35.3 percent respectively in 2006/7. [24]
- The measures announced for 2009/10 in the November 2008 Pre-Budget report will increase the incomes of the poorest fifth of households by 2.9 percent, compared with 1.8 percent for the richest fifth of households. [25]
- The effects are less pronounced when measured by the spending, rather than the income, of the bottom and top fifth of households—with increases of 2.4 percent and 1.9 percent respectively. [26]

Stimulate the economy and put money in the pockets of the poorest

Fiscal stimulus used to combat the recession should combine investment which promotes a transition to a green, environmentally sustainable economy with investment in the human and social infrastructure of society that is essential to the long-term eradication of poverty. Each has an important part to play in developing an economy based on sustainable, good-quality jobs, which help to reduce unemployment, tackle in-work poverty, and provide the broad infrastructure needed for future economic growth that is more equitably shared.

Many of the options for stimulating the economy while investing to create a more sustainable future have already become part of the public debate. For example, building a UK renewables industry and setting up a comprehensive nationwide energy-efficiency programme would create jobs and wealth, reduce poverty, and equip the UK better to mitigate the extent of climate change; [27] investing in a house-building programme would also reduce poverty.

The government should also invest in a similar manner in a substantial expansion of care provision. This could provide immense opportunities for reducing poverty, while preparing the UK for future challenges. While it is not physical infrastructure, it is an investment in social and human infrastructure. Workers in these sectors perform a vital role, but both child care and social care are expensive and in demand out of proportion to the availability of the provision. Increasing the availability of provision and making it free at the point of use would meet this challenge and improve the life chances of children and the quality of life of older and disabled people, while enabling their carers to pursue other options.

Not only would jobs be created as part of the immediate response to the recession, but it would also serve as a longer-term anti-poverty investment, enabling those with caring responsibilities, the majority of whom are women, to continue in or enter employment. As these are traditionally low-paid, low-skilled sectors, jobs created should be paid at above-market rates to raise the sector as a whole.

Box 2: Energy Efficiency

- The government is legally committed to eradicating all fuel poverty by 2016 and in vulnerable groups (such as elderly or disabled households) by 2010, but numbers of people living in fuel poverty have more than doubled in the past two years, to around 5 million households. [28]
- It is estimated that 3.1 million households need help with fuel bills because of a combination of energy-inefficient homes and rising fuel prices. The Warm Front scheme was launched in 2005, when 1.9 million households were estimated to be in need. [29]
- According to the National Audit Office, over half of Britain's poorest households are ineligible for help from the £852m Warm Front scheme, and £34m has been given to people who already have energy-efficient homes and are comparatively well off. [30]
- Customers using pre-payment meters for electricity and gas pay on average 17 percent more than the average for a direct-debit customer – with the gap doubling from £70 per annum in 2004 to £145 per annum in 2007. The gap between customers paying by cash or cheque and those paying by direct debit also more than doubled in the same period, from £36 per annum to £85 per annum.[31]

Box 3: Child and Social Care

- The EU has set a target for member states to provide child care by 2010 for at least 90 percent of children between the age of 3 years and the mandatory school age, and for at least 33 percent of children under the age of 3.
- British parents face the highest child-care bills in Europe, paying 75-93 percent of the cost of early-age provision. [32]

Contd...

- On average, child-care costs in the UK absorb around a quarter of a woman's earnings, regardless of whether she works full-time or part-time. [33]
- Only around 3 percent of workplaces provide on-site child-care facilities, and only 2.5-5 percent provide some financial assistance for child-care costs. [34]
- It is estimated that universal child-care provision for 1-4 year olds (with government paying 75 percent of the cost) would incur a net annual cost of £4.7 billion (around 0.5 percent of GDP) to the Exchequer, but a net benefit of £0.4 billion to the economy as a whole, rising to £40 billion over 65 years. [35]
- It is estimated that moving to a system where the state pays 80 percent of social-care costs–the remaining 20 percent being affordable for most individuals due to the Minimum Income Guarantee, thus minimising the need for means testing–would cost an extra £2 billion per year, or 0.2 percent of GDP. [36]

Increase the Incomes of the Poorest

The incomes of the poorest must be increased. Both for people who have relied on benefits for a long period and for those who are newly unemployed, there must be an emergency rise in all out-of-work benefits. The unique combination of the need for fiscal stimulus, the vastly reduced buying power of benefits compared with previous recessions, and a renewed public acknowledgement that unemployment is caused by structural factors outside the control of the individual means that a significant increase in unemployment benefits makes sense now more than ever. An increase of £15 per week in Jobseeker's Allowance would restore the gap between the benefit and average earnings to its 1997 level and help to protect newly unemployed people from some of the worst effects of a catastrophic fall in income. As well as supporting people in poverty, this will help to develop the key economic role of unemployment benefit as a fiscal stabiliser, ensuring that some degree of spending continues in a recession.

The government's current commitment to increasing the level of support available to people out of work is welcome and should be continued in spite of the economic downturn. People must not be condemned to long-term unemployment, as has been the case after previous downturns. But the continuing welfare-reform programme must be reviewed. The government must not increase conditionality in the benefits system at a time of recession, when fewer jobs are available. Conditionality and compulsion stigmatise poor people and undermine their rights, as well as shifting the blame to individuals and away from the systemic failure of the UK economy to provide an adequate living for all. Support given to people who are newly unemployed must not be given at the expense of those already unemployed. The newly unemployed may push the long-term unemployed, likely to be furthest from the labour market, to the back of the queue for help and support. This is especially likely as private companies delivering welfare services are offered incentives to get people into work, which could lead them to concentrate resources on those people who are easier to help into jobs.

An emergency increase in benefits levels should also act as a springboard towards a more realistic system for regularly up-rating benefits, with the aim that they become sufficient to keep recipients out of poverty. In the longer term, the government should examine the systemic problems and barriers faced by people living in poverty and the role that an inflexible benefit system has played in exacerbating these difficulties. [37] The UK requires a social-protection system which genuinely acts to alleviate poverty. Such a welfare state should ensure that people are able to undertake short-term or part-time work, and educational and training opportunities, as a step towards long-term, sustainable employment, without financial penalty, or a reduction in income security.

There should also be an emergency increase in tax credits, to support the working poor to manage the impact of the recession. In addition, both as a symbol of the government's determination not to allow the recession to derail its anti-poverty drive and as a practical help to millions of families, the government should invest in increased child benefit and tax credits, to ensure that it meets the target of halving child poverty by 2010. [38] And to tackle the enormous rises in energy costs and the consequent leap in levels of fuel poverty, the Winter Fuel Payment should this year be extended to all families in receipt of benefits and tax credits, to be reviewed next year once emergency increases in benefits and the minimum wage have been factored in.

Protect rights at work

And for those in work, effective enforcement of employment rights, including awareness raising, is essential to ensure that vulnerable workers do not face greater hardship or exploitation. Employers must be prevented from illegally singling out for redundancy part-time workers, those who are pregnant or are on maternity leave. As the risks of mistreatment increase, the government must make clear that the recession cannot be used as an excuse for denying staff their legal rights. In addition, the government must resist the siren call to retrench and reduce employment rights already in place or promised; for example, maternity leave and access to flexible working must be extended as intended.

Box 4: Out-of-Work Benefits

- Jobseeker's Allowance (JSA) for a newly unemployed person over the age of 25 is £60.50 per week (£47.95 for people aged 16-24).
- The gap between benefits and earnings has almost doubled since 1979, when benefit increases stopped being linked to earnings increases. [39]
- If that link was still in place, JSA in 2007 would have been £113.26 per week. [40]
- Increasing JSA in line with earnings since 1997 would give it a value of £75 per week. [41]

- Recent research by the Joseph Rowntree Foundation into minimum income standards has shown that a single working-age adult needs an income of at least £153 a week 'in order to have the opportunities and choices necessary to participate in society'. [42]

Box 5: Rights at Work

- In 2008, the TUC estimated that there were 2 million vulnerable workers in the UK. [43]
- HM Revenue and Customs is expected to enforce the NMW with a mere 89.5 inspectors – 5 percent of the number of inspectors available to the DWP benefit fraud unit. It has been estimated that the average employer could expect a visit from HMRC once every 320 years. [44]
- Employment Agency Standards Inspectorate has to enforce the law for agency workers with just 24 inspectors. [45]
- Only one in seven workers earning less than £7 an hour belongs to a trade union, compared with two-fifths of those earning £10 to £20 an hour. [46]
- 1 in 10 successful claimants in the employment tribunal system does not receive the due monetary award. [47]

Reduce Vulnerability to Financial Shocks: Affordable Credit

Paying for the cost of living on a very low income has driven many people living in or near poverty into unsustainable debt. Risky lending practices and a lack of financial regulation have been one of the causes of the present crisis. A maximum level of interest should be set, in order to prevent exploitation of people in vulnerable situations, with action taken to crack down on unscrupulous lending, including better regulation of sale-and-rent-back schemes. Government should promote and fund credit unions, and there should also be wider eligibility for social-fund hardship loans, making them more responsive to people's needs and providing a genuine alternative to commercial credit in emergencies.

Provide Secure Housing

Government housing policy should be focused on preventing people from falling into homelessness or temporary accommodation, and rebuilding the UK's housing stock for the future.

Having a secure and affordable home is crucial to lifting people out of poverty in a sustainable way. Oxfam welcomes the government's mortgage-rescue scheme, which will allow those struggling with mortgage payments to defer interest payments and stay in their homes. But the government must also act to protect private tenants whose landlords are at risk of repossession. This should include enforcement of a two-month notice period, and exploring options such as whole or part purchase of such properties by councils, housing associations, or the tenants themselves, in each case enabling the tenants to remain in their home.

But housing insecurity will never be ended while there are insufficient homes being built. Much of the government spending brought forward should be used to build more social housing, helping to fix one of the causes of the housing crisis: the lack of decent, affordable accommodation. In addition, this will help to make up the shortfall in private house building, tackling the long-term housing shortage, and protecting construction jobs in an environment where new construction starts fell by almost two thirds year on year during the three months from November to January. [48] Such housing should be in mixed developments, and with access to employment opportunities, to ensure that new 'sink' estates are not created. Finally, increased spending on improved energy efficiency for all homes can cut down on energy bills and reduce fuel poverty, as well as quickly providing new jobs.

Encourage Social Cohesion and Solidarity

The recession has the potential to bind people together through a common feeling of vulnerability and a shared desire for security. In particular, after a prolonged period of growth, the realisation that more people's livelihoods are insecure than previously thought offers space for government to make a renewed case for ending poverty and vulnerability, based upon a shared desire for security across society.

Box 6: Social Housing

- The government has a target of building 240,000 new homes a year in England, but only 141,900 new houses were built in 2008, a drop of 19 percent compared with the previous year, with new starts down 37 percent at 105,000. [49]
- 1.77 million households in England were on social-housing waiting lists in 2008, with a further 489,400 households living in officially overcrowded homes. [50]
- One in four local areas in England has seen its housing waiting list at least double in the last five years. [51]
- The government's Barker Review [52] estimated that 17,000 new social homes were needed per year just to meet the needs of new households, and a further 9,000 a year to make inroads into the backlog of need. In contrast, not one English region has seen a net increase in its social housing stock in the last five years. [53]

The emergence of 'new poor' people presents a challenge to the treatment of the existing poor. There may be increased empathy with those living in poverty, as the unavoidable effects of circumstance are demonstrated, but also a risk that the stigma of poverty will increase: for example, attitudes towards people claiming benefits have hardened in recent months. [54] The government must advocate renewed solidarity, ensuring through rhetoric and action that the newly poor are not portrayed as 'deserving' while those who were poor before the recession are seen as 'undeserving'.

However, as well as opportunities for combating negative attitudes, there are dangers that new divisions may arise and increase tensions. In particular, migrants and members of some black and minority ethnic communities may experience increased resentment and discrimination as unemployment rises. The government must redouble its public commitment to equality, anti-discrimination, and community cohesion, and ensure that it takes the opportunity to put equality at the heart of the renewed solidarity effort, rather than allowing it to drift off the agenda.

Conclusion

The current period of recession will exacerbate existing poverty and cause more people to fall into poverty. Already it is causing real suffering to people, and there is every likelihood that things will get worse. It is vital that the government deals with the short-term challenges that this crisis presents—but also vital that it does so in a way that is consistent with ending poverty in the long term.

The recession could be an opportunity to change thinking about poverty—in government and beyond. In tackling the economic crisis, government policy should seek to build the foundations for future recovery on a fairer, more sustainable basis. Through its actions and words, government should show leadership in working to renew people's sense of solidarity with one another, based on a shared need for security. The government must recognise its power to influence public attitudes as well as to change its policies, and use both to renew its commitment to ending all poverty in the UK.

Source: www.oxfam.org.uk
© Oxfam GB 2009. Reprinted with Permission.

Notes

1. The World Factbook, CIA, 5 March 2009.
2. When poverty is measured as living on an income of below 60 percent of median income: p. 37, Poverty and Inequality in the UK, Institute for Fiscal Studies, 2008.
3. From 14.2 million in 1992 to 13.2 million in 2006/7: source: Households Below Average Income, Department of Work and

Pensions (DWP) and Institute of Fiscal Studies (IFS).

4. Monitoring Poverty and Social Exclusion 2008, New Policy Institute.
5. Study by the IFS and Joseph Rowntree Foundation (JRF), June 2008, since updated in light of that failure to an estimate of £4.2 billion a year above current plans to meet the 2010 pledge (see Ending Child Poverty in a Changing Economy, Donald Hirsch, JRF, 18 February 2009).
6. Poverty and Inequality In the UK, Institute for Fiscal Studies, 2008
7. 57 percent of poor households have a household member in work, and the number of these households has increased by half a million in the past ten years, according to G. Cooke and K. Lawton, Working Out of Poverty: a Study of the Low Paid and Working Poor, IPPR, January 2008.
8. Office for National Statistics CPI First Release December 2008: http://www.statistics.gov.uk/pdfdir/cpi0109.pdf
9. 'Average inflation falls, but remains high for some', Institute for Fiscal Studies press release, 9th March 2009, which calculated the inflation rate for the poorest decile to be 5.4 percent, compared with 2.1 percent on average.
10. Consumer prices have risen for pensioner households in the poorest fifth by 20 percent, compared with 14 percent for non-pensioner households on average incomes, according to Monitoring Poverty and Social Exclusion 2008, New Policy Institute.
11. Labour Market Statistics First Release – March 2009, Office for National Statistics (18 March 2009).
12. http://www.cbi.org.uk/ndbs/Press.nsf/0363c1f07c6ca12a8025671c00381cc7/79d10a7e36bb511580257507005f5cf8?OpenDocument; Economic Outlook for Business, Winter 2009, Ernst and Young ITEM Club (http://www.guardian.co.uk/business/2009/jan/18/jobless-to-reach-more-than-3-million)
13. See, for example, Chapter 5: 'Income and wealth', and Chapter 6: 'Expenditure', Social Trends 38: 2008 Edition, Office for National Statistics (ONS).
14. The latest labour-market survey shows unemployment growing fastest among 18 to 24 year-olds: of the 137,000 rise in unemployment in the three months to October, 55,000, or 40

percent, were aged 18 to 24.

15. Hard Work Hidden Lives: the Final Report of the Commission on Vulnerable Employment, TUC, 2008.
16. Ending Child Poverty in a Changing Economy, Donald Hirsch, Joseph Rowntree Foundation, York, February 2009.
17. Department for Work and Pensions, Low Income Dynamics, 2002, based on the British Household Panel Survey, 1991–2000.
18. According to the Council of Mortgage Lenders, Housing Finance at a Glance, March 2009.
19. Figures rose from 900 to 1800: Possessions on Mortgaged Properties, Table AP5, Council of Mortgage Lenders (2008).
20. Communities and Local Government figures, released 22 January 2009.
21. Ending Child Poverty in a Changing Economy, Donald Hirsch, JRF, 18 February 2009.
22. http://www.timesonline.co.uk/tol/news/politics/article5601310.ece
23. The Effects of Taxes and Benefits on Household Income, 2006/07, Office for National Statistics (July 2008).
24. The Effects of Taxes and Benefits on Household Income, 2006/07, Office for National Statistics (July 2008).
25. The Distributional Effect of the 2008 Pre-Budget Report, Mike Brewer, James Browne, and David Phillips, Institute for Fiscal Studies (November 2008).
26. Ibid.
27. For example, A Green New Deal: Joined-up Policies to Solve the Triple Crunch of the Credit Crisis, Climate Change and High Oil Prices, New Economics Foundation (NEF), London, 2008.
28. Consumer Focus (press release, 2.10.2008) estimates that 5.5 million households are in fuel poverty.
29. The Warm Front Scheme, National Audit Office (February 2009).
30. Ibid.
31. Fuel Poverty Advisory Group (for England), Sixth Annual Report, 2007, Department for Business, Enterprise and Regulatory Reform (March 2008).
32. Reconciliation of Work and Private Life: A Comparative Review of Thirty European Countries, Chapter 2, 'Childcare services', European Commission (September 2005).
33. Reconciliation of Work and Private Life in the UK, Colette

Fagan, Rory Donnelly, and Jill Rubery, University of Manchester (March 2005).

34. Ibid.
35. Universal Childcare Provision in the UK – Towards a Cost-benefit Analysis, discussion paper by PricewaterhouseCoopers (August 2003).
36. Paying for Long-term Care: Moving Forward, Donald Hirsch, Joseph Rowntree Foundation (April 2006).
37. For a more detailed critique of welfare reform, see Oxfam's response to the DWP green paper, No-one Written Off.
38. For details of how this might be composed, see How to Halve Child Poverty by 2010, published by Barnardo's and the IFS.
39. Abstract of Statistics for Benefits, National Insurance Contributions, and Indices of Prices and Earnings, 2007 Edition, Department for Work and Pensions (2008).
40. Ibid.
41. Ibid.
42. A Minimum Income Standard for Britain: What People Think, Bradshaw et al., Joseph Rowntree Foundation (July 2008).
43. Commission on Vulnerable Employment Report, Trades Union Congress (May 2008).
44. Trades Union Congress, op. cit.
45. Employment Agency Standards Inspectorate – Annual Report 07/08, Department for Business, Enterprise and Regulatory Reform (December 2008).
46. Labour Force Survey, 2007 Quarter 4, Office for National Statistics (March 2008).
47. Justice Denied, Citizens Advice (October 2008).
48. National House-Building Council (2008): http://www.nhbc.co.uk/NewsandComment/Name,36958,en.html
49. House Building: December Quarter 2008, England, Communities and Local Government (February 2009).
50. Local Authority Housing Statistics, England: 2007/08: Housing Strategy Statistical Appendix (HSSA) & Business Plan Statistical Appendix (BPSA), Communities and Local Government (January 2009).
51. Home Truths 2008, National Housing Federation (July 2008).
52. Barker Review of Land Use Planning, HM Treasury (December 2006).
53. Home Truths 2008, National Housing Federation (July 2008).

54. See 'Growing support for tougher benefit rules' The Guardian, 8 December 2008.

10

The Current Crisis: A Challenge as well as a Chance to Implement Needed Reforms?

Amir Hadziomeragic

1. Robust Growth, Real Convergence and High Imbalances

The economy of Bosnia and Herzegovina (BiH) has been exhibiting robust growth (real growth averaged 6 percent annually between 2003 and 2008) coupled with a low inflation rate over the past five years. Considering its late start to transition and the devastating effects of the 1992–95 war, current level of per capita income in Bosnia and Herzegovina is remarkable. BiHs growth dynamics helped to put it on similar convergence path like other countries at a similar point in transition. Domestic demand has been primary engine of economic growth over the previous periods. Consumption was growing substantially over the whole period, while investment growth was uneven (even negative contribution to the GDP in 2006) over these years, but with significant acceleration in 2007 and 2008. The process of trade liberalization with the EU and within the region (SAA and CEFTA [1] agreements) has been very helpful for promoting trade and expanding the market for export. Privatization was not fully completed as planned due to a lack of political readiness and unresolved ownership rights.

However, privatized companies have been very active in raising new capital and creation of jobs, especially where strategic foreign investors found interest for long-term investing. The persistent imbalance on the external side has even widened in the last two years. The current account deficit reflects the absorption boom and insufficient domestic saving. The trade deficit has been very large (over 37 percent of GDP in 2007 and 2008) despite very pronounced export growth in the last three years. An important source of financing of the trade deficit has been workers' remittances from numerous BiH diaspora as well as workers compensation for temporary employments in the neighboring countries and the EU. Foreign official assistance has not been any more such a significant part of foreign capital inflows, but foreign direct investments (FDI) have become an important source of financing the current account gap. FDI inflows accounted for approximately 33 percent to 73 percent of the current account deficit, with exception in 2007 when large-scale privatization attracted FDI over 10 percent GDP.

Despite the large current deficit, international reserves were steadily growing due to large privatization proceeds and banking foreign borrowing till the last quarter of 2008. The external public debt is relatively low (18 percent in 2007 and 16.7 percent in 2008) and mostly under concessional terms. Thus the debt service does not pose a severe threat for external liquidity. Total public debt has been estimated [2] at 30 percent of GDP. Growth of the private external debt has been more intensive, since companies privatized with FDI were able to start foreign borrowing. Total foreign debt is estimated to be still below 50 percent of GDP, indicating no immediate problems related to foreign indebtedness in the coming period.

The real effective exchange rate has been quite stable and does not raise significant external stability concerns. Indicators of price and cost competitiveness vis-à-vis neighboring countries (being the most important trading partners) have been benign, while export growth has been remarkable over several years prior to the crisis. Constant-market-share analysis suggests that export growth between 2003 and 2006 can be mainly explained by the competitiveness effect. Relative to non-tradeables, average labor productivity of tradeables was much higher than that of main trading partners (euro area and neighboring countries).

Table 10.1: Key Macroeconomic Indicators 2004-2009

In Percent of GDP unless otherwise indicated	2004	2005	2006	2007	2008	2009
Real GDP Growth (Percent)	6.3	3.9	6.9	6.0	5.5	-3.0
CPI (Change in Percent, average)	0.4	3.8	6.1	1.5	7.4	2.1
Current account balance	-16.3	-17.3	-7.9	-10.4	-14.6	-9.3
FDI (Percent of Current Account)	42.8	32.8	73.9	132.7	36.7	25.0
General Government Balance	1.6	2.9	2.4	1.3	-1.5	-4.0
Reserve Cover (Months of Import)	3.7	4.0	5.2	5.4	4.4	5.5
Gross External Debt	47.5	52.6	48.0	48.5	40.5	42.0
Public Debt	25.5	25.6	21.2	18.1	14.6	16.0

Source: BiH authorities, IMF.

After the period of fiscal consolidation, the fiscal position has deteriorated in the last two years as a result of pro-cyclical fiscal policy. The large increase in public spending started in 2006 in the context of the fiscal space created by the introduction of the value-added tax (VAT). The general government surplus of 1.3 percent of GDP in 2007 was much lower than the surplus of 3 percent of GDP in 2006, which will lead to a deficit larger then 2 percent of GDP in 2008. Fiscal consolidation prior to 2008 alleviated pressure on external imbalance. Also, fiscal consolidation has been necessary to create space for settlement for resolving of accumulated arrears and liabilities from the pre-war period. Driven mainly by sharp increases of transfers to households, capital spending and public wages, government expenditures reached 50 percent of GDP. Strong revenue performance has continued even in 2008, but a gradual slowdown is expected even without effects of the current economic crisis. Tax reforms encompassed direct taxation as well, corporate and personal income taxes were streamlined and simplified in order to broaden the tax base and reduce the tax burden for employers. Results of these tax reforms are still not fully reflected in economic growth, but their positive impact is to be recognized soon.

The monetary regime based on the currency board with the peg to the euro has been successful in keeping inflation low. Inflation has been only slightly higher then in the euro area with the only exception in 2006. Due to a one-time price adjustment after introduction of the VAT, annual inflation in 2006 was substantially higher than in the previous years, but it proved not to have a prolonged effect. However, inflation dynamics abruptly changed in 2008, when inflation peaked at 9,9 percent in July due to an enormous increase of world energy and food prices. The nominal growth of wages has been much higher than inflation, so real wage growth was significant (10 percent in March 2009). Such a wage growth was partially underpinned with an increase of productivity in manufacturing, finances and the tradable sector. But wage pressure from the public has mounted in the recent period, after the government raised public wages to levels sometimes even higher than in the private sector.

Rapid financial deepening has been a key growth contributor and has been continuing for several years. After successful privatization and massive capital inflows in the banking sector credit flows have been very intensive in response to high demand from the private sector. Foreign-owned banks dominate the banking sector and liquidity management and financing is mostly managed through relation between local subsidiaries and foreign parent companies. Real credit growth for the period 2004–2008 averaged 19 percent, which led to an increase of the private credit stock to 57 percent of GDP at the end of 2008. Prolonged rapid credit expansion raised concerns about the widening current account deficit and about possible uncontrolled accumulation of credit risk by banks. Although the credit level was very low at the very beginning and credit expansion was understandable, it has become clear that such expansion may have negative macroeconomic consequences over time. The central bank was prompted to tighten reserve requirements in order to slow down credit growth. The last increase of the reserve requirement rate from 15 percent to 18 percent was introduced at the end of 2007. Simultaneously, supervision authorities introduced additional prudential measures with the aim for more reliance on domestic funding instead of foreign borrowing by banks. However, the effects of these measures have been limited in circumstances of high liquidity in the international markets and increased demand for loans.

Chart 1: Credit for the Private Sector (2004 – 2008)

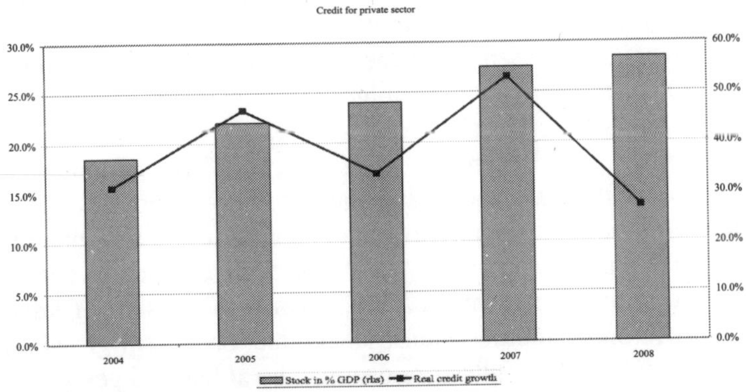

Source: CBBH statistics.

Banking supervisory activities have been focused on controls of both compliance with prudential regulations and business and financial operations on bank-by-bank basis. Supervision framework is still based on Basel I principles. Banking sector has grown steadily without any major banking crisis (only problematic banks are two insolvent banks without any active participation in the market) and need for fiscal remedies. Recently, more emphasis was given to the financial stability issues and systemic analysis of the banking sector. The central bank and supervisory authorities have been engaged in intensive coordination with the aim to ensure financial stability of the whole system. Cross-border supervisory cooperation has not been very effective, despite several bilateral and multilateral Memorandums of Understanding on supervisory co-operation. Some of the foreign supervisors have not been keen to establish effective co-operation and domestic supervisors have been deprived from access to key information about parent-banks consolidated balance sheet data and relevant supervisory assessment.

2. Crisis Impact and Untested Resilience

Over the first three quarters of 2008, real sector developments evolved pretty much according to the predicted scenario with a gradual slowdown in economic activities. However, the worsening of the financial crisis in September and October brought this benign scenario to an abrupt end. Industrial production and exports decelerated significantly in November and December, with a particularly pronounced decline in the base metal and the automobile industry. This deterioration of economic trends continued in the first quarter of 2009 and the output forecast has been drastically cut to around minus 2 percent for 2009. Thanks to a restart of large oil processing facilities industrial production is still growing, but almost all other industries declined by at least 15 percent to the first quarter of 2008. The export sectors have been suffering from weak metal [3] prices and import demand in the EU and CEFTA countries. For instance, aluminum prices fell nearly 40 percent from their peak in summer 2008 and prices of some steel products fell 30 percent. Moreover, EU import growth is projected to almost half in 2009 from 7 percent to 4 percent. The construction sector, except few large public infrastructures, is directly hit by the credit crunch, which will affect the demand for new business and residential buildings, as well as the ability to finance new projects. Finally, the retail sector has been affected by the slowdown of export earnings, reduced access to credit and reduced confidence on the side of consumers, so retail sales were down 10 percent in the first quarter to the same period last year.

Chart 2: Export Performance

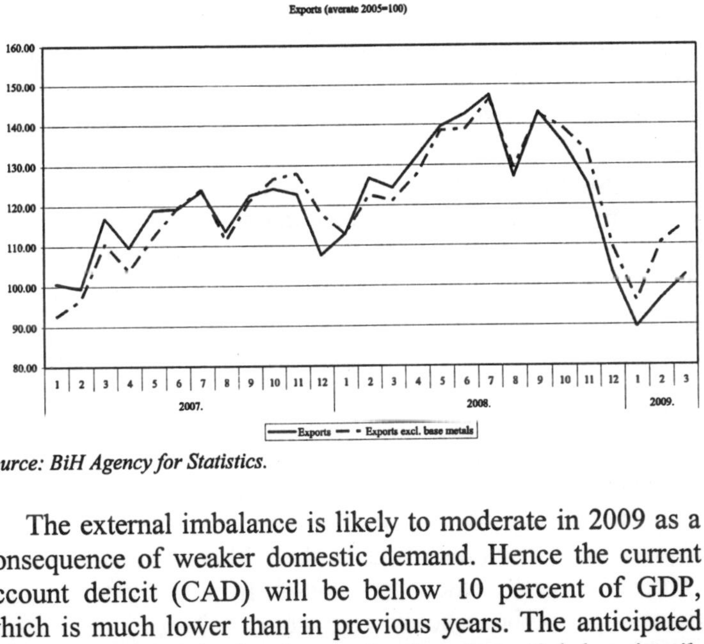

Source: BiH Agency for Statistics.

The external imbalance is likely to moderate in 2009 as a consequence of weaker domestic demand. Hence the current account deficit (CAD) will be bellow 10 percent of GDP, which is much lower than in previous years. The anticipated reduction of CAD is also the result of a substantial drop in oil, food, but also base metals prices, which together comprised around 44 percent of BH imports in 2008. The sources of CAD financing are more uncertain than previously. In 2008, less than half of the CAD was financed by FDI (5.7 percent of GDP), and another 10 to 12 percent by capital grants and drawings of loans by the government. Thus, about 40 percent of CAD depended on foreign borrowing by commercial banks and to a lesser extent private companies. In 2009, the FDI inflow is likely to decline relatively to previous years. (IMF WEO reports dramatic drop of 116 percent in capital inflows in the CEE) Moreover, the private sector is finding it increasingly difficult to borrow from abroad. Consequently, a larger portion of CAD financing may put pressure on foreign exchange reserves, which suffered a loss of 15 percent since October. The current level of foreign exchange reserves would be adequate to absorb this kind of shock in 2009, but there are realistic expectations that international financial institutions will provide additional financial assistance (Stand-by arrangement with the IMF has been recently discussed and other IFIs will likely make available additional sources for international reserves).

Inflation rates have been declining to 0.8 percent in March as a consequence of the slowdown in transport and food prices (drop of 3.5 percent). As the commodity prices and economic activity are on a downturn across the globe, BiH will not be importing inflation in 2009. Forecasted inflation in 2009 will be in the range of 2 to 3 percent and depend on the price of goods and services provided by the public sector, public sector wage policy, and the aggregate level of public expenditures.

The first wave of the ongoing crisis hit the banking sector when depositors started to withdraw deposits from the banks in October, when KM 814 millions or 6.3 percent of total deposits were taken out of the banks. Although resident banks were stable and without any losses from the international financial crisis, households were alerted with events in other countries and market downgrades for large international banks. The episode did not last too long and confidence in banks was restored after two weeks. The central bank of Bosnia and Herzegovina (CBBH) reacted promptly and reduced the reserve requirement rate from 18 percent to 14 percent in order to provide additional liquidity and compensate the withdrawn deposits. Also, the government increased the threshold for insured deposits from EUR 3,250 to 10,000 in early 2009. The CBBH continued with the relaxation of available monetary instruments, so reserve requirements have been further lowered to 10 percent for long-term liabilities (and 14 percent for short-term liabilities) and new foreign borrowings are totally exempted from the reserve requirements.

Despite all these measures, credit flows to the private sector dropped significantly in the beginning of 2009. (private sector credit growth was only 12.7 percent in March compared with 26.9 percent in September 2008), while lending rates increased significantly. Foreign subsidiaries have been facing a lack of foreign funding, since these banking groups are in a deleveraging process and can not provide much funding for their subsidiaries. Profitability of the banking sector for 2008 strongly deteriorated compared to 2007 (total profits are 43 percent lower and main profitability indicators declined accordingly), and even worse results are expected in 2009.

Chart 3: Rapid Credit Slowdown after Break-up of the Crisis

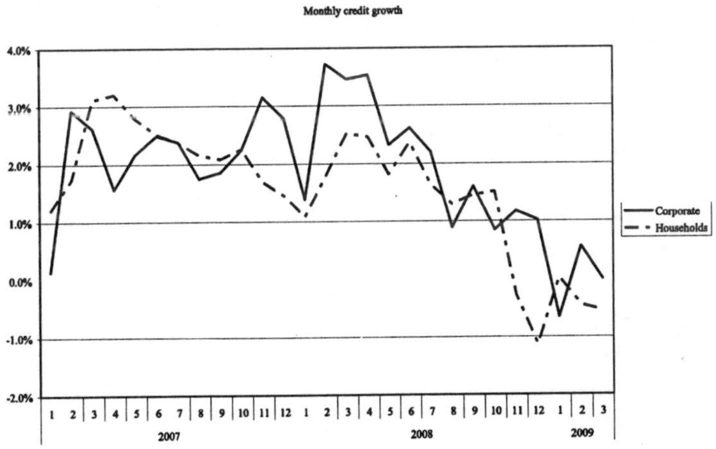

Source: CBBH statistics.

In the current global downturn the banking sector is likely to face a further deterioration and shocks on both sides of its balance sheet. In this environment, enhancing crisis preparedness and improving monitoring are key priorities.

Various authorities will work jointly on contingency planning arrangements and prepare for various crises scenarios. To this end, the creation of a Standing Committee for Financial Stability (comprising of fiscal authorities, banking agencies, deposit insurance agency, CBBH) has been under discussion. Its main task would be to review crisis preparedness and to discuss individual cases of significance and other developments relevant to financial stability.

The fiscal position has been very strained after the crisis started. The robust growth of tax revenue that was seen in recent years will not continue in 2009. The tax revenue will probably decline in nominal terms and also as percentage of GDP due to decreasing domestic demand and lower domestic and import prices. Under such circumstance, consolidated expenditures would need radical adjustment in order to run tolerable fiscal deficit (up to 4 percent GDP) in 2009. Authorities are keen to reduce current public consumption (especially public wages and social transfers) and continue necessary public investment. Even without any a fiscal expansion (such as a fiscal stimulus or bank bail-outs), the level of public debt is likely to grow as a result of the economic crisis.

3. A Need for Structural Changes and Different Growth Patterns

The existing monetary and exchange rate regime will be the cornerstone of future economic policies. The Currency Board Arrangement has served well over the past 12 years, ensured macroeconomic stability with low inflation, and has broad political and public support. The conservative financial system embedded in the currency board arrangement proved very beneficial as the financial crisis evolved and many other countries with more sophisticated countries were engulfed in credit problems, partly as a result of loose monetary policy. One of the main tasks for the next period is to secure the stability of the financial system. It would require further improvement of banking supervision, especially cross-border cooperation and approximation with the euro zone regulation and innovation. Also contingency planning and monitoring need to be further developed to ensure prompt and adequate reaction in the case of emergency. As it is likely that real sector circumstances deteriorate, banks will face further problems with asset quality.

Some of the main trading partners of BiH have recently experienced sizeable exchange rate deprecation, which might have an adverse impact on our competitiveness. It will necessitate to implement tools to prevent real appreciation of domestic currency. Wage flexibility needs to be maintained, and the government is determined to have a strict wage policy over the next 3 years. It is expected that wage restraint in the public sector will provide a strong signal for wage moderation in private sector settlements. Wages have been mostly negotiated at company level, which will facilitate necessary downward adjustment. However, some regulations of the labor market still need to be reformed in order to ensure more flexibility for employers (like part-time jobs, severance payment)

The current fiscal position has been very tight and does not provide space to finance fiscal stimulus from domestic sources. Ongoing reshuffling of public expenditures have been designed to reduce current consumption, without any increase in capital investment. It is, therefore, necessary to rely on external sources of capital for the stimulus aimed to boost domestic demand. Efforts should be made to secure additional funding for more projects from IFIs and foreign governments, since the access to international markets is severely constrained due to the low sovereign credit rating and increased risk aversion of foreign investors. After the worst part of the crisis is over, there is an urgency to ensure medium and long term fiscal sustainability. The level of public debt will rise over the next 2 to3 years, but it would require undertaking very bold steps to gradually reduce the debt level after the crisis is over. Future accession to the EU would impose strict rules on fiscal position and fiscal policies need to take it into account well before actual joining the EU. The limited room for fiscal maneuver underlines the importance to undertake the most effective measures including an increase in spending efficiency by e.g. cutting public administration costs, urging state-owned enterprises to devise saving plans or reducing the rate of public sector wage increases and pensions.

At the same time, public sector salaries and social benefits should not be presented as mandatory budgetary items. Only debt payments are mandatory items and even they could be postponed, although it would not be wise to suggest that at the moment. Increases in public sector salaries and social benefits are the consequence of long-term pressures from certain interested groups and future fiscal sustainability should be saved at any cost. So, the government should cut its current expenses on a more permanent basis and avoid temporary reduction (especially wages and social transfers).

Current government interventions are mainly aimed at preserving jobs and tempering output loss. To this end, governments have prepared, after a certain delay, a comprehensive action plan, but efficiency of these actions is still very limited. The main problems are a lack of fiscal space for massive interventions (subsidies, guarantees, capital injections and recapitalization) and complexity of structural reforms, which normally take a long time to complete.

Economic downturns are usually in times when existing economic policies and structure are being revised and new reforms are introduced. BH needs to prepare its economy for the post crisis resurgence and acceleration of European integration through tackling complex reforms. Governments and enterprises need accelerated economic reforms and increase efficiency to become more internationally competitive and able to achieve faster real convergence. Progress on structural reforms is uneven. BiH trails its best-performing peers on most structural and transition indicators and transition.

Private sector (still well below 60 percent of the economy) development has been hampered with burdensome regulations and weak institutions. Several international analyses [4] suggest that some of the reforms for more conducive business environment are important. The ongoing crisis will be an opportunity to address these deficiencies, which were frequently neglected during the periods of economic prosperity. It would enable to attract more foreign investments (which will be more difficult in the coming years) and to increase economic efficiency and lower production costs.

Source: http://www.oenb.at
Proceedings of OeNB Workshops No.15 "Recent Developments in the Baltic Countries – What Are the Lessons for Southeastern Europe,?" March 23, 2009. © The Oesterreichische Nationalbank. Reprinted with Permission.

The opinions expressed in this paper are those of the author and do not necessarily reflect the views of the central bank of Bosnia and Herzegovina.

Notes

1. Multilateral trade agreement CEFTA encompasses Bosnia and Herzegovina, Croatia, Macedonia, Moldova, Montenegro and Serbia.
2. Statistics on internal debt is still missing, so estimates of debt stock are necessary. Data have been quoted from IMF Article IV 2008.
3. Base metals export account for around 30 percent of total export.
4. Doing Business by the World Bank, EBRD transition indicators, Global Competitive Index, Corruption Perception Index.

References

Annual Report 2009, Central Bank of Bosnia and Herzegovina, March 2009.

Article IV Consultation for Bosnia and Herzegovina 2008, International Monetary Fund, August 2008.

Bosnia and Herzegovina 2008 Progress Report, European Commission, November 2008.

Financial Stability Report 2008, Central Bank of Bosnia and Herzegovina, September 2008.

Global Financial and Economic Crisis: Effects on the Bosnia and Herzegovina Economy, Mitigation, and Adaptation Measures, The World Bank and BH Directorate for Economic Planning, February 2009.

Recession in South East Europe, Is There Some Space for Policy Manoevre, Katarina Ott, IJF Newsletter May 2009.

Regional Economic Outlook: Europe, International Monetary Fund, 2009.

11

Spillovers of the Crisis: How different is Croatia?

Ljubinko Jankov

---

1. Overview

Central and Eastern Europe, a region which had been a recipient of massive capital inflows from Western Europe during the last twenty years, has been hit hard by the current global financial and economic crisis. After the collapse of Lehman Brothers it faced soaring risk premia and falling demand for its exports. The sharp downturn in real economic activity was accompanied by problems in the banking sector in some countries and the need for international official financial assistance.

The purpose of this paper is to explain why Croatia is one of the countries that have so far managed to cope with the crisis relatively well. The second section describes the causes of capital inflows and various measures adopted by the Hrvatska Narodna Banka (HNB) to slow them down, and stresses that it was almost an impossible mission for the HNB. The third section explains how these measures ensured the continued normal functioning of the Croatian banking system in the period of economic distress and suggests that avoiding the exchange rate and banking crisis was the key reason why the current decline in real economic activity is less pronounced than in peer countries. The fourth part admits that such policy is not without risks, particularly given that international competitiveness has been in decline for the last several years.

2. Main Features of HNB Policy after Obtaining EU Candidate Status

Since 2000, Croatia has significantly improved its political relations with the international community. Better political relations helped finalize negotiations on joining the World Trade Organization in 2001 and contributed to the signing of the Stability and Association Agreement with the European Union (EU) in 2002. Political integration was followed by higher foreign capital inflows to Croatia. When Croatia obtained the candidate status for EU membership in 2005, inflows intensified even further.

Foreign owned local banks were the main players moving foreign capital into Croatia. Their owners are major foreign banks that operate in the region, and most of them came to Croatia around 2000. They encouraged their local subsidiaries to increase domestic lending and financed the lending by foreign borrowing from other banks belonging to the same banking group. Making a profit on the difference between domestic and foreign interest rates has been the main motive of foreign banks' business in Croatia. Namely, while foreign interest rates fell to historically low levels in 2001 and remained there for several years, interest rates in Croatia have been much higher than abroad. Furthermore, the expectation that the nominal exchange rate would remain stable also supported capital inflows. Although the primary goal of the HNB is price stability, tight management of the nominal exchange rate of the Croatian kuna (HRK) against the euro has been the main feature of HNB monetary policy since 1993 and it has also proven to be successful in controlling inflation. This is a result of the fact that Croatia is a small open economy with a high degree of euroization (about 2/3 of bank deposits are in foreign currency).

Although capital inflows are considered positive, there were rising concerns within the central bank that Croatia receives, in the short run, too much of what is otherwise a good thing. Such concerns were supported by the fact that, on the one hand, the speed of economic growth was similar to other countries in the region, while on the other hand external vulnerabilities were materializing much faster. This was partly due to the fact that most of the new bank loans were granted to households, i.e. for consumption. The HNB recognized such trends as the seeds of future crisis, and decided to act. However, it had to do so within the following constraints: (1) the room for independent monetary policy was limited due to the exchange rate regime, (2) despite the HNB's legal power to impose capital controls, this was not possible due to the EU accession efforts, and (3) the cooperation with fiscal authorities was limited due to the large structural problems in the government budget. Therefore, the HNB's response to capital inflows was a combination of soft monetary policy and the adoption of various administrative and prudential measures. Such measures were introduced already in 2003, and were changed and gradually tightened afterwards. The choice of particular measures and changes in those measures over time were not simple and smooth processes because banks always tried to find ways to arbitrage them.

In 2003 the HNB introduced a speed limit to bank lending and a rule on minimum retained earnings if bank lending exceeds a certain threshold. The speed limit was set as the annual growth of banks' domestic credits of 16 percent. As the penalty for breaching it was high, banks formally met the limit, and the rate of growth of banks' credits to the non-government sector fell from 28.7 percent in 2002 to 11.8 percent in 2003. Because of the banks' attempts at arbitrage, the rate of growth of total domestic credits in the economy as a whole declined by much less. Banks actually adjusted to the limit by: (1) selling a part of their loan portfolio to affiliated Croatian leasing companies, securing the funding by borrowing abroad from the mother bank or other banks within the same banking group; and (2) selling the credit risk to the mother bank; under the accepted accounting standards banks can remove such loans from the balance sheet. The latter operation should had been recorded by statistics as foreign direct lending to non-bank clients (using the local bank credit office expertise), but it was not captured by statistics in 2003. The other measure adopted by the HNB was the requirement for fast-growing banks to retain a portion of earnings for three years. The purpose of such a requirement is to provide a cushion against possible deterioration of newly granted credits in the future.

The speed limit regulation was discontinued in 2004 and replaced by other measures believed to be better. The important new measure introduced in July 2004 was the marginal reserve requirement, which required banks to make additional non-interest bearing deposits with the HNB if their foreign liabilities increased above their value recorded at end-June 2004. The marginal required reserve rate was set in July 2004 at 24 percent. The rate was later gradually increased, reaching 55 percent at the end of 2005. Throughout that period, the HNB was also active in refining the regulation and closing all loopholes found by banks. For instance, marginal required reserves were also later applied to increases in liabilities to affiliated leasing companies, to off-balance sheet items related to the selling of credit risk and to debt securities issued. The latter were included because some banks started issuing debt securities by placing them privately with the mother bank. Prior to that, bank debt securities were not issued at all.

Marginal required reserves came in addition to the regular required reserves and the minimum foreign exchange liquidity requirement. Taken together, these three requirements reached their peak at the end of 2005, and—although there were some minor variations in the minimum foreign exchange liquidity requirement—remained there until October 2008. Banks were required to place 72 percent of the increase in foreign liabilities with the HNB, or in liquid foreign assets, while the remaining 28 percent was disposable for lending to clients (Table 11.1). In spite of extremely high reserve requirements, banks' domestic lending increased again. The annual rate of growth of banks' domestic credits was at 22.3 percent in 2005 and 23.9 percent in 2006. However, in 2006 banks' foreign liabilities started to decline because foreign borrowing as the source of banks' funds for domestic lending was replaced by raising new equity capital. At this time, incoming cash transfers from mother banks for the purpose of raising bank equity capital tripled relative to the previous three years' average.

Table 11.1: Required Reserves Set by the HNB

Source of Financing	Disposable for lending		Cost of financing (percent)		BEAIR (percent)*	
	2007	2009	2007	2009	2007	2009
Foreign Liabilities						
HRK (100)	28.0	86.0	4.30	5.87	15.04	6.73
HRK indexed to FX (100)	28.0	66.0	4.30	5.87	15.04	7.76
FX (100)	28.0	69.5	4.30	5.87	14.67	7.51
Household Deposits						
HRK (100)	83.0	86.0	2.80	6.65	3.27	7.65
HRK indexed to FX (100)	51.0	66.0	4.21	5.09	5.70	6.58
FX (100)	56.1	68.1	2.87	4.97	2.82	6.23
Average Interest Rate on New Placement	-		8.69	9.76	-	-

* BEAIR = Break Even Average Interest Rate
Source: HNB.

Furthermore, according to a survey of bank managers, changes in capital adequacy regulation also contributed to the increase in bank equity capital. As of mid 2006, risk weights applied to bank loans in foreign exchange or loans in kuna indexed to foreign currency, granted to un-hedged clients, have been higher than those required by Basel II. Applying such higher risk weights to a substantial part of bank assets (almost all households' loans are unhedged) caused a fall in banks' capital adequacy ratio by two percentage points.

Raising banks' reserve and capital adequacy requirements failed to weaken capital inflows. In 2005 and 2006, total domestic lending in the economy as a whole grew even higher than bank lending (24.6 vis-à-vis 23.1 annually), due to fast growth of direct foreign lending to non-bank enterprises. Creditors of non-bank clients were the same foreign banking groups. To discontinue such trends in domestic lending and the buildup of external vulnerabilities, the HNB decided to employ the speed limit to bank lending again in 2007. The regulation was prepared more carefully than in 2003, covering the selling of credit portfolio and credit risk. Loans granted by local bank affiliates were covered by the limit as well. The speed limit was set as the annual growth of bank lending of 12 percent. Penalties for breaching the limit were high, causing the annual growth of bank lending to fall to 15.3 percent in 2007. As bank lending is an important source of household credit, limiting it caused a significant decline in the growth rate of overall household credit, which fell from 23.5 percent in 2006 to 19.2 percent in 2007. On the other hand, the growth rate of credit to enterprises remained at 25 percent, because borrowing from domestic banks was replaced by foreign borrowing.

The speed limit was successful in restricting household credit, so the HNB employs it even today, although it is no longer binding. However, due to its obvious drawbacks, the HNB has also considered revoking the speed limit in the future, with the exit provided by linking bank capital adequacy with credit growth. Such a link was incorporated in the capital adequacy regulation at the beginning of 2008. According to it, banks growing at 12 percent annually have to satisfy a minimum capital adequacy rate of 12 percent, while banks growing faster than that face higher capital adequacy requirements. The HNB also tried to link the additional capital adequacy requirement negatively with the growth of core deposits. In addition, other supervisory regulation was also tightened prior to the crisis; weights used in the calculation of risk weighted assets were increased, as were the minimum retained earnings ratios for fast growing banks. Higher risk weights applied to bank loans in foreign exchange, as well as those in kuna indexed to foreign currency granted to unhedged clients, caused a decline in the banks' capital adequacy similar to that in 2006 and forced banks to raise more equity capital (see Chart 1). Consequently, by the end of September 2008 the ratio of banks' core capital to total assets reached almost the same value as bank capital adequacy, which was quite unique and high.

Chart 1: Capital Adequacy Ratios

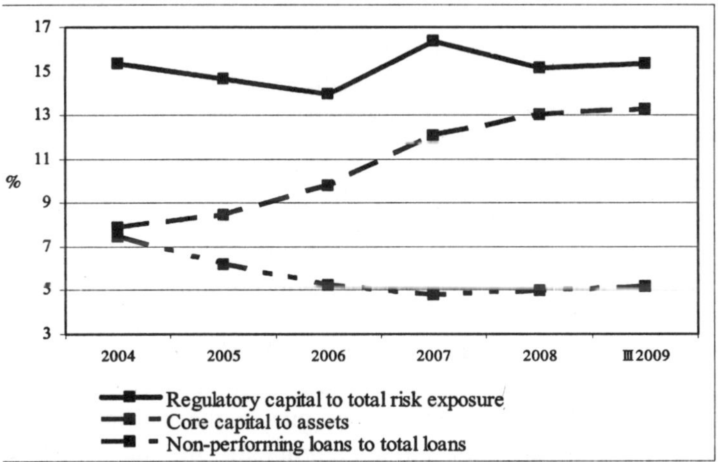

Source: HNB.

Looking back at the period preceding the global crisis from the point of view of a small transition country that has just started the accession process to the European Union, it turns out that it was extremely difficult to control the volume of capital imports. Due to the exchange rate regime, capital inflows forced the HNB to operate like a currency board and to build large international reserves. Various administrative and supervisory measures had to provide a cushion and slow down the buildup of external vulnerabilities. Applying such measures, the HNB managed, for the most part, to alter the structure of debt capital inflows—bank foreign borrowing from mother banks was replaced by enterprises' non-guaranteed direct foreign borrowing from the same creditors. This, in turn, altered personal consumption and private investments as more credit was provided to non-financial enterprises than to households. On the other hand, the cushion was provided by the high capital adequacy and high liquid assets held mostly in foreign currency, ensuring the soundness of domestic banks.

3. The Monetary Policy Response to the Global Financial Crisis

The bankruptcy of Lehman Brothers in September 2008 shook Europe. International capital flows to Central and Eastern Europe were suddenly viewed as extremely risky and the profitability of banking groups engaged in such transactions started to be questioned by their investors. The future trend of capital inflows to Croatia also became uncertain. In addition, expectations of future exports were revised downwards substantially due to rapidly declining foreign demand. The Croatian government was unprepared for the crisis; the budget was, until April 2009, based on unrealistic real growth projections, while the government's foreign currency debt obligations due in the coming period were high. Rumors of possible problems in mother banks caused an immediate reaction of Croatian depositors. In October 2008 they started withdrawing their funds from local banks, hoarding the withdrawn foreign currency cash mostly under mattresses. Although withdrawals had stopped already by the end of October 2008, they caused capital outflows in the amount of 2 percent of GDP in the last quarter of 2008. [1]

When the crisis started, the appreciation pressures that had previously been a common feature of the foreign exchange market were replaced by depreciation pressures. These exchange rate pressures were successfully contained. The

HNB acted by providing liquidity in foreign and tightening liquidity in domestic currency. It did this mostly by lowering required reserves in foreign currency, i.e. it avoided large direct market interventions. As it was in fact only repaying banks' required reserve deposits, its net international reserves did not decline. On the other hand, banks regulatory costs fell substantially (Table 11.1).

Defending the exchange rate was extremely complex due to the very large financial needs of the government. The required reserve reduction that took place from October 2008 to March 2009 was sometimes implicitly conditioned by granting new credit to the Croatian government. In fact, it turns out that within the same period an increase in banks' net claims on the government amounted to about 50 percent of funds freed by the reduction and 25 percent of the value of deposit withdrawals in October. In addition to providing foreign currency liquidity to banks by lowering required reserves, the HNB also tightened banks' liquidity in HRK, resulting in double digit overnight interbank lending rates as opposed to single digit ones prior to the crisis. The rates were extremely volatile and even reached 40 percent on a daily basis. However, the increase in lending rates to banks' clients was moderate due to lower regulatory costs (less than one percentage point), as well as the fact that the interbank market is not an important source of funds.

Although the money and foreign exchange markets stabilized as of March 2009, it is still early to judge the impact of the global financial crisis on Croatia. Based on the evidence of the last two quarters, it seems that there are some important positive trends: capital inflows to Croatia have continued, the banking system has remained stable, and the decline in real economic activity has been moderate relative to peer countries.

After the crisis had started, capital inflows continued as a result of a huge increase in domestic banks' foreign debt. The stock of non-bank enterprises' debt increased moderately as well (see Chart 2). This indicates that, thanks to earlier measures of the HNB, banks were well prepared for the crisis and had the opportunity to borrow abroad as much as was needed during the peak of the crisis. The total bank domestic lending rate continued its rapid growth. As new loans were mostly granted to the government, there was a sharp increase in banks' net claims on the government, while domestic bank credit to the private sector stagnated for the first time since September 2000, due to demand rather than supply factors.

Chart 2: Foreign Debt Stocks to Medium Term 2005 – 2008 Average

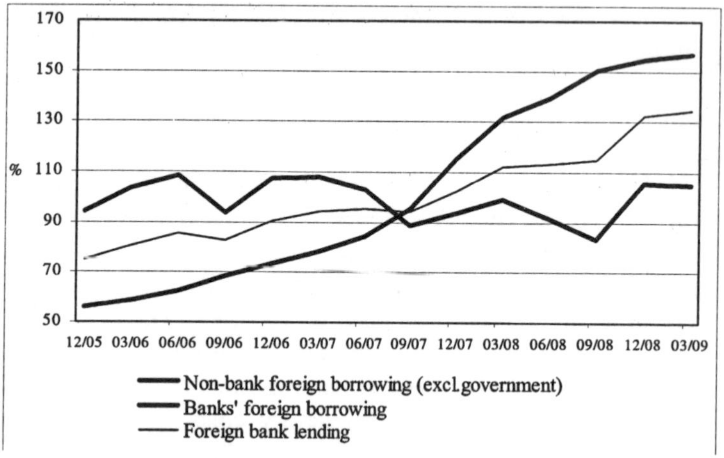

Source: HNB.

HNB policies aimed at maintaining exchange rate stability have also preserved the stability of the banking system. Banks remained profitable and loan loss reserves low (see Chart 1). As the HNB sets limits on banks' foreign currency exposure, banks are not directly exposed to foreign currency risk. However, since their clients are unhedged, the stability of the exchange rate is of crucial importance for banks. According to bank reports to the HNB, more than 90 percent of banks' claims in foreign currency, or claims in HRK indexed to foreign currency, are unhedged. Therefore the materialization of their clients' exchange rate risk could seriously lower the quality of banks' credit and provoke large losses. In addition, the large foreign debt of enterprises amplifies the exchange rate risk.

In general, the need to protect the exchange rate in bad times also means that the HNB monetary policy framework does not allow for the use of countercyclical monetary policy. Such a limitation of the HNB monetary policy framework has not proven to be important in this crisis. The fact that Croatia has been handling the crisis without having to clean the mess in its banking system ensures a less severe decline in real economic activity.

4. Challenges for the Future

The HNB policy of exchange rate stability is a long term concept. Building adequate official and bank reserves in good times has enabled the HNB to anchor expectations even in bad times, as well as to ensure the stability of the banking system. Although the HNB was willing to spend part of its international reserves in the crisis period, it was aware that they are not infinite, so it tightened monetary policy in order not to lose reserves in the future. In a longer-term perspective, the implementation of monetary policy will depend on future capital flows. If they continue to finance the current account deficit, there will be room for softer monetary policy; the less sufficient they are for the financing of the current account deficit, the tighter monetary policy will be.

The HNB policy of maintaining a stable nominal exchange rate of the kuna against the euro also means that the exchange rate is not used as a tool for the improvement of international competitiveness. The Croatian economy faces a number of structural weaknesses: low total factor productivity, low labor participation, a smaller share of goods exports in GDP than in peer countries, etc. Although the Croatian government tried to launch structural reforms to address some of these weaknesses, international competitiveness measured by relative unit labor costs started to worsen after Croatia became an EU candidate.

This presents a challenge for the implementation of economic policy in the long run. This trend in international competitiveness should be reversed by launching more structural reforms that increase the economy's long run growth potential.

The HNB has not questioned its exchange rate and monetary policy regime because of the changing international environment. In spite of low inflation since 1993, the moderate real appreciation of the HRK as well as regulatory banking costs which continuously favor deposits in HRK, financial euroization has not declined in the period prior to the crisis. During the crisis it has even increased further. Therefore, the main reasons for the existing exchange rate and monetary policy regime remain unchanged. Whether such a policy will continue to be as successful as it has been in the past remains to be seen.

Source: http://www.oenb.at
Proceedings of OeNB Workshop No.15 "Recent Developments in the Baltic Countries – What Are the Lessons for Southeastern Europe,?" March 23, 2009. © The Oesterreichische Nationalbank. Reprinted with Permission.

The author is Executive Director, Hrvatska Narodna Banka.

Note

1. In October the Government reacted quickly by raising the maximum insured deposit amount from HRK 100,000 to HRK 400,000, while the CNB provided foreign currency liquidity by revoking the marginal reserve requirement.

12

Central Asia and the Global Economic Crisis

Richard Pomfret

Introduction

In 2007 the EU published a Strategy for a New Partnership with Central Asia. In its initial stages the EU focused on developing new forums for dialogue with the Central Asian countries, and received some criticism for inadequate substantive actions. This Policy Brief argues that the current global economic crisis does not alter the priorities of the EU Strategy, but it does require the EU to stick to existing obligations and also provides an opportunity for fresh initiatives to better achieve the Strategy's fundamental goals.

A striking feature of the five Central Asian countries' economic strategies is that they followed divergent paths after becoming independent in 1991. Despite strong similarities in culture, history and economic structure, their transitions from Soviet central planning ranged from the most rapidly liberalising (the Kyrgyz Republic) to the most non-reforming (Turkmenistan) of all former Soviet republics. By the turn of the century, when the transition from central planning was essentially completed, the Central Asian countries had created vastly different economic systems. These differences had important implications for economic stability during the 1990s, for long-term growth prospects in the 2000s, and for the impact of the global economic crisis that gathered pace in 2008-9. The Central Asian countries are open economies in the sense that international trade is important, but they have all been suspicious of integration into the global economy and have embraced globalisation to varying degrees. In general terms, the more globally integrated an economy is the better its performance was over the last two decades, but the more exposed it was to crises. [1] In Central Asia this generalisation needs to be more nuanced; and Section 2 relates it to country-specific resource endowments and economic strategies.

The main implication for the EU Strategy is that what was desirable in 2007 is still desirable. Goals of strengthening human rights, rule of law, good governance and democratisation may be harder to achieve in straitened circumstances, but success is connected to the economic goals of promoting economic development, trade and investment and alleviating poverty. Finally, the Strategy's goal of strengthening energy and transport links may be easier in a period of low energy prices as long as the EU can turn the economic downturn into an opportunity rather than a threat.

1. The Central Asian Economies [2]

During the 1990s the Kyrgyz Republic was one of the leading reformers among former Soviet republics, *inter alia* the first to join the World Trade Organisation. Kazakhstan was also active in creating a market-driven economy. Both of these countries experienced disappointing economic performance over the decade, and just as they were emerging from the transitional recession both economies were severely hit by the 1998 Russian Crisis.

Uzbekistan and Turkmenistan were more cautious reformers. Gradualism was a good short-term strategy to minimize disruption from the end of central planning and the dissolution of the USSR. As the two largest cotton producers in the Soviet Union, both countries benefited from the ease with which cotton could be shipped to global rather than CIS markets and from buoyant world cotton prices in the first half of the 1990s. Uzbekistan was the best performing of all former Soviet republics during the 1990s, with the smallest decline in GDP and reasonably good social indicators. Turkmenistan, with a more autocratic leadership and negligible reforms, fared less well, despite revenue from cotton and gas exports, because the domestic economy was woefully inefficient.

Racked by civil war for most of the decade, Tajikistan's economic transition fell between these two pairs. The collapse of institutions led to rapid *de facto* privatisation, but limited the emergence of a well-functioning market economy. Tajikistan was a substantial exporter of cotton and aluminium, based on its hydroelectricity potential, but control over these key goods fluctuated in the civil war and maintenance of infrastructure such as irrigation systems was neglected.

By the start of the 21st century the five countries had differing potential for sustained growth. Uzbekistan in 1996 and Turkmenistan in 1998 implemented stringent foreign exchange controls after their export earnings declined due to falling world cotton prices, exacerbated in Turkmenistan's case by poor revenues from gas sales. The controls were symptomatic of suspicion of the price mechanism, and of a 'vent for surplus' view of foreign trade by which production of cotton and gas beyond domestic needs would be exchanged for imported goods. Trade was not part of a development strategy, and both countries promoted import-substituting industrialisation.

The negative consequences of these policies were recognized by Uzbekistan, but once in place they were hard to change because key individuals and groups benefited from exchange controls and barriers to imports (e.g. the state was able to manipulate prices to obtain a large share of cotton rents and owners and workers in inefficient industries were sheltered from competing imports). The controls were only gradually relaxed over the first decade of the 2000s. Consequently, Uzbekistan's economy grew sluggishly and in the face of growing discontent, the regime became more repressive–an outcome highlighted by the demonstrations and deaths in Andijan in 2005.

In Turkmenistan the response of President Niyazov, or Turkmenbashi the Great as he preferred to be known, was to retreat into autarchy. The approach was underpinned by the rise of world oil prices after 1998 which, with a time lag, filtered through into higher prices for Turkmen gas exports. The pipeline system continued to leave Turkmenistan dependent on Russian demand, but as the price paid by the EU for Russian gas soared, Russia was keen to ensure supplies of Turkmen gas for its own customers. Turkmenbashi's only international trip in the last years before his death in December 2006 was to China, driven by a desire to diversify gas export routes. More active foreign policy has been a keynote of the early years of the presidency of Gurbanguly Berdymukhamedov, Niyazov's successor, with promises of increased gas exports to Russia, China and the EU, but the seriousness of these commitments and of pronouncements about economic reform are still to be tested. [3]

Kazakhstan and the Kyrgyz Republic were better placed for sustained growth over the last decade because central planning had been replaced by better functioning market-based economies than in Uzbekistan or Turkmenistan. However, their relative economic fortunes would be dominated by energy market developments.

Kazakhstan's recovery from the 1998 crisis, with a large devaluation stimulating export growth in 1999, was overshadowed by oil exports. Kazakhstan's huge oil reserves in the Caspian Basin were finally starting to flow in large quantities. The first alternatives to the Russian Transneft pipeline were being constructed, and oil prices were starting a climb from under US$ 10 a barrel in 1998 to a peak of almost US$ 150 in 2008. Kazakhstan was one of the fastest growing economies in the world in the decade starting in 1999. The oil boom fuelled confidence, government spending, a credit boom and an asset bubble centred on construction in the two main cities, Almaty and Astana. The financial sector, already the most dynamic in Central Asia became internationalised as banks sought funds from abroad to meet the insatiable demand for credit domestically. [4] Signs of a banking crisis started to emerge in 2006 and 2007, before the global crisis but with similar roots to the US sub-prime crisis (i.e. over-exuberant borrowing and lenders paying less and less attention to borrowers' creditworthiness or the value of collateral).

In the absence of hydrocarbons or other major exportables apart from a single goldmine, the performance of the Kyrgyz economy was weaker, and the political situation was plagued by uncertainty. All of the Central Asian countries have established super-presidential regimes, but parliament is least weak in the Kyrgyz Republic. Moreover, alone among the Central Asian countries, the Kyrgyz Republic has experienced a political succession not associated with civil war or bereavement. Nevertheless, the domestic political situation remains unstable, with rampant corruption and a disappointing economic performance. Internationally, Kyrgyzstan has been the most consistently pro-Western of the countries and hosts the last remaining US base in Central Asia, although at the time of writing the base's future is limited. [5] Northern Kyrgyzstan is increasingly economically dominated by its richer neighbours to the north, with many workers migrating to Kazakhstan or Russia and a financial system dominated by Kazakh banks since the 1998 crisis.

For Tajikistan peace and the authority of the central government were established between 1997 and 2001, but many institutions remain weak. A huge percentage of the male population works abroad, mainly in Russia, and remittances are the country's major source of foreign exchange; although data are sketchy, the share of remittances in GDP is perhaps the highest in the world. [6] The resident population remains desperately poor.

2. Globalisation and Central Asia

The Central Asian economies are open but they are not integrated into the global economy in particularly complex ways. Kazakhstan as the richest and most developed economy in the region has the most complex relations to globalisation, but even there suspicion of losing autonomy (reflected in the slow progress of WTO accession negotiations) has limited the degree of globalisation of the Kazakhstani economy. The main channels of globalisation, and hence for contagion from the global economic crisis, run through (1) the financial sector, (2) trade, and (3) migration and remittances. The last is important because hundreds of thousands of workers from Tajikistan and to a lesser extent the Kyrgyz Republic and Uzbekistan are working abroad and their prospects will be directly influenced by economic conditions in Russia and elsewhere.

2.1 Finance: Over the last decade Kazakhstan's economy has been the success story of Central Asia. Among the jewels of the market-driven economy have been the banks, sometimes claimed to be the most efficient in the CIS, and expanding first into the Kyrgyz Republic, where over 70 percent of the assets of the banking sector are Kazakh-owned, and more recently into Tajikistan. Kazakhstan's banks became increasingly integrated into global financial markets. As Almaty and Astana in the mid-2000s experienced a real estate boom, banks lent to borrowers eager not to miss out in the property market and as demand for credit outran domestic savings the banks borrowed in international markets. By 2006, Kazakhstan's banks were raising large amounts of capital abroad, where the cost was less than the double-digit interest rates that they could charge borrowers at home. In the first half of 2007, medium - and long-term debt-creating capital inflows more than doubled, largely due to external borrowing by the banking sector. The maturity mismatch between the foreign assets and the banks' loan portfolios caused problems when the foreign institutions began to worry about Kazakhstan's external obligations and when loosening of the exchange rate peg caused domestic banks to reassess their foreign currency exposure. [7]

In 2007 Kazakhstan's banks started to compete in making deposits more attractive and substantially increased the interest rates on loans, which by year's end had reached about 20 percent, double the rates of two years' earlier. In November

2007, the government provided support of around US$ 4 billion, targeted at construction projects in danger of being abandoned half-finished, and the central bank raised the official refinancing rate, which had been unchanged at 9 percent since July 2006, to 11 percent. [8] In late 2007, Standard and Poor's downgraded Kazakhstan's sovereign debt to BBB - the lowest grade above speculative.

By 2008, Kazakhstan's financial sector problems were coinciding with the emergence of a global financial crisis, but the origins of the domestic financial crisis were home-grown. The banks' problems arose from loan portfolios overweighted in domestic real estate projects, not from buying over-risky financial assets in the global market. Kazakhstan's banks had been borrowers in the global financial markets rather than investing in toxic assets coming out of the US financial system. Moreover, although the banking crisis will have substantial economic costs, they are not unbearable because the authorities are well-placed to finance an economic stimulus using the earnings accumulated during the 1999-2008 oil boom.

The financial sectors of the other Central Asian countries are even less exposed to turmoil in global financial markets. The Kyrgyz financial sector is dominated by Kazakh banks, so its financial sector worries are largely tied to Kazakhstan's. The banking sector in Uzbekistan is dominated by state banks which are conservative in their international activities. Turkmenistan's financial sector is even more repressed and the only significant transactions are processing revenues from gas and cotton exports and transferring remittances. Tajikistan is too poor to have an internationally integrated financial sector beyond transferring remittances.

2.2 Trade: The Central Asian countries have high export/GDP ratios (Table 12.1), except for Tajikistan whose ratio would be much higher if exports of labour services were included (remittances are guesstimated to be equal to about a third of GDP). Despite efforts to diversify their economies by using revenues from energy, mineral or cotton exports or through import-substituting policies or other measures, the Central Asian countries' exports remain heavily concentrated in a small number of commodities.

Table 12.1: Openness and Major Exports

	Exports/GDP percent		Major Exports
	2006	2007	
Kazakhstan	51	49	Oil, Minerals, Iron and Steel, Grain
Kyrgyz Rep	42	45	Gold, Cotton
Tajikistan	23	21	Aluminium, Cotton
Turkmenistan	72	63	Gas, Cotton
Uzbekistan	38	40	Cotton, Gold, Gas

Source: World Bank, World Development Indicators at www.worldbank.org (accessed 27 April, 2009).

The commodity concentration of exports is high in all five countries, although it fluctuates as world prices change and, especially in Tajikistan's case, due to volatile quantities. For Kazakhstan, oil accounted for over 60 percent of exports by the height of the oil boom, up from just under 40 percent in 1999, when grains, various minerals and iron and steel products were all major export items. Turkmenistan's data are non-transparent, but natural gas and to a lesser extent oil have come to almost totally dominate exports as cotton production declined. Gold and cotton fibre account for about 45 percent of Kyrgyz exports. Cotton fibre, gold and natural gas accounted for 68 percent of Uzbekistan's exports in 1999 and, despite efforts at export diversification, their share has remained over 60 percent. Over 80 percent of Tajikistan's exports in 2004 consisted of aluminium and cotton, but the output of both commodities varies substantially from year-to-year. [9]

Thus, apart from demand for migrant labour, the primary channel through which the global financial crisis is likely to hit Central Asia is through reduced demand for key commodities and this impact will be country-specific. In 2008 and early 2009, the impact has primarily been felt by the energy exporters, Kazakhstan and Turkmenistan. Adjusting to the end of the oil boom and the bursting of an asset bubble is a major problem for Kazakhstan, but with its much higher income levels and accumulated reserves Kazakhstan is the Central Asian country best-placed to tighten belts. Turkmenistan has been less exposed to global energy market developments because gas prices are less volatile than oil prices. Turkmenistan under new leadership may also be well-placed to weather an energy-price bust, if better economic management leads to increasing gas output and if pipeline routes can be diversified to reduce dependence on Russian routes.

Figure 1. World Cotton Prices, 2004-9

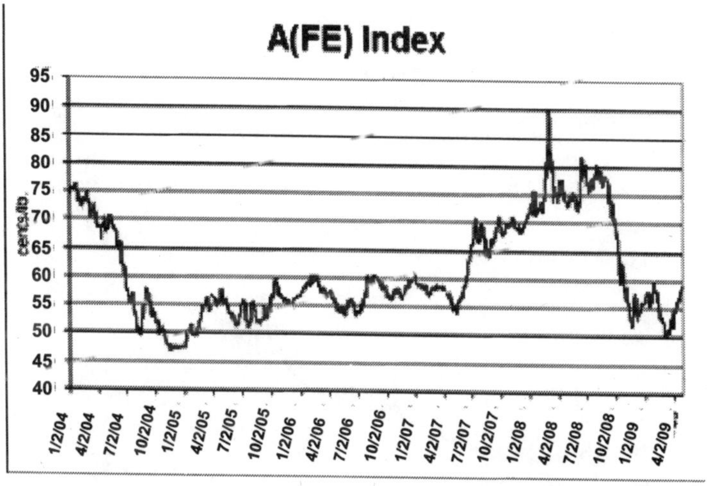

Source: Cotlook A(FE) index, graph from the National Cotton Council of America at http://www.cotton.org/econ/prices/cotlook-a-indices.cfm\ (downloaded 30 April 2009.)

Grain prices fell in 2008 from a short-term peak. This should help the poorest countries, which are net importers of food. Kazakhstan is a major grain exporter, but Kazakhstan's farmers benefited in the 2000s from an improved policy environment which left them with a larger share of net revenues. [10]

World cotton prices are of importance to all Central Asian countries, and especially to Uzbekistan, which is the world's fourth largest exporter. Although world cotton prices fluctuate, there was no clear trend during the 2000s. There was an upturn in 2007-8 but this corrected in the third quarter of 2008. [11]

For the region's gold exporters (the Kyrgyz Republic and Uzbekistan) concerns about a global recession have a positive impact on export earnings. Gold prices, which were languishing around US$ 300 per ounce in the early 2000s, began to surge in mid-decade and as financial concerns mounted in 2007 they rose above US$ 900. Despite a dip in 2008, gold prices have returned to these highs in 2009 (see Figure 2).

Figure 2. World Gold Prices, 1999-2009

Source: Gold Price Australia, at http://goldprice.org/charts/history/gold_10_year_o_usd.png (accessed 27 April 2009.)

Tajikistan's main exporter is the Talco aluminium smelter utilising the country's abundant hydro resources. Aluminium exports normally account for over half of the country's export earnings, although earnings suffered a precipitous decline in 2008-9 as global prices for aluminium collapsed (*see Figure 3*). Tajikistan should have benefited from surging world prices during the 2000s, but output was often disrupted and whether the proceeds from the smelter benefit the country is unclear. The IMF has publicly stated that data on the flow of funds have been falsified. Talco revenues accrue to a company registered in the British Virgin Islands, and large amounts have been siphoned off by well-connected individuals; a corruption trial is in progress in London. [12] This is symptomatic of Tajikistan's institutional problems, which make it close to being a failed state.

Figure 3. World Aluminium Prices, 1999-2009

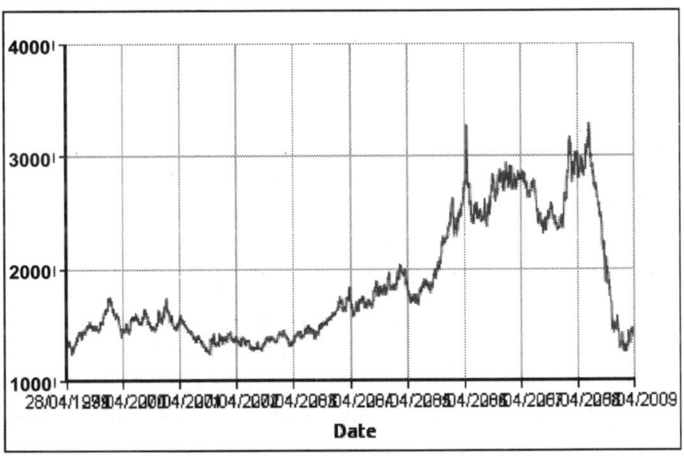

Source: London Metal Exchange at http://www.lme.co.uk/aluminium_graphs.asp (accessed 27 April 2009.)

3. Implications for EU Policy

The implications from the above analysis are that the global economic crisis should have little influence on EU economic policy towards Central Asia. What would have been desirable in the absence of the crisis is still desirable. At the same time, while the impact of the global economic downturn may be comparatively benign in the region, it will raise important challenges that will affect the EU Strategy in the region. Growing unemployment and poverty may increase social tensions and even be the source for conflicts. This suggests that the EU and international organisations should re-examine some of their existing programmes in the areas of poverty alleviation and conflict prevention in light of the changed circumstances

EU members should keep their borders open to imports from Central Asia. The Central Asian countries' exports remain heavily concentrated in a few commodities, but all governments recognise the desirability of export diversification and this should not be hampered by closed doors in Europe. All EU countries claim commitment to avoiding protectionism, but all are under domestic pressure to protect domestic producers, and weak trading partners are the softest targets. The EU must ensure that members do not undermine European relations with Central Asia by throttling non-traditional export opportunities.

EU can help Central Asia by living up to its commitment to promote regional cooperation. The BOMCA/CADAP programme, which in its early years focused too much on restricting the drugs trade, now plays an unspectacular, but worthwhile role in improving border management and facilitating trade. Trade facilitation is most vital to the two poorest and most geographically isolated countries, Kyrgyzstan and Tajikistan. Such measures should be in cooperation with multilateral agencies, e.g. through CAREC. [13] The EU can provide a European dimension by supporting initiatives to develop trade corridors such as the E40 Tashkent–Berlin road, which for hundreds of kilometres is little more than a dirt track through the desert.

EU's commitment to poverty alleviation in Central Asia requires that resources be made available to Kyrgyzstan and Tajikistan, the region's two poorest countries and the ones most severely hit by the global crisis. Domestic labour markets in these countries will be destabilised by returning migrants unable to find work in Russia or Kazakhstan. Aid will be necessary to help provide domestic employment and for humanitarian reasons.

Perhaps most imaginatively, **the EU could use an era of subdued energy prices to put together a coherent long-term strategy towards energy security and relations with Central Asian producers**. It is important to place EU support for specific projects in the context of changing attitudes towards renewable energy and changing technology (e.g. liquefaction technology that may transform the economics of gas pipelines). Nevertheless, the headlines in the near future will concern pipeline routes and their geopolitical undertones; especially where pipelines might be mutually exclusive, as with the Russian-favoured South Stream and the US-backed Nabucco route, it is important to develop a coherent approach in the best interest of the EU and Central Asia.

4. Conclusions

The global recession's impact has been relatively benign for Central Asia. Kazakhstan, the country most integrated into the global economy and potentially most harmed by the global crisis, is the country best-prepared for negative financial and trade effects. Uzbekistan and Turkmenistan have foregone economic benefits from global integration, but by the same token are relatively insulated from external shocks other than through commodity prices. The Kyrgyz Republic is in an intermediate position, but its major export commodity, gold, often does well during recessions and 2008-9 has been no exception. A more significant transmission for the poorer countries is migration, and the direst negative impact is through the reduced flow of remittances to Tajikistan, the poorest country in the region.

Recession is a threat to Central Asia, as economic hardship may lead to increased repression, challenging the EU's commitment to human rights and democratisation in the region. However, global recession also presents opportunities. So far the EU has played a minor role in Central Asia. Despite grand overarching statements in the 2007 Strategy and high level meetings in 2008, questions remain about the EU's ability to deliver on its promises to foster a broad range of engagements with Central Asia. [14] The shifting positions of other interested parties offer an opportunity to change this. China is using the commodity bust to buy into resources. Russia is more subdued than when oil prices were high. The US has a new administration. Iran has upcoming elections. The EU is committed to pursuing the Central Asia Strategy through the Swedish Presidency until the end of 2009, and in 2010 Kazakhstan will chair the OSCE. The EU should keep nimble in these shifting circumstances.

Source: www.eucentralasia.eu
© EUCAM. Reprinted with Permission.

This EU- Central Asia Monitoring (EUCAM) Policy Brief is part of a mini series of three publications on the impact of the global slowdown on Central Asia and its relations with the European Union.

Dr. Richard Pomfret has been Professor of Economics at the University of Adelaide since 1992. He was previously Professor of Economics at the Johns Hopkins University School of Advanced International Studies in Washington DC, Bologna (Italy) and Nanjing (China).

Notes

1. See R. Ranciere, A. Tornell and F. Westermann (2008), "Systemic Crises and Growth", *Quarterly Journal of Economics,* 123(1); pp. 359-406 provide evidence of a positive relationship between crisis prone economies and growth.
2. For more details see The Economies of Central Asia, (Princeton University Press, Princeton NJ, 1995) and The Central Asian Economies since Independence (Princeton University Press, 2006).
3. R. Pomfret, "Turkmenistan's Foreign Policy", The China and Eurasian Forum Quarterly 6(4), November 2008, pp. 9-34 (available at http://www. isdp.eu/cefq).

4. The first substantial foreign investment in the banking sector was in November 2007 when the Italian bank UniCredit paid US$ 2.1 billion for a 91.8 percent stake in ATF Bank, Kazakhstan's fifth largest bank.
5. In February 2009 the Kyrgyz Republic gave the USA six months' notice to vacate the airbase.
6. See A. Kireyev, The Macroeconomics of Remittances: The Case of Tajikistan, IMF Working Paper 06/2, January 2006.
7. For more details see R. Pomfret, "Kazakhstan's Banking Problems", Central Asia Caucasus Analyst, 20 February 2008 (e journal available at http://www.cacianalyst.org/?q=issueachive).
8. The full amount owed by Kazakhstan's banks to foreign creditors is unclear. According to the Financial Times, in October 2007 Kazakh banks' international borrowings totalled US$ 40 billion, and conservative estimates put the banks' foreign debt due in 2008 at around US$ 12 billion.
9. The numbers in this paragraph draw on the Asian Development Bank report Central Asia: Increasing gains from trade through regional cooperation in trade policy, transport, and customs transit (Manila 2006).
10. Estimates of producer support to farmers are contained in R. Pomfret, "Kazakhstan", in Kym Anderson and Johan Swinnen (eds), Distortions to Agricultural Incentives in Europe's Transition Economies, World Bank, Washington, D.C., 2008, pp. 219-63.
11. According to the 'Cotlook A' price index, which is the average of the lowest five of nineteen prices for cotton delivered in Asian ports, cotton prices reached a peak at 92 US cents/lb in 1994/95, after which they fell by more than half to 42 cents/lb in 2001/02 before recovering to 68 cents in 2003/04. On 27 April 2009 the index stood at 59 cents.
12. See J. Helmer, "IMF blows Whistle on Tajik Corruption", Asia Times Online, 26 March 2008 (www.atimes.com/atimes/Central_Asia/JC26Ag01. html – accessed 30 April 2009). The London trial, in which Talco is trying to recoup US$ 500 million from two former employees, is estimated to be costing about 5 percent of Tajikistan's GDP ("Tajikistan: Aluminum Plant embroiled in Protracted Expensive Legal Case", *Eurasianet*, 14 November 2008).
13. Central Asia Regional Economic Cooperation (CAREC)

involves eight countries and an alliance of multilateral institutions comprising Asian Development Bank, European Bank for Reconstruction and Development, International Monetary Fund, Islamic Development Bank, United Nations Development Programme, and World Bank.

14. N. Melvin and J. Boonstra, The EU Strategy for Central Asia @ Year One, EUCAM Policy Brief No. 1, October 2008.

13

Measuring the Pulse of Africa in Times of Crisis

OECD

Introduction

Only a year ago Africa's economic growth prospects seemed historically bright. But what effect has the global crisis had? The international environment facing Africa [1] has turned decisively negative. GDP in the OECD countries is expected to contract by 4.3 percent in 2009 and to be virtually flat in 2010. Growth in emerging economies is also expected to slow dramatically. In turn, world trade is expected to contract by 13.2 percent in 2009—its first decline in 60 years. For Africa this means that growth projections for 2009 have fallen to 2.8 percent after four consecutive years above 5 percent.

The hardest hit African economies are those that are heavily reliant on commodity exports. Most commodity prices have fallen back to their 2005 or 2006 levels, many of them registering declines of 40 percent or more. Net oil importing African countries face a different set of challenges, with GDP growth in many of them expected to fall sharply in 2009 and 2010. For many countries in the region, the persistence of high prices for internationally traded food continues to contribute to a food crisis, especially for the urban poor.

Meanwhile, inflation continues to rise, although at a more moderate pace. This is mainly due to a more complete pass-through of international oil price increases to consumers combined with increases in the international prices of grains and vegetable oils.

Politically, the need to promote good governance in Africa

is as important as ever, as several years of improved political and social stability came to an end in 2007 and worsened in 2008. The deterioration of the economic situation could jeopardise some of the advances made toward greater democracy and better governance. More needs to be done to nurture an environment that is conducive to private-sector development, especially in further reducing corruption. That said, some progress is being made. The AU/NEPAD African Peer Review Mechanism has begun to provide a candid assessment of African countries and, thus, to foster progress in governance.

The promising news is that despite these economic strains and social disruptions, Africa is in better shape to survive the global economic crisis than it would have been ten years ago. With the right combination of domestic policy reforms, and with donors' willingness to compensate for drops in trade revenues, the continent can continue to grow.

This *Policy Brief* presents some of the main findings of the *2009 African Economic Outlook.*

How Will the Economic Crisis Affect Africa's Growth?

Not surprisingly, the outlook for Africa has been adversely affected by the global recession. Economic growth in Africa is expected to be only 2.8 percent in 2009, less than half of the 5.7 percent estimated for 2008. It is then expected to rebound partially to 4.5 percent in 2010. Growth in oil-exporting countries, which continued to outpace that of oil importers by a substantial margin in 2008, is slowing as well, and is expected to be 2.4 percent in 2009 compared to 3.3 percent for the net oil importers. Moreover, some countries continue to face particularly serious problems—including the humanitarian catastrophe in the Darfur region of Sudan, the economic collapse in Zimbabwe, conflicts and political unrest in Guinea, Guinea-Bissau, Equatorial Guinea, Madagascar and Somalia—that are likely to further impede economic progress.

The hard-won macroeconomic stability achieved recently

in African countries was also affected by food price inflation in the first three quarters of 2008 and could be challenged further by worsening economic conditions. A slowdown of investment in oil and mineral production is also expected to be a drag on growth in 2009 and 2010.

However, Africa is better equipped to withstand an economic crisis than it was ten years ago. Wiser macroeconomic policies have strengthened fiscal positions and reduced inflation, while recent multilateral debt-relief operations have improved the debt burden and eased financing constraints. This should help many countries to avoid drastic spending cuts and to afford small budget deficits. Structural reforms have led to an improved business environment both for domestic and foreign operators, as shown by improved scores on the World Bank Doing Business indicators. In addition, the increased importance of Asian and Latin American emerging markets as development and trade partners is reducing the continent's vulnerability to the economic performance of OECD countries. A prolonged international crisis, however, could pose a risk to these advances, making 2010 crucial for medium-term macroeconomic prospects.

Figure 1.
REAL GDP GROWTH

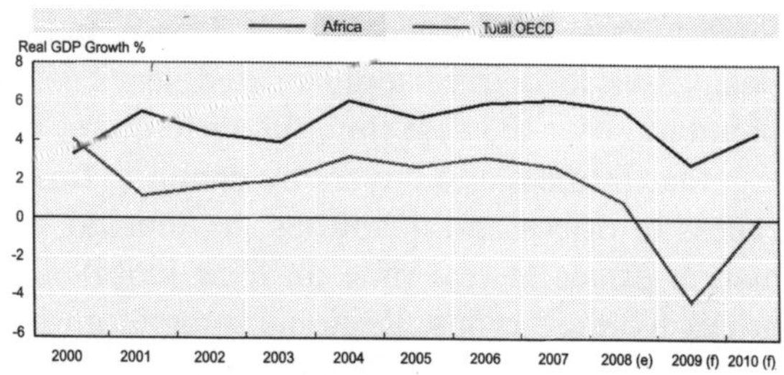

Source: OECD Development Centre/World Bank, 2009.

How Can the Region's Governments Safeguard the Progress Made in Recent Years?

It will not be easy. The balance sheets of African governments are suffering from falling revenues linked to the economic slowdown and falling commodity prices. As early as

2007, oil-importing countries began to suffer from rising import costs and the implementation of costly tax exemptions and subsidies in response to food and fuel price increases. Today, however, it is oil and mineral exporters who are experiencing the sharpest fall in their fiscal and current account balances due to the slump in oil prices. African governments will have to find a balance between insisting on macroeconomic fundamentals, such as public expenditure streamlining, real exchange rate depreciation to reinstate competitiveness, and inflation control, and continuing with structural reforms, including infrastructure development, institutional improvements and actions to reduce poverty.

What Role Can Information and Communication Technologies (ICTs) Play?

Innovative use of ICTs is vital as it is breaking down long-standing barriers to market development. Four out of ten Africans have a mobile phone line, and mobile-banking solutions are quickly scaling up on a continent with low levels of bank users. For example, in Kenya, where only 26 percent of the population has a bank account, mobile-payment services have attracted over five million users in less than two years. Such high levels of access to ICTs are making it possible for businesses to deliver sophisticated services to the continent's population for the first time. In agriculture, ICTs have brought together farmers and buyers by enabling timely and affordable access to prices and quantities. In Senegal, farmers can check market prices in real time on their mobiles to obtain the best prices for their crops. Regional integration is being reinforced as more inland broadband links are built. Pan-African operators are already offering free roaming services across 12 countries. Africa is the only region in the world where this innovative business model exists.

Figure 2.
HARD COMMODITIES
(BASE 100 IN 2000)

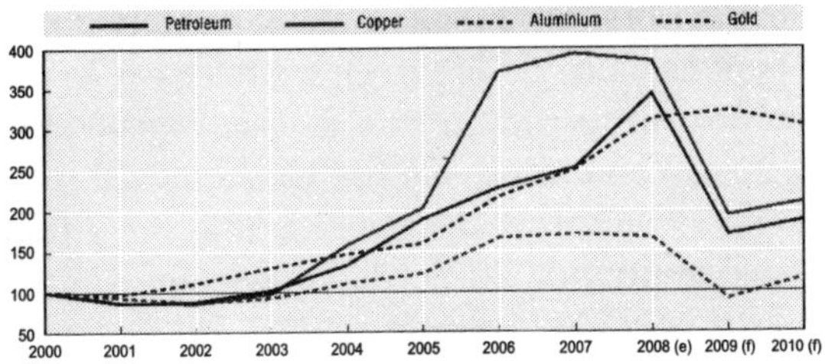

Source: OECD Development Centre, based on World Bank, 2009

What Must Donors Do Now?

Official development assistance to Africa, which was driven largely by debt relief and emergency assistance, fell by 18 percent in real terms in 2007, mostly due to the end of exceptional debt relief operations. However, global aid reached a record high in 2008, and may well grow, albeit slowly, in 2009 and 2010. Africa may benefit more than other regions. There is a risk that ballooning fiscal deficits and dwindling political support for greater aid in major donor countries could trigger a downward revision of aid levels. Donors must therefore increase efforts to honour their Gleneagles commitments to double aid to Africa by 2010, as OECD Secretary-General Angel Gurría, and the Chair of OECD's Development Assistance Committee, Eckhard Deutscher urged in their "Aid Pledge" initiative in October 2008.

African countries need donor support to continue investing in infrastructure and structural reforms. To abandon such reforms would mean jeopardizing gains in poverty reduction and future growth prospects. In a context where foreign private capital flows and government revenues are drying up, ODA should not only be maintained, but also scaled up and used counter-cyclically against the downturn. Taking into account the economic difficulties in donor countries, the focus should be on front-loading aid spending, and improving effectiveness, particularly by reducing fragmentation as a way to streamline ODA and increase its impact.

Finally, Africa needs help in restoring trade financing which has also dried up. One strategy is to create mechanisms for donors to play a role in that regeneration. For example, cash-rich countries, such as China, could set up facilities with regional multilateral agencies, like the African Development Bank, to provide the needed financing.

Figure 3.
POLITICAL STABILITY INDICATOR
Civil tensions

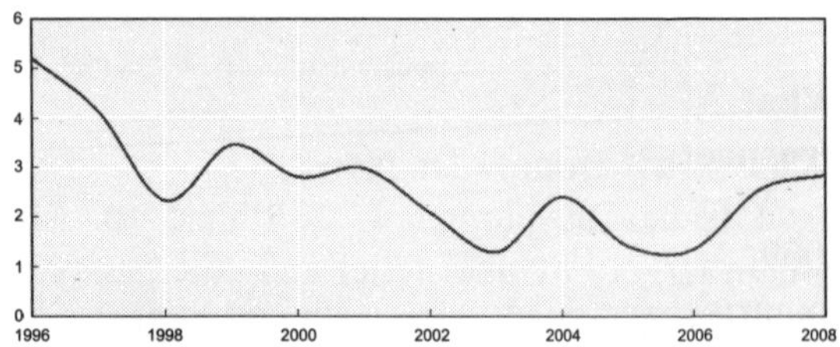

Civil tensions: Occurrence of strikes, demonstrations, violence and *coups d'état*. Qualitative data obtained from *Marchés Tropicaux et Méditerranéens*.
Source: OECD Development Centre, 2009.

Can the Crisis Pose Setbacks for Political and Social Stability?

Yes, and maintaining social stability will be a challenge. Since the end of 2007, when rising living costs triggered a series of disturbances, authorities have worked to strike a careful balance between adopting measures to control unrest and avoiding a shift to authoritarianism. With some exceptions, governments responded constructively. The challenge will now be to continue this approach during a time of decreasing public resources and uncertain donor support.

There are promising signs however. Increased political awareness among the population has made some governments more accountable. They now convene regular electoral consultations and implement structural reforms in public administration, which have improved governance and increased transparency. In addition, some countries have shown improvements in macroeconomic management and the regulatory environment, and conflicts have begun to subside. Positive signs also come from regional co-operation on governance in the framework of the African Union and in the

African Peer Review Mechanism. According to the OECD Development Centre Political Stability Indicator however, social instability worsened overall in Africa between 2007 and 2008, as it did in other parts of the world. Many African governments responded with tough measures, reflecting the rise in social tension common during periods of economic stress.

What Must Africa do to improve its Long-Term Growth Prospects?

While most OECD countries will experience a recession in 2009, Africa has an opportunity to continue growing. To do so, countries need to promote domestic growth based on greater investment and consumption. Suggestions include:

Macroeconomic Policy

- Strike a balance between insisting on macroeconomic fundamentals (public expenditure streamlining, real exchange-rate depreciation to reinstate competitiveness, and inflation control) and investing in structural reforms (infrastructure development, institutional improvements, poverty-reduction programmes).
- Adopt sustainable fiscal policies that increase government revenue while creating a business environment conducive to domestic and foreign private investment.

Political and Economic Governance

- Prioritise transparency (electoral consultations, public administration reforms) and regional co-operation on governance.

Private Sector Development

- Work with businesses to remove the hurdles to ICT infrastructure development; improve regulation; and invest in scaling-up innovative applications for social services.
- Eliminate bottlenecks for the domestic private sector, such as inadequate infrastructure and poor access to credit.
- Promote domestic production and diversification.

Regional Economic Integration

- Strengthen the role of regional actors, including financial institutions.

ODA

- Lobby donor governments to scale-up aid commitments, use aid counter-cyclically, especially in highly aid-dependent countries, and avoid protectionism.

The implementation of these measures will not only reduce present and future vulnerability, but also help lay a stronger basis for future growth and development.

Source: Policy Brief, May 2009, www.oecd.org
© OECD 2009. Reprinted with Permission.

Note

1. This *Policy Brief* presents some of the main findings of the *2009 African Economic Outlook*. The 47 countries examined in this eighth edition of the OECD's *African Economic Outlook* are classified by sub-region: in North Africa: Algeria, Egypt, Libya, Mauritania, Morocco, Sudan and Tunisia; in West Africa: Benin, Burkina Faso, Cape Verde, Côte d'Ivoire, the Gambia, Ghana, Guinea, Liberia, Mali, Niger, Nigeria, Senegal, Sierra Leone, and Togo; in Central Africa: Cameroon, Chad, Central African Republic, the Republic of Congo, the Democratic Republic of the Congo, Equatorial Guinea, and Gabon; in East Africa: Burundi, Djibouti, Ethiopia, Kenya, Rwanda, Seychelles, Tanzania and Uganda; in Southern Africa: Angola, Botswana, Lesotho, Madagascar, Malawi, Mauritius, Mozambique, Namibia, South Africa, Swaziland and Zambia.

14

The Global Financial Crisis and its impact on the Asia-Pacific Region

Anwar Nasution

1. Introduction

It is impossible to predict the nature and extent of the damage that the current global economic crisis will inflict or how long the world and the Asia-Pacific economies will suffer from the ensuing low economic growth. The recession will hit the economies of this region hard through falls in commodity prices, declining trade, capital outflows and lower remittances from citizens working overseas. As this region has neither sufficiently robust domestic demand, nor large intra-regional trade to offset the impact of falling exports to the United States and Europe, countries in Asia-Pacific should adopt a two-pronged approach to the crisis. Internally, they should foster closer policy cooperation to make better use of the region's financial resources and relatively large domestic markets in order to speed up economic recovery. In the long term, the expansion of potentially large domestic markets can gradually replace the current export oriented development strategy of many countries in this region. Globally, this region should work hand-in-hand with other regions, particularly with the relevant authorities in their main export markets in the US and Europe, to promote world economic growth in line with the APEC ethos of open economies, and resist the temptation of protectionism. All of these require closer cooperation on monetary, fiscal and exchange rate policies, both regionally and globally. Otherwise, Asia-Pacific may well experience a "lost decade" like that suffered by Indonesia following the Asian financial crisis in 1997-98 or by Japan in the 1990s.

The crisis has been strengthening the position of the U.S. as the global financial superpower. US financial institutions are now consolidating to become giant financial conglomerates. The U.S. Treasury and the Federal Reserve Bank are able to issue billions of dollars in debt at close to zero nominal interest rates-lower than inflation rates. Negative real interest rates mean that rather than paying an interest rate, the U.S. Government actually gets paid for borrowing money. People around the world are now so averse to risk, and the scramble for both safety and liquidity so strong, that they are hoarding the safer U.S. dollar, U.S. Treasury bills and U.S. long-term government bonds. Massive capital inflow has allowed the U.S. to finance its budget and balance of payment deficits, and provide funds for rebuilding its financial system, stimulating its economy, recycling funds to provide dollar liquidity to foreign central banks through the Federal Reserve Bank's bilateral currency-swap facilities, and for financing its expensive wars in the Middle East.

The world economic downturn is being exacerbated as all sectors in the economy stop spending. Deterioration in borrowers' balance sheets due to faltering mortgages and stock markets, foreclosures and bankruptcies have worsened credit risks and made the problems of adverse selection and moral hazards more prominent. Both banks as well as companies need to deleverage in order to improve their liquidity positions, reduce dependency on wholesale funding and rebuild profit margins. As a result, banks have stopped lending, businesses have stopped investing and lending to each other and households are refusing to spend. All of this has reduced the velocity or turnover of money-to-service transactions in the economy. At a given money supply, the fall in the velocity of money will reduce gross domestic product, which is the multiplication of the two monetary variables.

The rest of this note is organized as follows. Section 2 analyzes the evolution of the global financial crisis and contrasts it with the Asian financial crisis of 1997-98. Section three examines the current economic situation in the Asia Pacific region. Section four describes global and regional responses, and the final section sets out my recommendations for policy coordination in the region aimed at promoting global economic recovery.

2. The Global Financial Crisis

Like the Asian financial crisis of 1997-98, the current sub-prime mortgage debacle, which erupted in the United States in the summer of 2007, was precipitated by a crisis of confidence among short-term creditors that caused them to withdraw funds from the shadow banking system. Over the years, the shadow banks relied on short-term collateralized lending in the form of repurchase agreements. [1] The shadow banking system includes finance companies, hedge funds and investment banks that buy mortgages and loans from banks, as well as corporate bonds and other assets, like credit card receivables, automobile and student loans, and repackage and sell them in sophisticated but arcane ways to financial investors around the world.

The increase in the delinquency rates of sub-prime mortgages eroded the collateral value of the assets of the highly leveraged shadow banks and, at the same time, caused maturity mismatches on their balance sheets as they borrowed short and lent long. The drop in market prices and liquidity adversely affected the capital and solvency of shadow banks, raised the funding needs of all financial institutions and reduced their access to lending markets. The supply of funds further diminished as creditors and uninsured depositors pulled their funds from risky institutions and transferred them to safer bets. This made the financial institutions vulnerable to runs and resulted in their hoarding their liquidity, as well as in interest rate surges in the short-term money markets. Gridlock in the markets for certain asset-backed securities occurred, as institutions were unable to pay their obligations because others were not paying theirs. On the other hand, the demand for credit by companies and households decreased due to the economic recession and the reduced value of their assets.

A number of policies were adopted to deleverage the balance sheets of the shadow banks, such as tightening lending standards, improving credit quality, reducing the volume of loans, and selling assets. However, these simultaneous attempts to deleverage by so many institutions depressed asset prices and produced additional losses. As it is nearly impossible to determine market prices for certain asset-backed securities, such securities cannot be used as collateral for new funding to borrowers.

The credit crunch in the U.S. financial markets spread quickly around the globe. By mid-September 2008, after 13 months of market stress, short-term credit markets froze and the interbank markets of many countries were disrupted as the banks stopped lending to each other. The process of flight to safety began with the hoarding of cash by investors, the pulling of capital from perceived weak institutions and the shifting of portfolios to government bonds, mainly U.S. Treasury bills. Short-term interest rates surged, far above central banks' targets, on fears that many leveraged financial institutions might collapse due to a lack of short-term credit. Some banks in the U.S. (Wachovia) and Europe (Northern Rock, IKB, Bradford & Bingley and Fortis) were either taken over by stronger institutions or nationalized. Bank of Asia of Hong Kong experienced a small bank run. Bank Century, a small bank in Indonesia, was taken over by *Lembaga Penjamin Simpanan* (Indonesian Deposit Insurance Corporation) on the November 21, 2008, and PT Bank IFI went bankrupt. Four banks in the Philippines were taken over by the Philippines Deposit Insurance Corporation (PDIC), in addition to 9 small banks placed in PDIC receivership by order of the Central Bank of the Philippines.

The credit crunch has reduced the flow of financing for economic activities of both companies and households, which has exacerbated the economic downturn, and in turn weakened financial institutions and intensified the credit crunch. Uncertain about demand for their products, both in domestic and export markets, and unsure about how to finance their activities, non-financial firms reduced production and cut demand for inputs, including raw materials, oil and labor. The credit crunch and high interest rates have encouraged such firms to repay debt, reduce spending and put investment plans on hold. At the same time, the credit crunch has also left households with fewer resources to finance spending.

3. The Current Situation

At the end of their meeting in Lecce, Italy, on the June 13, 2009, Finance Ministers of the Group of Eight issued a cautiously optimistic statement on the progress of policies to address the present economic turmoil. They have seen positive signs of stabilizations in major economies including a recovery of economic growth and stock markets, a decline in interest rate spreads and improvements in both business as well as consumer confidence. As monetary policy has been more aggressive in the US and the size of the fiscal stimulus there has been greater, the American economy is expected to recover faster than that of Europe. The progress has allowed the authorities to begin discussing a framework for unwinding the lax monetary policy and massive fiscal stimulus in order to maintain fiscal sustainability, combat inflation, prevent currency realignments, and avoid high long-term interest rates once a recovery is certain. The statement warns, however, that the positive signs remain very weak and that uncertain and significant risks remain to economic and financial stability. Even after economic growth begins picking up, unemployment is, however, expected to continue to rise, partly due to the process of restructuring of major industries and companies, such as General Motor. This includes restructuring its expensive employee health and pension costs.

The negative effects of the crisis filtered into the export-oriented Asia Pacific economies through the current and capital accounts of the balance of payments. Foreign demand for this region's exports fell sharply as the deeply interconnected world economy began to show signs of having entered a dangerously downward spiral: recession or low economic growth, falling commodity prices, rising unemployment, faltering stock markets, realigning of exchange rates, collapsing property values, imploding hedge funds as well as foreclosures, bankruptcies, write-offs, and a credit crunch. The fall in demand has resulted in unsold stocks piling up, higher excess capacity and signs of deflation.

Until recently, international and regional banks and institutions have been revising their economic forecasts downward with depressing frequency. The IMF forecast for world economic growth for 2009 was revised downward to 0.5 percent in January 2009 from 2.2 percent in November 2008. The group of advanced economies is forecast to contract by 2 percent over the course of 2009. The Japanese economy is predicted to shrink by 2.6 percent. Because of the global economic crisis and, in particular, the fading demand for mining resources, the Australian economy is projected to contract by 0.2 percent in 2009. The highly export dependent economy of Singapore is expected to shrink between 2 percent to 5 percent in 2009. This is mainly due to the falling demand for its export products, such as petrochemicals and electronics. China is projected by the IMF to grow by 6.7 percent this year, lower than the average annual rate of 9 percent over the past few decades. This is lower than the minimum rate of growth of 8 percent required to absorb new entrants into the labor market. The Newly Industrialized Asian Economies are predicted to contract by 3.9 percent and ASEAN-5 is expected to grow by 2.7 percent.

Euler Hermes [2], a subsidiary of Allianz Insurance of Germany, is predicting that corporate bankruptcies in the advanced economies of Europe, the U.S. and Japan will hit a record high this year. The highest annual increase in company failures in 2009 will be in the U.S. at 50.4 percent, followed by

Western Europe at 16.7 percent and Japan at 7.9 percent. A number of airline and automobile companies around the world, including General Motors, have received equity injections from governments to keep them in operation. General Motors finally declared bankruptcy on the June 1, 2009 and applied for Chapter 11 protection from its creditors. Toyota, the best run and most profitable car producer, suffered its first loss since it began its financial reporting 68 years ago [3] in 2008 and some of its assembly plants have been temporarily closed. Labor disputes and riots are increasing in China as a result of the closure of labor intensive export-oriented manufacturing firms, and the ensuing redundancies resulting from this.

The economies of the emerging countries in this region are very much driven by foreign capital inflows. This is because of the high dependency of companies, the banking system and, to some extent, the public sector on foreign financing. The emerging economies in this region are also prone to capital outflows. Benefiting from the economic and commodities boom, they had regained the confidence of international investors after the Asian financial crisis of 1997-98. At the beginning of the crisis, however, private investors pulled their funds out of South Korea, Taiwan, Thailand, Indonesia, and the Philippines.

Falling commodity prices and export revenues, along with rising unemployment in labor importing economies have dealt a triple blow to commodity dependent and labor surplus emerging economies, such as Indonesia and the Philippines. Political instability has hit the tourism industry in Thailand. Sharply reduced revenues from both exports and labor remittances, together with capital outflows, mean that these countries will need to cut spending and let their currencies depreciate. The rise in unemployment in labor importing economies, and the ensuing deportation of foreign workers from these countries, has increased the pressure on the labor markets of the labor surplus countries. Unemployment, healthcare and job-retraining assistance are practically nonexistent in these countries, which mainly have emerging economies. Prolonged economic hardship could cause political instability and social unrest in densely populated countries that could end up being exported globally.

The crisis has also seriously affected banking systems in this region and has eroded the value of foreign assets and external reserves. The stronger capital bases, better supervision of the banking system, and larger external reserves that have been developed since the Asian financial crisis of 1997-98 have proved inadequate to overcome foreign exchange illiquidity, particularly with regard to the U.S. dollar, with the result that settlements of international transactions have been affected. Fortunately, the exposure of financial institutions in this region to U.S. collateralized debt obligations (CDOs) arising from sub-prime mortgages is relatively small. This has saved the region from the sort of bank failures that have occurred in Europe. In addition, the homegrown sub-prime market is relatively small in this region, as household debt is insignificant and the shadow banking system is underdeveloped.

4. Responses

The first policy response of all countries to overcome the crisis has been to restore the flow of credit so as to avoid a deeper recession and stabilize the financial system. As the financial sector is closely interlocked with the real sector of the economy, financial resources have not only been made available to help the financial sector but also extended to major clients such as AIG insurance and General Motors as well as to local governments in the United States.

The second policy response has been to prevent any further deterioration in economic activities by expanding aggregate demand. As traditional monetary policy has proved ineffective in promoting the expansion of consumption and investment, central banks are now switching to monetary easing and a greater reliance on fiscal policy as an instrument for restoring economic growth. It is interesting to note the contrast between the US policy to address the crisis and the policies adopted by the EU member countries. The US has adopted a policy of larger stimulus spending and more vigorous practices to restructure its financial system and manufacturing industries. In contrast, the Europeans have adopted a more cautious stance. Their view is that the use of fiscal policy will cause an unprecedented budget deficit and is only a temporary solution while fixing the dysfunctional credit markets caused by the uncertain value of asset-backed securities. This is because not all government spending is desirable or necessary and much of it is wasteful. Prolonged large deficit spending can reignite inflation, raise long-term interest rates, and have a detrimental effect on the solvency of the economy.

The third policy response has been to dampen liquidity pressures. To dampen international liquidity pressures that have seriously affected international trade and investment, central banks have moved together to provide currency swap facilities amongst themselves. Cooperation and coordination to enhance the effectiveness of policies aimed at addressing the crisis are not the only steps to have been taken by central banks. Fiscal programs across major economies are also now better coordinated.

The fourth policy response has been to increase the financial resources available and to reform the IMF. Major countries have agreed to increase their contributions to the augmented New Arrangements to Borrow (NAB) at the IMF. An agreed to portion of gold sales of the IMF is to be used to support low-income countries. Capital resources of multilateral development banks are to be strengthened so as to enable these banks to play a counter-cyclical role in responding to the global financial crisis by providing financial resources to member countries for mitigating capital outflows and reduced exports.

The fifth policy response has been to make the market

work more effectively by strengthening market fundamentals to protect individual property rights. This includes the strengthening of regulatory and supervisory systems as well as the promotion of transparency and business ethics.

4.1 Restoring Credit Markets

With the non-functioning of short-term credit and inter-bank money markets, commercial banks around the world have turned to central banks as the lenders of last resort for liquidity. A central bank is a powerful monetary authority, which controls the supply and demand for high-powered money, or the monetary base. The source of this monetary base consists of gold and foreign exchange reserves administered by central banks as well as their outstanding loans to governments, commercial banks and, during crises, directly to businesses. There are two principal uses of the monetary base, namely; currency and bank deposits with central banks. The central bank has a monopoly right over the issuing of bank notes and coins, and also sets the minimum reserve requirements for commercial banks. The reserve requirement ratio requires commercial banks to keep a certain fraction of their deposits as reserves. Just like a tax on bank deposits, this therefore reduces their capacity to lend and invest. Normally, central banks expand the money supply by buying short-term government papers, such as Treasury bills, and paying for them by printing money. To contract the money supply, central banks sell government papers and withdraw money from circulation. Central bank activities designed to affect the money supply through the buying and selling of government papers are referred to as open market operations (OMO). In the absence of short-term government securities, as is the case in Indonesia, the central bank creates its own short-term debt instruments. As the bankers' bank and lender of last resort, a central bank also offers short-term credit facilities to commercial banks.

At the beginning of the crisis, the U.S. Fed encouraged

banks to borrow using the discount window facility which lowered the penalties on such borrowing. The discount window is used as an instrument to influence the reserves of the commercial banks and hence money supply. The facility is backed by government securities and has a very short-term maturity, usually overnight. Through the discount window, central banks can set their policy rates, discount rates, fees for loans and quantity of loans. However, banks are reluctant to borrow from the discount window, as very often market participants will perceive them as being in trouble and may begin to pull out their funds. In December 2007, four months after the crisis erupted, the U.S. Fed introduced three new lending facilities with wider collateral requirements and longer maturities.

On the international front, the U.S. Fed has coordinated its monetary policy with other leading central banks so as to provide liquidity to the globalized inter-bank and money markets, and has also cut its nominal discount rates to close to zero at the present time. In addition, the U.S. Fed has established temporary bilateral currency swap facilities with 14 central banks to allow participating institutions to draw down balances denominated in the U.S. dollar to meet their needs in that currency. [4] Governments, banks, companies and investors outside the U.S. have borrowed huge amounts in dollars. However, renewing these loans and rollover corporate and sovereign debts has become more expensive, especially for emerging economies. The combination of rising interest rates and tightened lending standards has made it more difficult for these economies to repay the debts. This problem is likely to continue after the crisis. Similar swap facilities have also been established by the ECB and, in line with the Chiang Mai spirit, by central banks in this region. South Korea has received a currency swap facility from Japan and China. China has increased the number of currency swap facilities made available to Indonesia.

Similar to credit lines from international and regional

financial institutions, bilateral currency-swap facilities add to the foreign exchange reserves of the recipient countries. Such currency-swap facilities are designed to expand lending facilities and cut policy rates, to revive frozen credit markets and stagnant bank lending both to businesses as well as to consumers, and to effect lower interest rates spreads. During the early stage of the crisis, Taylor and Williams reported that central bank target interest rates had become disconnected from overnight rates. This was partly because the markets were uncertain about U.S. policy regarding the losses on sub-prime mortgages, with the result that inter-bank interest rates and the cost of borrowing have been pushed up. [5]

As normal procedures have proved ineffective in restoring the proper functioning of inter-bank money markets, the U.S. Fed has revised its procedures by switching to monetary easing. However, pumping liquidity into the economy has not worked because of the liquidity trap as nominal interest rates are now close to zero and already negative in real terms. As interest rates have nearly hit the zero mark, the Fed cannot push them much lower. When interest rates near zero, Treasury bills are transformed into the equivalent of cash as both of them become perpetual government bonds that carry no interest. In this liquidity trap, the demand for money is infinitely elastic. Because of this, people prefer cash to bonds as any future rise in interest rates would consequently cause a fall in bond prices. Therefore, like the Bank of Japan in the 1990s, the U.S. Fed is now purchasing financial assets outright, starting with the longer term Treasury bonds and securities issued by government-sponsored enterprises, such as Fannie Mae and Freddie Mac. The types of securities that can be purchased by central banks can also be expanded to include corporate bonds, state and local government bonds or even the sovereign bonds of foreign countries.

4.2 Stabilizing the Financial System

To stabilize the U.S. financial system, on October 14,

2008, the U.S. Congress authorized the Treasury to establish TARP (Troubled Assets Relief Program) funds amounting to US$ 700 billion. The TARP facility is being used to address solvency problems in the banking system and in other financial institutions by injecting capital into them, and by removing toxic assets from their balance sheets. To avoid any further erosion in the financial condition of banks, including their Tier 1 or core capital, Securities and Exchange Commissions around the world have banned short selling of shares of financial institutions and their clients.

Panic withdrawals of deposits from the banking system have been stopped by restoring trust and confidence through broadening the coverage and increasing the size of guaranteed liabilities of insured institutions by deposit insurance companies. Similar blanket guarantees on bank deposits have been introduced all around the world, including in this region. To avoid disruption of foreign trade and investment, some emerging economies, such as South Korea, have provided guarantees for foreign currency borrowings by their private sectors.

The process of bank consolidation in the U.S., backed by the government, started with the provision of emergency financing by the New York Fed to JP Morgan on March 14, 2007. This enabled JP Morgan to take over the financially distressed Bear Stearns, a large and well-regarded investment bank. The availability of TARP funds has accelerated the process of consolidation through mergers and the conversion of many non-bank financial institutions (NBFI) into regular commercial banks. In return for closer scrutiny by the central bank, the commercial banks are entitled to receive liquidity support from the bankers' bank.

Through capital injections, loans, and guarantees on commercial debts, the U.S. government has effectively nationalized the financial sector and automobile industry in the United States. The Treasury allocated US$ 250 billion of the TARP funds for recapitalizing large banks (US$ 125 billion each for 9 large banks), smaller local banks, savings associations, and certain bank, savings and loan holding companies. The large banks that have received TARP funds include JP Morgan, Citigroup and Wells Fargo. A number of small and financially weaker institutions have been taken over by financially stronger ones. The NBFIs in the U.S. that have received approval to become regular commercial banks include industrial loan companies, such as GMAC, IB Finance Holding Companies, CIT Group, the American Express Company and the American Express Travel Related Service Company (AMEX). Owned by General Motors, GMAC has been a primary source of financing to customers and dealerships seeking to purchase and lease GM vehicles. AMEX provides charge and credit payment-card products as well as travel related services all over the world.

One hundred billion of the TARP funds have been used to purchase direct obligations of three housing-related government sponsored enterprises, namely; Fannie Mae, Freddie Mac and the Federal Home Loan Bank. Meanwhile US$ 500 billion has been allocated for the purchase of mortgages guaranteed by these quasi-governmental companies. The American International Group (AIG), a large insurance company, received a capital injection of US$ 40 billion in TARP funds. The financially distressed car makers, General Motors, Ford, and Chrysler, are seeking US$ 25 billion in financial support from the TARP funds.

After rigorous stress testing, 10 of the financially sound US banks in early June 2009 repaid US$ 68 billion of the TARP funds back to the Treasury. These banks include JP Morgan-Chase, Goldman Sachs, Morgan Stanley, US Bankcorp and Amex. Other giants such as Citicorp, Bank of America and Wells Fargo remain in the program. Compensation for the executives of financial institutions under the TARP Program is subject to the scrutiny of the Treasury in order to protect the interest of shareholders and tax payers and to reinforce the stability of firms and the financial system.

The Eurozone, with its single currency for 15 sovereign member countries, possesses neither a single supervisory authority nor integrated supervision of Euro area banks with lender of last resort facilities, either of which would help prevent a recurrence of the present financial turmoil. Neither does the Eurozone have a concerted plan to deal with the failure of systematically important cross-border European banks. Each member country supervises the financial institutions within its own jurisdiction and acts individually to resolve the liquidity and solvency problems of its own home banks. After the collapse of the Icelandic banks, it became clear that both supervision and support on the part of the Icelandic central bank were insubstantial.

To protect their financial systems, authorities around the world have developed programs similar to the U.S. recapitalization bailout program. There are three ways in which governments have injected capital and removed toxic assets from bank balance sheets. Firstly, the public sector directly purchases the toxic assets from the financially distressed banks. This was the U.S. Treasury's original plan. Secondly, governments provide asset guarantees in return for warrants, the way the U.S. Treasury rescued Citigroup. The third way is to establish bad banks to purchase toxic assets from financially troubled financial institutions. This plan has been abandoned as it turns out that it is not easy to buy toxic assets due to the difficulty in assessing their value in a time of crisis and this can expose taxpayers to losses.

4.3 Fiscal Policy

Fiscal policy, including both tax cuts and expansion of government spending, has been the most powerful policy instrument to expand aggregate demand after the credit crunch made monetary policy ineffective in expanding consumption and investment expenditure which lead to increasing economic growth. A fiscal stimulus is expected to cause an incremental increase in aggregate demand. This only happens, however, if the recipients, both households and businesses, are willing to spend more money than they would otherwise have spent. Because of this condition, the structure of a fiscal stimulus is very important as it impacts not only aggregate demand but also income distribution. Another important element of fiscal policy is the timing of both tax cuts and expenditure expansions.

A fiscal policy that causes an unprecedented budget deficit is, however, only a temporary initiative and cannot be continuously relied upon as it can negatively affect a country's solvency. Government borrowing from both domestic and international financial markets to finance budget deficits raises interest rates and crowds out private investment. Such a slowdown in private sector investment reduces productivity and the standard of living. The gross public debt of the G-20 economies is expected to reach 106 percent of GDP in 2009 as compared with just 78 percent in 2007. Servicing domestic and foreign debt requires higher future taxes to pay both the principal as well as the interest on that debt. The resulting higher tax rates distort economic incentives. Servicing external debt requires an increase in export revenues and causes transfer problems that weaken economic performance.

The large number of issuers of sovereign bonds for financing fiscal stimuli increases competition for a limited pool of international savings. This leads to an increase in interest rates in international markets. In turn, this reduces the access of both the corporate sector and the governments of many countries to international credit markets. In January 2009, Standard & Poors downgraded the sovereign credit ratings and long-term sovereign debts of many countries, including Greece, Spain and Portugal, because of their deteriorating public finances and exports. During this time of crisis, government tax revenue is declining and government social spending is increasing. A combination of a shrinking supply of funds, rising credit risk, increases in interest rates, and the downgrading of sovereign credit ratings as well as bonds of emerging economies has ended the era of easy credit and has given way to a withdrawal of funds from less advanced economies. Political pressure, government regulations and 'moral suasions' are increasingly putting pressure on financial institutions to give priority to home markets. For example, state support for financial institutions in many countries is increasingly provided on condition that these institutions lend support to businesses and jobs at home, not abroad. Banks themselves are retreating from overseas markets to minimize credit risks. Credit risks in home markets are perceived to be much easier to manage than in overseas markets. In his remarks recently at the World Economic Forum in Davos, Lord Adair Turner, the Chairman of Britain's Financial Services Authority, calls the reflux of capital from foreign markets to home ones as "the risk of new mercantilism" centered on credit availability.

At the November 2008 summit in Washington D.C., the G-20 group recognized the need to coordinate sporadic fiscal policy initiatives to overcome the present global crisis. In reality, however, there has been no effective global fiscal policy response to magnify the combined impacts of coordinated national stimuli. The Eurozone also lacks a central fiscal authority. Fiscal policy coordination in the EU is dependent on the government budget deficit rule (no higher than 3 percent of the GDP) and debt rule (no more than 60 percent of the GDP), as set out in the Maastricht stability pact of 1991. The EU (European Union) proposed a 200 billion Euro economic stimulus program on November 27, 2008, which amounted to 1.5 percent of the EU's GDP. Most of the funding (170 billion Euro) is expected to come from contributions by the EU's 27 member states in the form of tax cuts and expansion of infrastructure expenditures. Some member states, however, are unwilling to make large commitments.

Table 14.1 shows fiscal stimulus packages in leading economies as of the first week of December 2008.

Table 14.1: Fiscal Stimuli for FY 2009 in Leading Countries

<table>
<tr><td rowspan="2">Country</td><td colspan="2">Size of stimulus</td></tr>
<tr><td>In nominal terms</td><td>As percent of GDP</td></tr>
<tr><td>United States</td><td>US$ 500 to 700 billion</td><td>3 to 5</td></tr>
<tr><td colspan="3">Usage of Stimulus Funds
• Income tax cuts for consumers and temporary increases in food stamp payments for lower income groups.
• US$ 136 billion in infrastructure projects that are “ready to go”.
• Investments in renewable energy projects and other “green jobs” initiatives.</td></tr>
<tr><td>Germany</td><td>31 billion euros</td><td>1.25</td></tr>
<tr><td colspan="3">Usage of Stimulus Funds
• 15 billion euros for new lending to companies through the state-owned bank KfW.
• New government investments and contracts in infrastructure and transport.</td></tr>
<tr><td>Britain</td><td>£20 billion</td><td>1.2 percent</td></tr>
<tr><td colspan="3">Usage of Stimulus Funds
• Tax cuts and £ 3 billion of capital spending.
• Cut in VAT (sales tax) to 15 percent from 17.5 percent.
• Tax repayments where business can offset current losses against past profits, and tax exemptions for companies’ foreign dividends.</td></tr>
<tr><td>France</td><td>26 billion euros</td><td>1.3</td></tr>
<tr><td colspan="3">Usage of Stimulus Funds
• 10.5 billion euros on infrastructure, research and development, and financing for local authorities.
• Aid for the auto industry with a 1,000 euro subsidy for car buyers to scrap their old vehicles and buy new, more environmentally-friendly models.
• 11.4 billion euros to help companies by early reimbursement of state debt due to them, spending to create or safeguard jobs.
• 1.8 billion euros for more zero-interest housing loans and public housing schemes</td></tr>
</table>

Contd...

Russia	US$ 20 billion	1.5
Usage of Stimulus Funds • Cut in tax on profits to 20 percent from 24 percent and a new depreciation mechanism that will allow firms to reduce the profit tax further. • Billions of dollars of soft funding from state-run banks to support industry.		
Japan	**5 trillion yen**	**2.0**
Usage of Stimulus Funds • 2 trillion yen in direct cash payouts to families, tax breaks on mortgages, a bank rescue scheme involving 2 trillion yen in public fund injections, and tax relief for small firms.		
China	**4 trillion yuan**	**16**
Usage of Stimulus Funds • 1.8 trillion yuan on large-scale infrastructure projects such as railways, roads, and airports. • 1 trillion yuan to rebuild areas ravaged by May's Sichuan earthquake. • Lower-income housing, large-scale environmental clean-ups, rural infrastructure, and industrial restructuring.		
Australia	**A$ 15.4 billion**	**1.2**
Usage of Stimulus Funds • Spending on hospitals and schools to generate 133,000 jobs		
South Korea	**14 trillion won**	**1.5**
Usage of Stimulus Funds • Wide range of tax cuts including corporate tax and income tax over five years. • 8 trillion won to help the construction industry including buying firms' unused land and unsold new homes.		
Taiwan	**NT$ 483 billion**	**3.5**
Usage of Stimulus Funds • A NT$ 82 billion shopping voucher handout-or NT$ 3,600 for every one of its 23 million citizens. • NT$ 58.3 billion in infrastructure spending to create 100,000 jobs by mid-2009. • Subsidies to low-income households and tax cuts for private investment.		

Contd...

Singapore	S$ 2.9 billion	1.2
Usage of Stimulus Funds • Enhancing existing business financing schemes by giving bigger loans, raising government risk sharing of loan defaults and extending schemes to all local enterprises. • S$ 600 million worth of packages over two years to enhance job training programmes and increase training subsidies for workers.		
Hong Kong	**HK$ 19.3 billion**	**1.2**
Usage of Stimulus Funds • 66 small-scale projects to create over 12,000 jobs. • Construction brought forward to 2009 from 2010 on a mega bridge to link Hong Kong, Zhuhai, and Macau.		
Malaysia	**RM 7 billion**	**1.1**
Usage of Stimulus Funds • RM 5 billion for construction and upgrading of infrastructure such as schools, high speed broadband, hospitals, roads, low-cost housing, and government buildings. • Fuel subsidies and a cut in employees' pension fund contributions to 8 percent from 11 percent. • RM 600 million for worker training programmes.		

Source: The Straits Times, Saturday, December 6th 2008, pages A12-A18.

The Table illustrates the already-mentioned contrast between the size of the US fiscal policy with that of the policies of members of the European Union. For example, the fiscal stimulus in Germany, the leading economy in the Eurozone, only amounted to below 4 percent of its annual GDP for the Fiscal Year 2008-10. Most of the fiscal stimulus in Germany is to be spent on infrastructure investment. In contrast, the stimulus packages in the United States and Taiwan were both around 5 percent of their GDP, while the figure in Japan is 2 percent. On January 22nd 2009, Singapore announced a larger fiscal stimulus totaling SIN$ 20.5 billion, equivalent to 8 percent of its GDP, partly financed by withdrawing US$ 4.9 billion from its fast external reserves. The objectives of the Singaporean stimulus program are to save jobs, help viable companies to stay afloat, provide support to low income groups and finance long-term sustainable projects such in the fields of health, education, green transport and energy. On January 28, 2009, the U.S. House of Representatives passed a US$ 787.2 billion economic stimulus plan containing emergency spending initiatives and tax cuts as proposed by the new administration of President Barack H. Obama who had just come to power on January 20, 2009.

China is one of the countries in this region that has had both huge budget and large current account surpluses for many years. The country has also accumulated nearly US$ 2 trillion in foreign exchange reserves. All this allows China to step up domestic spending to fill the gap left by a major drop in exports due to recession in its main export markets, namely the U.S., Europe and Japan. In China, cash rebates for low income groups are likely to be more effective in promoting expansion of aggregate demand than tax cuts. Tax rebates for middle and high income groups in thrifty China are unlikely to work as people will simply save the money. This is because household tax is either nonexistent or very light in China.

The recently announced fiscal stimulus package in China, amounting to four trillion Renminbi (US$ 586 billion), or 16 percent of the GDP, is unlikely to be enough to maintain the minimum economic growth of 8 percent needed to absorb new entrants into the labor force. The structure of the stimulus package will not encourage domestic spending as it focuses on modernizing railways, building roads and airports, rebuilding the rural areas devastated by the Sichuan earthquake in May last year, and other infrastructure projects that may be useful to support short-term economic growth but not long-term productivity. Only about 1 percent of the fiscal stimulus will be spent on expanding social services to cope with the economic downturn by easing the burden on families as regards education, healthcare, old age and unemployment.

Australia, Japan, South Korea and Taiwan can also afford to expand domestic aggregate demand to ease the global crisis.

Benefiting from the commodities boom, Australia has enjoyed budget surpluses and ballooning external reserves since the mid-1990s. Japan, while it has large external reserves, also has a large government debt. South Korea and Taiwan also have financial resources. As is the case in China, exports of sophisticated manufacturing products from Japan, South Korea and Taiwan are also suffering from falling demand in their traditional markets of the U.S. and Europe. South Korea announced a 33 trillion won fiscal stimulus in its 2009 budget. Australia unveiled a large stimulus plan on February 3, 2009 totaling 41.5 billion Australian dollars or US$ 26.19 billion over the next four years in the form of a combination of cash handouts, infrastructure spending and tax breaks. Low income workers, farmers and students in Australia are to be given cash handouts of AUS $1,000 each to spend. The fiscal stimulus in Taiwan includes shopping vouchers worth NT$ 3,600 (US$ 107) per person.

Weak fiscal balances and small amounts of fiscal surplus and external reserves limit the capability of developing and emerging economies to introduce fiscal stimuli. Raising funds through selling sovereign bonds is difficult while raising tax revenue is likely impossible due to the economic recession and weak tax administration. As Indonesia's experience in the early sixties proved, printing money for financing government spending causes a high inflation rate with disastrous consequences. At the same time, widespread tax evasion makes the provision of tax breaks a useless policy to stimulate economic growth. Most of the fiscal stimulus in Indonesia is in form of tax relief. Expenditure increases are mainly financed by using unused expenditure from the previous budget and from government borrowings.

5. Recommendations for Regional Policy Coordination and Cooperation

The economies of the Asia-Pacific are sitting on huge foreign exchange reserves, which are mainly invested in U.S.

dollar denominated assets, particularly U.S. Treasury papers. As of November 2008, six of the top ten countries in terms of foreign exchange reserves in this region were-- China (US$ 1,885 billion), Japan (US$ 977 billion), Taiwan (US$ 292 billion), South Korea (US$ 212 billion), Singapore (US$ 162 billion) and Hong Kong (US$ 155 billion). This list doesn't include Russia (US$ 441 billion), which is a member of APEC, and India (US$ 239 billion) in South Asia. Learning from the experience of the Asian financial crisis of 1997-98, the countries of the region have long been accumulating foreign currency as a shield to ward off speculators. This region has generated savings from both exports and the boom in commodity prices. The money, however, is unevenly distributed.

Well endowed with huge amounts of foreign exchange reserves, the Asia-Pacific economies can implement five forms of economic cooperation and coordination in order to achieve common goals.

Firstly, national economies should be stimulated through the expansion of both public sector spending and private consumption expenditures. As pointed out earlier, in the long-term, the export-led development strategy of many Asia-Pacific economies can gradually be replaced by a domestic oriented growth strategy. This is particularly true in the countries with potentially large domestic demand. The usefulness of tax rebates is limited in the emerging economies of this region due to the general thriftiness of the population, the low number of effective taxpayers, and rampant tax evasion and avoidance. Coordinated and well-structured efforts in Asia Pacific are capable of amplifying sporadic national programs for mutual benefit. Part of the economic stimulus should be for the building of modern infrastructure, something which is desperately needed for further growth in this region.

The program to stimulate national economies with large external reserves includes the expansion and strengthening of domestic demand by correcting government policies that suppressed both the share of wage income relative to GDP as well as domestic household consumption. To raise the share of wage income relative to the GDP, there is a need to correct government policies that are biased towards manufacturing industries and particularly favor capital-intensive industries. The program to ease the burden on families by increasing social service expenditure on things such as health, education, old age and unemployment benefits, also requires the modernization of the financial system including developing social security, health insurance and pension funds. Policies that favor capital intensive manufacturing and export oriented development programs should take into account subsidies and tax breaks, interest rates and exchange rate policies.

Secondly, the huge external reserves of this region should be used for expanding the bilateral currency swap arrangements under the Chiang Mai Initiatives (CMI) so as to facilitate intra-regional private sector investment and trade in the Asia-Pacific region. The CMI can be expanded by increasing the number of participating countries, increasing the number of currency swaps, and by making use of swap facilities in a more flexible manner. Ideally, the funds should be multilaterally pooled as a kind of collective initiative to help neighbors to meet their liquidity needs. These pooled financial resources could be used to lend directly to member countries in need. The facility could also be used as a way of enhancing or guaranteeing credit in order to facilitate member countries in borrowing in the regional and international financial markets. This would help them to overcome the growing financial mercantilism. The recent trilateral summit between Japan, China and Korea that resulted in the provision of a currency swap for Korea provides a good reference point for reforming the CMI. This currency swap facility, and a currency swap facility provided by the U.S. Fed, will allow Korea to address the urgent issue of capital flight because of the high dependency of both its private sector and banking system on foreign funding.

To operate a multilateral pooling of exchange reserves, the Asia-Pacific region needs to establish macro-economic surveillance. At present, this region relies on input from the Asian Development Bank, the only regional financial institution in the Asia-Pacific region.

Thirdly, financial resources should be provided to emerging countries in this region, in order to limit the adverse effects of the global crisis on their economic growth and employment situation, due particularly to adverse capital outflows and a decline in exports. This can be done through bilateral mechanisms and/or through multilateral financial institutions such as the ADB, IMF and the World Bank. The recent pledge by Prime Minister Taro Aso of Japan at the World Economic Forum in Davos to provide aid amounting to 1.5 trillion yen (US$ 17 billion) to emerging economies in Asia is a welcome initiative. This financial assistance would be used for building infrastructure projects in the recipient countries.

The London Summit of the G-20 in April 2009 pledged to raise the fiscal stimulus to US$ 5,000 billion. Of this, US$ 500 billion was allocated for IMF funding, US$ 250 billion for Special Drawing Rights, another US$ 250 billion for trade finance, and US$ 100 for increasing the capital of all development banks in order that they provide aid to the poorest sectors of society. In addition, Japan and the United States have each committed to contribute US$ 100 billion to the augmented New Arrangement to Borrow at the IMF.

Aside from increasing the capacity of regional and international financial institutions to lend, the prevailing principles for borrowing from these institutions need to be changed. Loan conditions for those countries facing difficulties due mainly to adverse external circumstances rather than their own mistakes should be relaxed. On the other hand, stringent conditions should be applied to those countries with policy inadequacies.

Fourthly, regional cooperation to avert the threat of financial mercantilism should be strengthened. Closer regional economic cooperation on financial issues can be started by encouraging closer cooperation between banks and financial market regulators in terms of sharing information on the management of liquidity by banks, total leverage and assessment of risk-weighted assets. Because of the sensitivity of issues such as sovereignty and diversity in the levels of economic development and social systems in this region, the creation of a single supervisory authority for cross-border banks and financial markets is not feasible at the present time.

Lastly, policy coordination should also be strengthened to ward off the return of trade mercantilism that would only serve to deepen the recession. This requires close coordination on issues such as exchange rate management, the environment, state aid, agriculture, trade and investment.

Source: www.bpk.go.ld
© Dr. Anwar Nasution. Reprinted With Permission.

Anwar Nasution is Professor of Economics at the University of Indonesia and Chairman of the Supreme Audit Board of Indonesia (*Badan Pemeriksa Keuangan Republik Indonesia*). e-mail address: anwar_n42@yahoo.com

This is a revised note originally prepared for the International Public Sector Convention 2009, Certified Public Accountant Australia, Sydney Convention and Exhibition Centre, Darling Drive, Darling Harbour, New South Wales, March 18-20, 2009.

Notes

1. See Brunnermeier, Markus K. 2008. "Deciphering the 2007-08 Liquidity and Credit Crunch". *Journal of Economic Perspectives* (forthcoming). Draft. May 19, and David Greenlaw, Jan Hatzius, Anil Kayshyap and Hyun Song Shin. 2008. "Leveraged Losses: Lessons from the Mortgage Market Meltdown". *US Monetary Policy Forum Conference* Draft. www.chicagogsb.edu/usmp/docs/usmp/2008confdraft.pdf.
2. "Company crashes set to hit record next year". *Financial Times*. Monday, December 8, 2008. Companies and Markets. p. 19.

3. "Toyota to suffer first loss in 68 years", *Financial Times*, Asia, Tuesday, December 23, 2008. page 1.
4. The central banks are those in Australia, Brazil, Canada, Denmark, ECB (the European Central Bank), Korea, Japan, Mexico, New Zealand, Norway, Singapore, Sweden, Switzerland, and the United Kingdom.
5. Taylor, John B. and John C. Williams, 2009. "A Black Swan in the Money Market". American Economic Journal Macroeconomics. 1(1). January. Pgs. 58-83.

15

The Global Financial Crisis, Developing Countries and India

Jayati Ghosh

The Global Context

It is now evident that this is an unprecedented phase in the history of global capitalism. The still-unfolding financial crisis has already moved well beyond the predictions of more pessimistic observers. Several potential "Minsky moments" of pure meltdown in the core capitalist economies appear to have only just been averted, but the dangers persist. Across the world, real economies are being affected by the financial distress in direct and indirect ways, associated with sharply slowing economic activity and rising unemployment. Of course, this particular crisis reflects contradictions at the heart of the capitalist system, including those emanating from its dependence upon inelastic expectations about the value of money, which are inherent to the smooth functioning of capitalism (Patnaik 2008). There is also little doubt that the financial deregulation of the 1980s and 1990s, aided by the incentives to finance provided by successive governments, is essentially responsible for the current mess (Kregel 2008, Crotty 2008).

Several features make this different from the various financial crises that have emerged in different parts of the world, especially in emerging markets, in the phase of globalisation: the origin of the crisis in the core of capitalism, the US economy, rather than in emerging markets that are typically seen to be more vulnerable; the intensity of the crisis, as panic and counterparty risk arising out of complex financial entanglement have made even supposedly healthy institutions look extremely fragile; the rapid and extensive global spread of the crisis to economic agents, sectors and economies that were previously perceived to be relatively immune.

In addition, there are other features that are "new" and therefore mean that the historical analogies that are frequently made (for example, to the Great Depression in the 1930s, or to the collapse of Soviet-style socialism at the turn of the 1990s) are at best very inexact guides to the present or to the immediate future. The current global financial crisis does not exist in a vacuum, but rather is superimposed and intimately related to a broader set of economic processes that were already reaching crisis point. There are several economic imbalances that cannot be sustained and must be addressed in the medium term for effective recovery to be possible.

First, there is the imbalance between finance and the real economy, which has two important aspects. To begin with, the financial sector had stopped playing its basic role of intermediating between savings and investment, and transferring resources from capital-rich to capital poor economies. Instead, financial liberalisation generated a life of its own, with a proliferation of instruments and transactions that expanded often without reference to any real economy requirements. Financial flows then determined both balance of payments and domestic patterns of investment and consumption, by creating asset bubbles that were then associated with consumption booms and drive investment accordingly. The particular combination of open capital accounts (with the related increase in external vulnerability) and export dependence of emerging markets, then led to a situation in which developing countries accumulated reserves based on either current or capital account surpluses. Since these reserves were then largely placed in supposedly "safe havens" such as US Treasury Bills or Wall Street securities, the developing world transferred net financial resources to the North (and particularly to the US) even though its own requirements for capital remained pressing. The large macroeconomic imbalances between deficit and surplus economies that have emerged as a result obviously cannot continue beyond a point, which means that the US cannot remain the engine of global growth in the same way that it was in the recent past, and that cross-border financial flows also must take new forms and find different trajectories.

In addition, the consumption-led growth based on asset market bubbles led to an immense overhang of debt, especially private debt in the form of personal loans and corporate borrowing. Such over-borrowing is of course a standard feature of the "euphoria" phase of financial cycles described by Kindleberger (1978); however, the scale and rate of expansion of such debt was historically unprecedented. This was especially so in the world's largest economy, which served as the growth engine for the rest of the world. Outstanding debt in the US now amounts to more than 3.5 times the GDP, most of which is private debt (303 percent of GDP in 2008). While public debt in 2008 was below the total GDP, it still amounted to nearly US$ 11 trillion. These excessive debt positions will have to be brought down, by both public and private sectors. In particular private debt – and household debt – will have to be wound down. Some of this is happening already through the housing defaults and other shakeouts being witnessed in the US financial sector, but much more is required and will necessarily occur in the medium term. This will clearly have an impact on aggregate consumption and production patterns. The obvious response is therefore to increase public spending, which is reflected in the projected US government budget deficit of 12.5 percent of GDP in 2009 (which is likely to be even higher as GDP has probably been overestimated) but this strategy too has limits for the US given the large external public debt overhang. This therefore affects the prospects for and nature of the recovery in the US and in other advanced economies such as the UK. Other countries – including developing and emerging markets that were unlucky enough to follow that same track even though to a much lesser degree, and therefore have high total debt to GDP ratios–are more likely to have painful adjustment measures forced upon them, with associated falls in income and employment. The adverse economic effects of private debt deflation are likely to extend over a protracted period and require ever larger fiscal stimuli to counteract them.

It should also be noted that the recent global boom involved another growing imbalance – that between the nature of economic growth and natural resources. Issues of climate change are only one among the many environmental problem generated by such growth. The boom involved rapacious natural resource extraction, over use and degradation, and has been associated with increasing stress of pollution and congestion especially in developing countries. Soil quality has deteriorated rapidly in many countries, adversely affecting agricultural productivity; water supplies have become more tenuous, polluted and fought over; forests and mineral resources have been pillaged and over-extracted with adverse ecological and socio-economic consequences; pollution, overcrowding and congestion have not only affected production but also quality of life, especially in the rapidly urbanising developing world.

Financial Liberalisation in Developing Countries

Developing countries are no strangers to financial crises, which have marked the history of some regions such as Latin America for more than a century (Eichengreen 1991) but became particularly prevalent since the early 1980s. The proclivity to crisis and to financial boom-bust cycles was especially evident in more financially open and deregulated developing economies. It is now well known that financial liberalisation has resulted in an increase in financial fragility in developing countries, making them prone to periodic financial and currency crises, not just internal banking and related crises, and currency crises stemming from more open capital accounts. Greater freedom to invest, including in sensitive sectors such as real estate and stock markets, ability to increase exposure to particular sectors and individual clients and increased regulatory forbearance all lead to increased instances of financial failure. In addition, the emergence of universal banks or financial supermarkets increases the degree of entanglement of different agents within the financial system and increases the domino effects of individual financial failures. Indeed, the major financial crises of the recent past in the developing world–the 1982 Latin American debt crisis, the 1994 Mexican crisis, the Southeast Asian financial crisis of 1997-98, the 2001 Argentine crisis - can be described as endogenous market failures resulting from under-regulated and excessively liquid financial markets (Palma 1998).

In addition, open capital accounts generate tendencies whereby capital movements occur because of unpredictable changes in investor confidence (Ghosh and Chandrasekhar 2008). This affects both inflows and outflows in ways that the governments concerned cannot control. Onc vcry common conclusion that has been constantly repeated since the start of the Asian crisis in mid 1997 is the importance of "sound" macroeconomic policies, once financial flows have been liberalised. It has been suggested that many emerging markets have faced problems because they allowed their current account deficits to become too large, reflecting too great an excess of private domestic investment over private savings. This belated realisation is a change from the earlier obsession with government fiscal deficits as the only macroeconomic imbalance worth caring about, but it still misses the basic point. With unregulated capital flows, it is not possible for a country to control the amount of capital inflow or outflow, and both movements can create consequences which are undesirable. If, for example, a country is suddenly chosen as a preferred site for foreign portfolio investment, it can lead to huge inflows which in turn cause the currency to appreciate, thus encouraging investment in non-tradeables rather than tradeables, and altering domestic relative prices and therefore incentives. Simultaneously, unless the inflows of capital are simply (and wastefully) stored up in the form of accumulated foreign exchange reserves, they must necessarily be associated with current account deficits. Thus, it was no accident that all the emerging market economies that received substantial financial capital inflows also experienced property and real estate booms, as well as stock market booms around the same time, even while the real economy may have been stagnating or even declining. These booms, in turn, generated the incomes to keep domestic demand and growth in certain sectors growing at relatively high rates. This soon resulted in signs of macroeconomic imbalance, not in the form of rising fiscal deficits of the government, but a current account deficit reflecting the consequences of debt-financed private profligacy.

Large current deficits are therefore necessary by-products of the surge in capital inflow, and that is the basic macroeconomic problem. This means that any country which does not exercise some sort of control or moderation over private capital inflows can be subject to very similar pressures. These then create the conditions for their own eventual reversal, when the current account deficits are suddenly perceived to be too large or unsustainable. What all this means is that once there are completely free capital flows and completely open access to external borrowing by private domestic agents, there can be no "prudent" macroeconomic policy; the overall domestic balances or imbalances will change according to the behaviour of capital flows, which will themselves respond to the economic dynamics that they have set into motion. This knowledge is at least partly responsible for the paradoxical tendency of developing countries across the globe to hold excess reserves, even when they reflect capital inflow, rather than use such resources to increase domestic absorption. This strategy of increasing reserves not only builds a cushion against capital flight in the event of a change in investor confidence, but also prevents the currency from appreciating. But it creates the bizarre global result of financial liberalization, that poor countries end up financing the expansion and consumption of the richest economies, especially the US, rather than investing in their own development. That is why the current liberalised system did not provide for a net transfer of resources to the developing world. In the past six years, there has been a net flow of financial resources from every developing region to the North, primarily the US, even as global income disparities have increased.

In addition to creating the conditions for greater internal and external fragility, financial liberalisation has generated a bias towards deflationary macroeconomic policies in developing countries. To begin with, the need to attract internationally mobile capital means that there are limits to the possibilities of enhancing taxation, especially on capital. Typically, prior or simultaneous trade liberalisation already reduces indirect tax revenues, and so tax-GDP ratios deteriorate further. This then imposes limits on government spending, since finance capital is generally opposed to large fiscal deficits and fear of capital flight will restrict governments from running deficits in such a context. This not only affects the possibilities for countercyclical macroeconomic stances of the state but also reduces the developmental or growth-oriented activities of the government.

Such a tendency is exacerbated by the fact that financial deregulation can lead to the dismantling of the financial structures that are crucial for growth and development (Chandrasekhar 2008a). While the relationship between financial structure, financial growth and overall economic development is complex, the basic issue of financing for development is really a question of mobilising or creating real resources. In the old development literature, finance in the sense of money or financial assets came in only when looking at the ability of the state to tax away a part of the surplus to finance its development expenditures, and the obstacles to deficit-financed spending, given the possible inflationary consequences if real constraints to growth were not overcome. By and large, the financial sector was seen as adjusting to the requirements of the real sector. But this need not happen when the financial sector is unregulated or covered by a minimum of regulation, since market signals then determine the allocation of investible resources and therefore the demand for and the allocation of savings intermediated by financial enterprises. This aggravates the inherent tendency in markets to direct credit to non-priority and import-intensive but more profitable sectors, to concentrate investible funds in the hands of a few large players and to direct savings to already well-developed centres of economic activity. The socially necessary role of financial intermediation therefore becomes muted. This certainly affects employment-intensive sectors such as agriculture and small-scale enterprises, where the transaction costs of lending tend to be high, risks are many and collateral not easy to ensure. The agrarian crisis in most parts of the developing world is at least partly, and often substantially, related to the decline in the access of peasant farmers to institutional finance, which is the direct result of financial liberalization (Patnaik 2005). Measures which have reduced directed credit towards farmers and small producers have contributed to rising costs, greater difficulty of accessing necessary working capital for cultivation and other activities, and reduced the economic viability of cultivation, thereby adding directly to rural distress. In India, for example, there is strong evidence that the deep crisis of the cultivating community, which has been associated with to a proliferation of farmers' suicides and other evidence of distress such as mass migrations and even hunger deaths in different parts of rural India, has been related to the decline of institutional credit, which has forced farmers to turn to private moneylenders and involved them once more in interlinked transactions to their substantial detriment (Ramachandran and

Swaminathan 2005).

It also has a negative impact on any medium term strategy of ensuring growth in particular sectors through directed credit, which has been the basis for the industrialisation process through much of the 20th century. Indeed, it is hard to think of any country that has reached "developed" status without relying to greater or lesser extent on directed credit. For late industrialisers, the necessity is even more evident, because capital requirements for entry in most areas are high; because technology for factory production has evolved in a capital-intensive direction from its primitive industrial revolution level; because of competition from established producers within and outside the country.

Impact of the Current Crisis on the Developing World

The past months have made it clear that the developing world is far from immune to the storms raging in financial markets in industrial countries. Stock prices in emerging markets have gone on similar roller coaster rides to those in New York and Europe, in a manner reminiscent of the behaviour of stock indices in the last major international financial upheaval in 1929/30–the Great Depression. The credit crunch and freezing of interbank lending have been only too evident even in developing countries whose economic "fundamentals" were apparently strong and whose policy makers believed that they could de-couple from the global trends.

This almost immediate diffusion of bad news is partly the result of financial liberalisation policies across the developing world that have made capital markets much more integrated directly through mobile capital flows, and created newer and similar forms of financial fragility almost everywhere (Akyuz 2008). But the international transmission of turbulence is only one of the ways in which the global financial crisis can and will affect developing countries.

A medium-term implication is the impact on private

capital flows to developing countries, which are likely to reduce with the credit crunch and with reduced appetite for risk among investors. The past five years witnessed an unprecedented increase in gross private capital flows to developing countries. Remarkably, however, this was not accompanied by a net transfer of financial resources, because all developing regions chose to accumulate foreign exchange reserves rather than actually use the money. Thus, there was an even more unprecedented counter-flow from South to North in the form of central bank investments in safe assets and sovereign wealth funds of developing countries, a process which completely shattered the notion that free capital markets generate net financial flows from rich to poor countries.

The likely reduction of capital flows into developing countries is generally perceived as bad news. But that is not necessarily true, since the earlier capital inflows were mostly not used for productive investment by the countries that received them. Instead, the external reserve build-up (which reflected attempts of developing countries to prevent their exchange rates from appreciating and to build a cushion against potential crises) proved quite costly for the developing world, in terms of interest rate differentials and unused resources. While some developing countries may indeed be adversely affected by the reduction in net capital inflows, for many other emerging markets thus may be a blessing in disguise as it reduces upward pressure on exchange rates and creates more emphasis on domestic resource mobilisation.

Similarly, it is also very likely that the crisis will reduce official development assistance to poor countries. It is well known that foreign aid is strongly pro-cyclical, in that developed countries' "generosity" to poor countries is adversely affected by any reversal in their own economic fortunes. But in any case development aid has also been experiencing an overall declining trend over the past two decades, even during the recent boom. In fact, the developed countries were extremely miserly even in providing debt relief to countries whose development prospects have been crippled by the need to repay large quantities of external debt that rarely contributed to actual growth. Notwithstanding the enormous international pressure for debt write-off, the G-8 countries have provided hardly any real debt relief. When they have done so, they have provided small amounts of relief along with very heavy and damaging policy conditionalities and in a blaze of self-serving publicity. So the speed and extent of the debt relief provided to their own large banks by the governments of the US and other developed countries, even when these banks have behaved far more irresponsibly, has not gone unnoticed in the developing world.

One major source of foreign exchange that is already strongly affected is remittance incomes, especially from workers based in Northern countries. Already, the Inter-American Development Bank estimates that 2008 will be the first year on record during which the real value of inward remittances will fall in Latin America and the Caribbean. Remittances into Mexico (which are dominantly from workers based in the US) in August were already down 12 percent compared to a year previously, and this will only get worse. There is also evidence of declining remittances from other countries that relied strongly on them, such as the Philippines, Bangladesh, Lebanon, Jordan and Ethiopia. In India, where around half of inward remittances currently come from the US, the same pattern of decline is likely.

Exports of goods and services, like remittances, are going to be affected by the global economic downturn. For most developing countries, the US and the European Union remain the most important sources of final export demand, and as they inevitably tip into recession, exports to these markets will also decline. All the loose talk of China emerging as the alternative engine of growth for the world economy has died down after China's exports contracted in the last two months of 2008 and domestic manufacturing stagnated. Chinese growth, which has pulled along many other Asian developing countries in a production chain, has been largely export-led. The US, EU and Japan together account for more than half of China's exports, and as their economic crisis intensifies, it is bound to affect both exports and economic activity in China. Even if China's policy makers respond by shifting to an emphasis on the domestic economy, for example through expansionary fiscal policy of along the lines suggested by the declared fiscal stimulus of US$ 340 billion over two years, this is unlikely to generate levels of international demand that will come anywhere near to the meeting the shortfall created by recession in the developed countries. China's share of global imports is still too small for it to serve as a growth engine on the same scale.

Across the developing world, one additional detrimental effect of the current crisis is likely to be the postponement or even cancellation of large investment projects whose ultimate profitability is now in doubt. This will have negative multiplier effects, as cancelled orders and lost jobs further reduce demand. The construction sector has already been hit, and many large projects are being cancelled even in economies that are still growing. The aviation sector is going through a major shakeout, which is evident even in India where there has already been a tendency towards mergers and worker retrenchment. The tourism and hospitality sector, which had emerged as an important employer in many developing countries, is facing cancellations and declining demand across both luxury and middle class segments.

The recent crisis has also signaled the end of the commodity boom, which is bad news for those developing countries dominantly reliant on commodity exports, and good news for commodity-importing developing countries. This follows a period of unprecedented increase in oil and other commodity prices, led largely by speculative investor behaviour. For example, world oil prices, which had increased to nearly US$ 150 per barrel in early July, fell to less than US$ 40 per barrel by December 2008. (Brent Crude futures) fell to less than US$ 70 per barrel from nearly US$ 150 in early July. One important index of commodity prices, the Reuters-Jefferies CRB index, in early December was more than 5o percent below its all-time high in July. While speculative behaviour was clearly behind the volatility in commodity prices over the past year, it is likely that such prices will continue to decline or stagnate at low levels for some time now because of the broader economic slowdown.

This may provide some breathing space in terms of inflation control for importing developing countries, especially oil importers. But the food crisis still rages for possibly a majority of the population of the developing world, and the current global economic crisis will certainly not make it better. While world prices of important food items have also declined in the recent past, they are still too high for many developing countries with low per capita incomes and a large proportion of already hungry people. And retail prices of food have hardly declined in most developing countries. Indeed, the financial crisis may actually make it more difficult for many governments of poor developing countries to secure adequate commodity supplies to meet their people's needs.

These are forces that will affect all or most developing countries, but they will be felt differently in different places. In particular, the extent of financial contagion and possible local financial crisis depends on how far the developing country concerned has gone along the road of financial liberalisation. Countries with large external debts and current account deficits will face particular problems. Already, it is apparent that financial markets are estimating the risk of default (in the form of the price of credit default swaps) for countries such as Pakistan, Argentina and Ukraine as high as 80 percent or more. Sometimes, as in Kazakhstan and Latvia, it is because of their highly leveraged banking systems.

In other cases, as for Turkey and Hungary, it is because of the very high current account deficits. The developing countries that have gone furthest in terms of deregulating their financial markets along the lines of the US (for example Indonesia) have been the worst affected and may well have full blown financial crises of their own. By contrast, China, which has still kept most of the banking system under state control and has not allowed many of the financial "innovations" that are responsible for the current mess in developed markets, is relatively safe. In India, which still has a nationalised banking system and greater degree of regulation, is better off than Indonesia, but recent reforms that the NDA and UPA government have pushed through despite Left protests, along with the growing current account deficit, have rendered the Indian economy more fragile and potentially vulnerable than China.

Of course, developing countries are still bit players in this global drama. This particular financial crisis has so many ramifications mainly because it is occurring in the very core of capitalism, and originated in the US, the country that had the global power and influence to impose its own economic model on almost all of the rest of the world. And the depth and severity of the crisis are likely to signal global political economy changes that will shape the world for the next few decades. Geopolitical shifts are likely to result from such glaring exposure of economic vulnerability in the global hegemon. Large bailouts and the planned Obama fiscal stimulus in the US will lead to a big increased in the US public debt. It will also make it harder for the US to maintain its military dominance, which has been a major source of the strength of the US dollar.

While the drama is still being played out and the ultimate denouement is still unclear, what cannot be denied is that US dominance of world economics and politics is now under severe question, and has suffered a blow from which it may not recover. The changes in the world in the next decade will not be linear or unidirectional, and there are bound to be savage conflicts over resources and much else, but the recent pattern of global imperialism has been severely disturbed. But even more than the geopolitical or economic shift, a bigger shift may come about from the clear failure of the economic model of neo-liberalism. The notions that markets know best, and that self-regulation is the best form of financial regulation, have now been completely exposed as fraudulent. And so this pervasive financial crisis, which is still to fully play out and work through in real economies, may have create a genuine opportunity not only for questioning the economic paradigm that has been dominant for far too long, but also replacing it with more progressive and democratic alternatives.

International Financial Architecture and the Role of IMF

Progressive change will require fundamental changes in the system of organising global finance and the institutions that govern trade and finance. But such changes will not come easily. The global financial and trading system is one that for many generations has been almost exclusively determined by the governments of western former colonial powers, and their writ still runs large in all the global institutions. Thus, the G-7 which leaves out Russia and China, not to mention India and Brazil, still presumes that it has the right to redesign the international financial architecture. The Financial Stability Forum of the Bank for International Settlements excludes any representation from developing countries. The tiny countries of Belgium, Netherlands and Luxembourg, with a total population of less than 28 million, have more votes in the IMF than China, Brazil or India.

The role of the IMF has once more assumed significance in this changed context. It has been some time now since the IMF lost its intellectual credibility, especially in the developing world. Its policy prescriptions were widely perceived to be rigid and unimaginative, applying a uniform approach to very different economies and contexts. They were also completely outdated even in theoretical terms, based on economic models and principles that have been refuted not only by more sophisticated heterodox analyses but also by further developments within neoclassical theory.

What may have been more damning was how out of sync the policies proposed by the IMF have also been with the reality of economic processes in developing countries. The 1990s and early 2000s were particularly bad for the organisation in that respect: their economists and policy advisers got practically everything wrong in all the emerging market crises they were called upon to deal with, from Thailand and South Korea to Turkey to Argentina. In situations in which the crisis had been caused by private profligacy they called for larger fiscal surpluses; faced with crisis-induced asset deflation they emphasised high interest rates and tight money policies; to address downward economic spirals they demanded fiscal contraction through reductions in public spending. The countries that recovered clearly did so despite their advice, or in several cases because they actively pursued different policies. And the recognition became widespread among governments in the developing world that IMF loans were too expensive because of the terrible policy conditions that came with them. So returning IMF loans early became something of a fashion, led by some Latin American countries.

In the past few years an even more terrible fate had befallen the IMF: that of increasing irrelevance. From 2002 onwards, the IMF and the World Bank became net recipients of funds from developing countries, as repayments far exceeded fresh loans. The developing world turned its attention to dealing with private debt and bond markets, which is where the action was. Less developed countries found new sources of aid finance and private investment from other sources, as China, Southeast Asia and even India to a limited extent, began investing in other developing countries.

So the IMF was not really a significant player in the international economic scene in the recent past, and the reasons for its very existence were often called into question. However, every crisis is also an opportunity, and the IMF has been quick to seize on the current global financial crisis as an opportunity to increase its own influence, by offering its services to emerging markets. As the crisis spreads and engulfs developing countries, and as global credit markets seize up and create credit crunches, more and more developing and transition countries are going to need access to emergency liquidity. Already several countries have lined up for this and signed agreements with the IMF: Pakistan, Ukraine, Hungary, Iceland. Some European governments have called for a strengthening of the IMF and even implored surplus countries like China to put more money into the IMF's coffers.

But with its current personnel and ideological framework, such strengthening of the IMF will only mean that the conditionalities it imposes will make things much worse for the developing world. The guiding principles of IMF lending are clear: countries in the midst of financial crisis must undergo fiscal contraction, however painful and regardless of whether the crisis was caused by public or private overspending. When the government account is in deficit, it must be reduced or converted into a surplus: when it is already in surplus, that surplus must be increased. This is obviously pro-cyclical and can cause the crisis to spread to the real economy and create a sharp economic downswing, but this is essential medicine and necessary pain to ensure the eventual recovery. Acceptance of these principles explains why so many developing countries have experienced even sharper and more prolonged economic downturns after turning to the IMF.

However, this argument is apparently valid only for developing economies, whose place is low in the international financial pecking order. In the World Economic Outlook for October 2008, the IMF clearly exposes very blatant double standards for industrial and developing countries. Contrary to its past prescriptions, countercyclical macroeconomic policy is seen to be acceptable for industrial countries. "Macroeconomic policies in the advanced economies should aim at supporting activity, thus helping to break the negative feedback loop between real and financial conditions, while not losing sight of inflation risks...Discretionary fiscal stimulus can provide support to growth in the event that downside risks materialise, provided the stimulus is delivered in a timely manner, is well targeted, and does not undermine fiscal sustainability." (IMF 2008:34, emphasis added.) But for developing countries, who have this time been caught in a crisis that is not of their own making, the same advice is not tenable at all. "While emerging economies have greater scope than in the past to use countercyclical fiscal policy should their economic outlook deteriorate ...this is unlikely to be effective unless confidence in sustainability has been firmly established and measures are timely and well targeted. More broadly, general food and fuel subsidies have become increasingly costly and are inherently inefficient." In fact, the IMF believes that in developing countries, despite the economic slowdown, there is room for tightening on all fronts, both fiscal and monetary! "Greater restraint on spending growth, including public sector wage increases, would complement tighter monetary policy, in the face of rising inflation, which is particularly important in economies with inflexible exchange regimes." (IMF 2008: 38)

So the IMF seems to have one rule for industrial countries in crisis, no matter how irresponsible the run-up to the crisis; and another rule for developing countries, even the most prudent and fiscally "disciplined" of them. Given this clearly unbalanced and potentially disastrous approach of the IMF, the need to examine alternative and less destructive sources of emergency finance for crisis-affected developing countries is urgent, as is the need, over the medium-term, to create a more democratic and less rigid international financial regime.

The Crisis and India

When the crisis first broke internationally, within India there was much talk of how the Indian economy is less likely to be affected and how the Indian financial sector will be relatively immune to the winds from the international financial implosion. But it is clear that important elements of the balance of payments and the domestic financial sector have been affected. There are significant implications for domestic banking, which are already reflected in the credit crunch that has dramatically affected access to credit especially for small and medium enterprises. There are effects on some important macroeconomic prices, in particular the exchange rate. And there are direct and indirect effects on employment, with falling export employment generating negative multiplier effects.

Despite all this, Indian policy makers still seem to be caught in some complacent time-warp, whereby they proudly point to the GDP growth rate (now spluttering, but still high by international standards) and to the supposed "resilience" of the domestic financial sector. Of course, neither of these is as positive as the government would like to make out. The current slowdown in GDP is sharper than the government would like to admit, and more significantly it has been accompanied by a much steeper than expected reduction in employment, especially in export sectors. Domestic banking is still generally secure, especially because nationalised banking remains the core of the system, largely thanks to resistance from the Left parties to government attempts to privatise it. Even so, there are clear signs of fragility and inadequacy within the banking sector: the recent rapid growth of often dodgy retail credit, associated attempts to securitise such debt, the emergence of a credit crunch in the face of macroeconomic uncertainty, and the inability or unwillingness of the banking system to provide loans to medium and small borrowers other than in the form of personal credit.

Beyond these implications, the effects of the global crisis have directly impacted upon some important macroeconomic variables. Three such indicators stand out in terms of their quite sudden deterioration since the middle of last year: the decline in the foreign exchange reserves held by the Reserve Bank of India; the fall in the external value of the rupee, especially vis-à-vis the US dollar; and the decline in stock market indices.

Chart 1 shows how foreign exchange reserves, which had been increasingly steadily over the past few years, started declining after June 2008. It must be noted that the earlier build-up of reserves did not reflect any real macroeconomic strength, since unlike China it was not based on current account surpluses. Instead, the Indian economy experienced an inflow of hot money, especially in the form of portfolio capital of FII investment. Domestic macro policies combined with the need to prevent exchange rate appreciation to prevent increased domestic absorption of such resources, as a result of which these were largely added to reserves. Since they were based on hot money inflows, it was only to be expected that they would reverse with any bad news, and that is essentially what has happened over the past eight months, with the bad news coming from the US and other developed markets rather than from the Indian economy.

Chart 1: Foreign exchange reserves

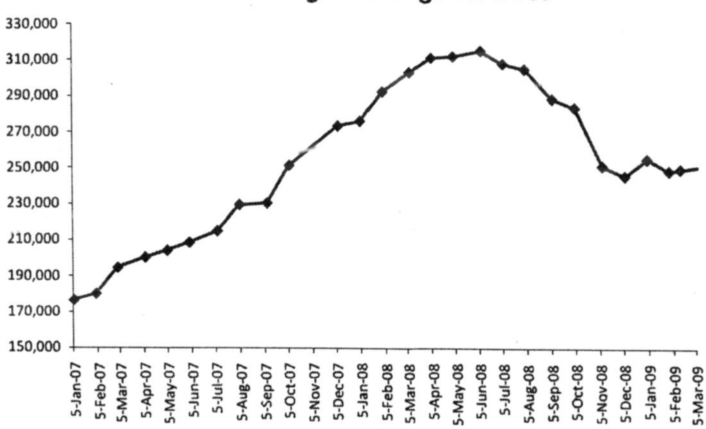

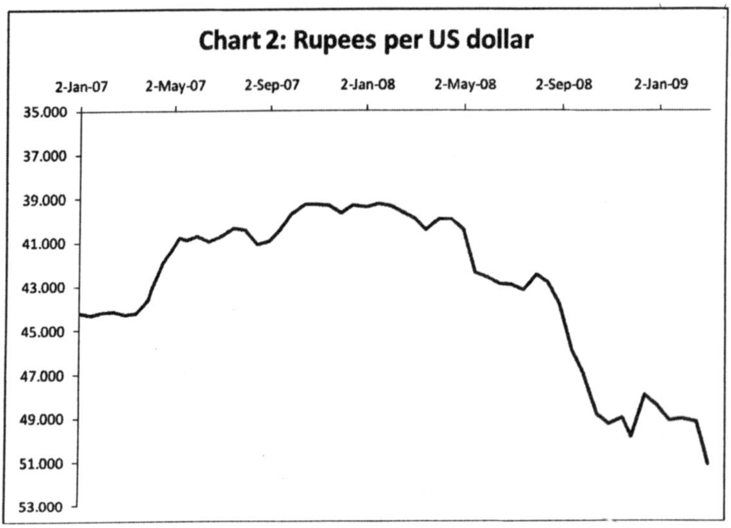

This movement of foreign institutional investors was in turn related to the sudden collapse of the rupee, shown in Chart 2. Early in March 2009 the rupee even breached the line of Rs. 51 per dollar, and currently continues to fall. There are those who argue that this depreciation is positive since it will help exports, but conditions prevailing in the world trade market, with falling export volumes and values, does not give rise to much optimism in that context. India currently has a current account deficit including a large trade deficit and also quite significant factor payments abroad. The falling rupee implies rising factor payments (such as debt repayment and profit repatriation) in rupee terms, which has adverse implications for many companies and for the balance of payments.

Associated with all this is the evidence of falling business confidence expressed in the stock market indicators. The Sensex, shown in Chart 3 had reached historically high levels in the early part of 2008, capping an almost hysterical rise over the previous three years in which it more than tripled in value. But it has plummeted since then, with high volatility around an overall declining trend, such that its levels in early March were below the levels attained in December 2005.

Chart 3: Daily movements in the Sensex

How much of all this is due to the behaviour of foreign investors, rather than domestic investors? Chart 4 tracks the changes in total foreign investment, split up into direct investment and portfolio investment, over the period since April 2007. It is evident that both have shown a trend of increase followed by decline. FDI has been more stable with relatively moderate fluctuations (even though it does include some portfolio-type investments that get categorised as foreign direct investment). It peaked in February 2008 and thereafter has been coming down but is still positive. Portfolio investment (which includes both FII investment in the domestic share market and GDRs/ADRs) has been extremely volatile and largely negative (indicating net outflows) since the beginning of 2008, and this has dominated the overall foreign investment trend.

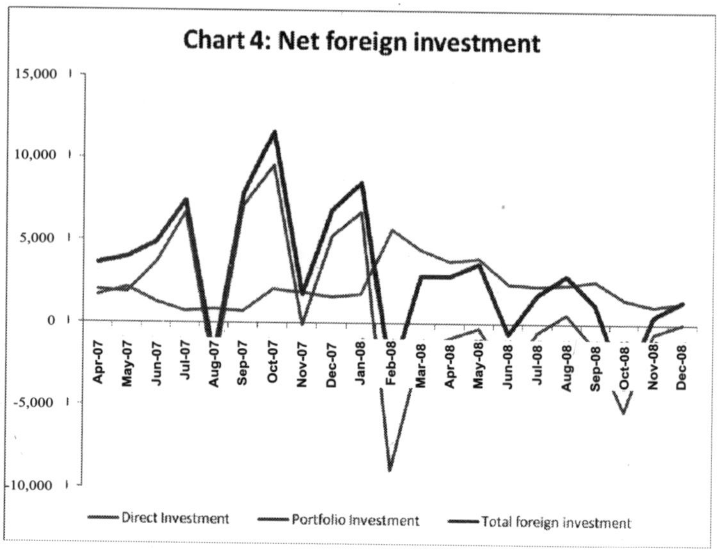

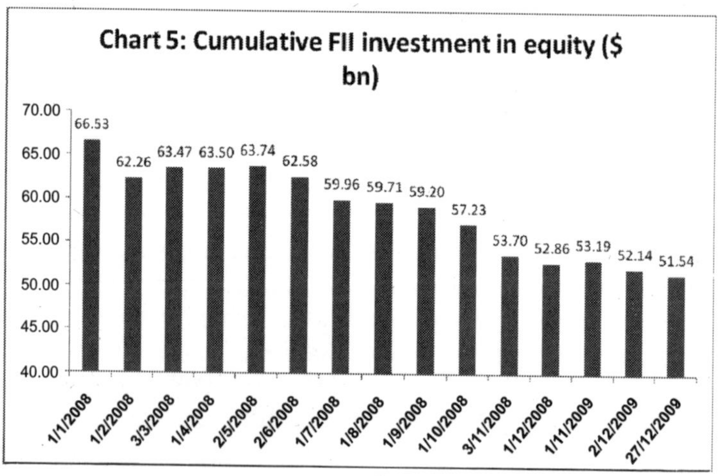

As a result, as Chart 5 shows, the cumulative value of the stock of Indian equity held by FIIs fell quite sharply, by 24 percent between May 2008 and February 2009. This is not likely to be due to any dramatically changed investor perceptions of the Indian economy, since if anything GDP growth prospects in India remain somewhat higher than in most other developed or emerging markets. Rather, it is because portfolio investors have been repatriating capital back to the US and other Northern markets. This reflects not so much a flight to safety (for clearly US securities are not that safe anymore either) as the need to cover losses that have been incurred in sub-prime mortgages and other asset markets in the North, and to ensure liquidity for transactions as the credit crunch began to bite.

Whatever the causes, the impact on the domestic stock market has been sharp and direct. Since the Indian stock market is still relatively shallow, and FII activities play a disproportionately strong role in determining the movement of the indices, it is not surprising that this outward flow has been associated with the overall decline in stock market valuations. As Chart 6 shows, the Sensex has moved generally in the same direction as net FII inflows. In fact movements in the latter have been much sharper and more volatile, suggesting that domestic investors have played a more stabilisng role over this period.

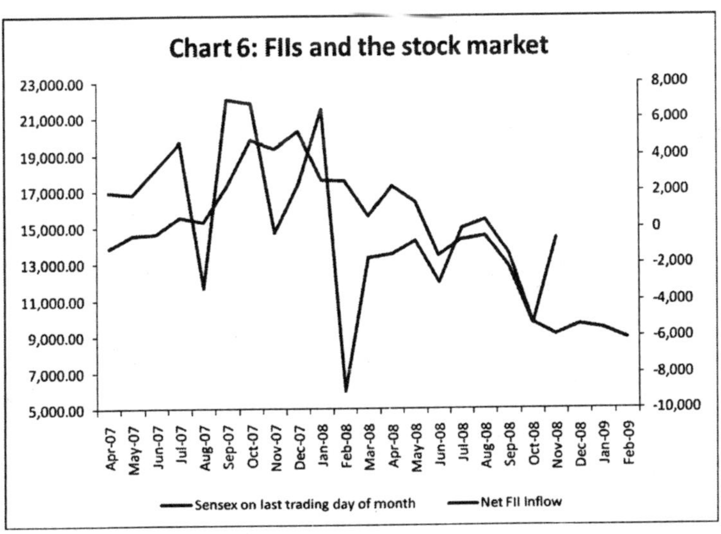

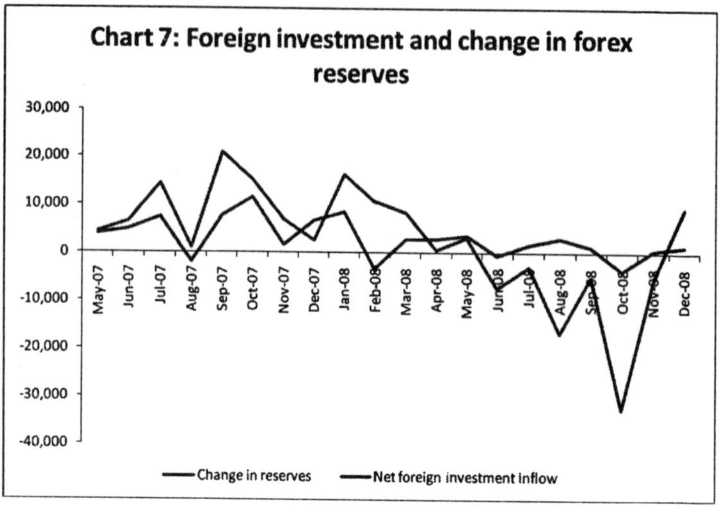

Overall foreign investment flows (including not just FII but direct investment) have also, predictably, played a role in determining the level of external reserves. Chart 7 shows the pattern of aggregate net foreign investment and change in reserves since April 2007. Once again the two move together. In this case, however, foreign investment has been less volatile than the change in reserves, suggesting that other components of the balance of payments have been important as well. The changes in external commercial borrowing are likely to have been significant.

In addition, the possibilities of domestic investors moving their funds out should not be underestimated. As Table 8.1 shows, the recently liberalised rules for capital outflow by domestic residents have led to outflows that are not insignificant, even if still relatively small. Liberalised rules for capital account transactions by Indian residents seem to be increasing the vulnerability that derives from India's dependence on foreign investment flows. This an aspect of India's external payments that policy must address, especially since there are constraints set by WTO membership on using tariffs and quantitative restrictions on reducing foreign exchange outflows that occur on account of imports.

Table 15.1: Outward Remittances under Liberalised Rules (US$ mn)

	2004-05	2005-06	2006-07	2007-08	Apr-Jul 2008
Deposits	9.1	23.2	19.7	1	12.8
Purchase of immovable property	0.5	1.9	8.5	39.5	26.9
Investment in equity/debt	-	-	20.7	144.7	54.4
Gifts, donations and others	0	0	23.9	232.3	126.6
Total	9.6	25.0	72.8	440.5	220.7

At the same time, exports dropped sharply, declining by 17 percent in November 2008 compared to the same month in the previous year. Aggregate growth projections were continuously revised downwards by both official and other analysts, as the expectation that GDP growth would remain above 7 percent for the year 2008-09 was tempered by the realisation of a likely sharp decline in the second of the year. The impact on employment was immediate: in early December it was estimated that more than 1 million jobs had already been lost, especially in the construction and small-scale export manufacturing sectors. Agriculturalists, especially those producing export crops whose prices had collapsed, faced growing difficulties on top of their existing financial problems. Real–and sometimes even nominal–wages of workers in industry and services have been falling, and the incomes of the self-employed who constitute half the work force are also under threat. Small scale producers in all sectors are being squeezed by the pincer movement of falling demand and credit crunch. Investment projects are being curtailed by the liquidity trap conditions in which banks are willing to lend only to the most secure borrowers, who in turn are unwilling to invest because of greater uncertainty. State governments' tax receipts have fallen and so they are increasingly strapped for cash and unable to meet even essential spending on basic services, not to mention development.

The Indian Government's Response

The initial responses of the government focussed on the financial side of the current crisis. There were measures to infuse liquidity into a banking system that had become very constrained by reducing the Cash Reserve Ratio and the Statutory Liquidity Ratio, to reduce interest rates by bringing down repo and reverse repo rates, and to provide some relief to non-bank financial institutions, particularly insurance companies. These were confidence-building measures that became necessary not because the international contagion was spreading to the banking system but because the Indian banking system had (in a less extreme form) several of the fragilities that undermined the US banks. But these monetary all proved to be lacking and did not ease credit conditions in any meaningful way. This was of the liquidity trap characteristics of the situation: banks were unwilling to lend to any but the most credit-worthy potential borrowers, but such potential borrowers were unwilling to borrow because of the prevailing uncertainties and expectations of slowdown. Meanwhile, all other enterprises, even those who desperately required working capital just to stay afloat, found it increasingly difficult to access bank credit even as they faced more stringent demand conditions. Some of the measures seemed to be more designed to push up the stock market than to revive the real economy, but even this was unsuccessful because of dampened expectations of real revival.

In such a situation, reducing interest rates does not solve

the basic problem of tightened credit provision, even though it may marginally reduce costs for those who are able to access bank credit. And the real economy cannot be revived through such measures in the absence of a strong fiscal stimulus. It is well known that there is really no alternative to the standard Keynesian device of using an expansionary fiscal stance to create more economic activity and demand, and thereby lift the economy from slump. Even so, the Government of India took an inordinately long time to announce the required fiscal stimulus, and when the much awaited fiscal package was finally announced, it turned out to be relatively small. It allowed for only up to Rs. 20,000 crore of direct additional spending through the Planning Commission in unspecified areas. This would be less than 0.5 percent of GDP, a tiny fiscal input which is too small to be really countercyclical or even to change the expectations of private agents in any meaningful way.

This direct spending was combined with a tax cut measure, on domestic duties–reducing the ad valorem Cenvat rate by 4 percentage points. But the point about such economic situations is that price responses do not work, and therefore output has to be addressed directly through spending. In any case, even price changes would not necessarily follow, since tax cuts would have an impact in terms of supporting economic activity only if producers respond by cutting prices, and such price cuts generate demand responses. But neither is inevitable. For example, the Government of India cut the administered price of aviation fuel in October 2008, but this was not passed on to consumers by the airline companies, and even two months later only one carrier–the public sector Air India - promised to reduce the aviation fuel surcharge. So that particular measure simply became an additional subsidy to shore up profits of airline companies. Across the world, governments have been finding that in these times of economic uncertainty, tax cuts are much less effective in stimulating activity than direct government expenditure. Similarly, measures that try to provide additional export incentives (such as interest reductions for export credit) to exporting sectors such as textiles, garments and leather would not counteract the effect of big losses of export orders as the major markets start shrinking. What is required was a more serious and systematic attempt to allow these industries to keep producing at technologically efficient levels and shift demand to other markets.

But what is even more significant is what the stimulus package announced in November 2008 left out. Not only was the overall size of the package too small to have much effect, but some of the most critical areas of spending were ignored or neglected. These areas include resource allocation to state governments, direct investment to ensure mass and middle-class housing, interventions to improve the livelihood conditions of farmers and enlargement of employment schemes to provide relief to working people as well as a macroeconomic stabiliser with positive multiplier effects.

The Interim Budget of the UPA government–the last chance to provide some macroeconomic stimulus to counteract the downturn, was even more disappointing. For the first four months of 2009-10, the UPA has proposed hardly any increase in expenditure, along with a recovery of revenues, such that the fiscal deficit is actually projected to come down to 5.5 percent of GDP compared with the current year. What is even worse is that while the amount of revenue receipts that state governments are projected to receive is even less than was budgeted for the current year, there is hardly any proposed increase in central assistance to state plans compared to the current year.

Similarly, there is no evidence of particular attention to employment-intensive sector like construction, which surely could have benefited from a large dose of public investment for affordable housing. The chance of a proper relief package for agriculturists to cope with the price shocks appears to be remote when the total expenditure for the Ministry of

Agriculture is projected to be flat. Food has emerged as a critical issue, and central PDS allocations to the states have been cut at a time when food prices are very high. Yet the allocation for the Department of Food and Public Distribution, which manages the food distribution and accounts for the food subsidy, has actually been reduced, falling from an estimated Rs. 45,536 crore in the current year to a budgeted Rs. 44,744 crore in the coming year! Despite the claim that an impetus would be provided to rural infrastructure through additional spending, the Ministry of Rural Development is actually slated to receive less money in 2009-10 than it is getting in the current year.

By the middle of 2008, state governments had already started feeling the resource constraint as their tax revenues were affected by the economic downturn. Yet they are responsible for most of the public services that directly affect people, such as those relating to agriculture and rural development, health, sanitation, education and so on, but unlike the Centre, the States face a hard budget constraint. So the overall conditions of life of the citizenry are likely to be affected. Yet the Centre could so easily have announced some measures to provide fiscal relief to the States to help them cope with the adverse effects of the downturn. Such measures could include reducing interest rates, providing more central funds and most of all relaxing fiscal responsibility norms that are inappropriate for the current situation and which the Centre itself has already discarded.

Similarly, the food crisis has been forgotten in all the excitement about the financial crisis, but food insecurity remains widespread and may even be spreading, given the significant rise in prices over the past two years. While overall inflation has been easing, food inflation in India continues despite large food grain stocks. And the real incomes of workers and cash crop cultivators have not kept pace with this. Poor or inadequate nutrition is already a big problem, which will deteriorate as the downturn worsens. A major positive role of crisis management would be played if it involved the allocation of significantly increased resources towards expanding, universalising and improving the functioning of the Public Distribution System. This would at least partly alleviate the problems of those who are already at the margin of survival, as well as those who could be tipped over into poverty by recent economic processes. Similarly, specific interventions are required to ensure the financial viability of cultivators, especially those who have been hit by falling output prices even as their own costs have kept rising.

The construction industry is a major employer and it has been hard hit already by the downturn. Yet the shortage of affordable housing remains acute across our cities and towns. Part of the problem is that private developers have increasingly focussed on the luxury segment of the market, without addressing this very obvious and basic need. It is important to expand the provision of middle class and mass housing, which is easily possible through public sector organisations, and can even be done through schemes that will be largely self-financing.

While monetary policies are not sufficient to address the current economic problems in India, this does not mean that the financial sector can be neglected. In particular, what is most obvious is that financial sector liberalisation has to be reversed, given the knowledge of the huge imperfections in such markets and the ability of unregulated finance to create massive scams that also destabilise real economies. Across the world, and especially in the major industrial countries, banking and insurance institutions are being effectively nationalised–yet in India there are moves towards more privatisation! The UPA government in mid-December actually placed a bill in Parliament that would raise the cap on FDI in the insurance sector to 49 percent, along with several other liberalising moves, even though the need is so obvious to exercise strong and effective regulation on insurance companies and prevent private domestic savings from being misused and exported out of the country. Further, the rapid expansion of retail credit since the early 2000s–with very large volumes of often unsecured lending in the form of housing loans, vehicle loans and credit card debt–provokes concerns about domestic financial fragility, especially as the economic slowdown bites into incomes and employment.

What is to be done?

It is more than obvious that the current global crisis provides a real opportunity to initiate and develop alternative policies, both internally and domestically. A change in economic paradigm is essential; without it the international economy will continue to lurch from crisis to crisis and the developing world will not be able to advance and provide basic needs to citizens. The need for more state intervention in economies is now recognised everywhere: the concern now is to ensure that such state involvement is more democratic and more accountable to the people.

Everyone now recognises the need to reform the international economic regime. But the idea should not simply be to fix a system that is obviously broken: we need to exchange it for a better model. That is because, as noted above, the current financial architecture has failed to meet two obvious requirements: of preventing instability and crises, and of transferring resources from richer to poorer economies. Not only have we experienced much greater volatility and propensity to financial meltdown across emerging markets and now even industrial countries, but even the periods of economic expansion have been based on the global poor subsidising the rich. These global failures are so immense that they constitute enough reason to abandon this system. But there are other associated failures in terms of what the regime has implied within national economies: it has encouraged pro-cyclicality; it has rendered national financial systems opaque and impossible to regulate; it has encouraged bubbles and speculative fervour rather than real productive investment for future growth; it has allowed for the proliferation of parallel transactions through tax havens and looser domestic controls; it has reduced the crucial developmental role of directed credit.

So we clearly need a new system, even if the goals remain the same as that of the original Bretton Woods: to ensure currency stabilisation through international monetary co-operation; to encourage the expansion of international trade in a stable way; and to promote development by facilitating productive investment. To achieve this in the current context, four elements are crucial. First, the belief that self-regulation supported with external risk assessment by rating agencies is an adequate way to run a financial system has been blown sky-high. There is no alternative, therefore, to systematic state regulation of finance. Second, since private players will inevitably attempt to circumvent regulation, the core of the financial system-banking-must be protected, and this is only possible through social ownership. Therefore, some degree of the socialisation of banking (and not just socialisation of the risks inherent in finance) is also inevitable. In developing countries it is also important because it enables public control over the direction of credit, without which no country has industrialised. Third, to cope with the adverse real economy effects of the current crisis, fiscal stimulation is essential in both developed and developing countries. Enhanced public expenditure is required to prevent economic activity and employment from falling, to manage the effects of climate change and promote greener technologies (Pollin 2008), and to advance the development project in the South. Fourth, the international economic framework must support all this, which in turns means that capital flows must be controlled and regulated so that they do not destabilise any of these strategies.

In India too, a major change in economic paradigm is required along these lines. But first of all, it is necessary to ensure that Indian economic policy makers remember the basic Keynesian principles that are now back in fashion everywhere else in the world, such as that direct public spending is the best countercyclical measure, especially in a situation of liquidity trap. Such public spending will be more economically effective and more welfare -improving if it is directed dominantly towards employment schemes, social spending and rural and urban infrastructure for mass use. This will also enable more progress towards meeting developmental goals, but this also requires that government spending be made more democratically accountable and more directed towards altering consumption and production patterns in more sustainable directions.

Source: www.networkideas.org
© International Development Economics Associates. Reprinted with Permission.

References

Akyuz, Yilmaz (2008) "The global financial crisis and developing countries", Resurgence, December, Penang: Third World Network.

Augar, Philip (2006) The Greed Merchants: How the investment banks played the free market game", New York: Penguin Books.

Chandrasekhar, C. P. (2008a) "Global liquidity and financial flows to developing countries: new trends in emerging markets and their implications", G-24 Working Paper, available on http://www.networkideas.org/featart/jul2008/fa29_G24.htm

Chandrasekar, C. P. (2008b) "India's sub-prime fears" Economic and Political Weekly

Crotty, James (2008) "Structural causes of the global financial crisis: A critique of the international financial architecture", http://www.networkideas.org/featart/oct2008/fa24_Financial_Architecture.htm

Eichengreen, Barry (1991) "Historical research on international lending and debt", Journal of Economic Perspectives 5 (2): 149-169.

Ghosh, Jayati and C. P. Chandrasekhar, eds. (2008) A Decade After: Financial crisis and recovery in East Asia, New Delhi: Tulika Books, forthcoming.

International Monetary Fund (2008) World Economic Outlook, Washington, D.C., October.

Kindleberger, Charles (1978) Manias, Panics and Crashes: A history of finance crises, New York: Basic Books.

Kregel, Jan (2008) "Using Minsky's 'cushion of safety' to analyse the crisis in the US sub-prime mortgage market", IDEAS Working Paper 04/2008, http://www.networkideas.org/working/jun2008/wp18_04_2008.htm

Palma, Gabriel (1998) "Three and a half cycles of manias, panics and (asymmetric) crash: East Asia and Latin America compared", Cambridge Journal of Economics 22: 789-808.

Patnaik, Prabhat (2005) "The illusionism of finance" http://www.networkideas.org/featart/jan2005/fa27_Illusionism_Finance.htm

Patnaik, Prabhat (2008) The Value of Money, New Delhi: Tulika Books.

Pollin, Robert (2008) "How to end the recession" http://www.networkideas.org/news/nov2008/news10_Recession.htm

Ramachandran, V.K. and Madhura Swaminathan, eds. (2005) Financial Liberalisation and Rural credit in India, New Delhi: Tulika Books.

16

Risk Management in the Midst of the Global Financial Crisis

D. Subbarao

Thank you for inviting me to be the keynote speaker at this Financial Management Summit. The global economy is passing through its deepest financial and economic crisis of our time. Protecting the Indian economy from the worst impact of the crisis has been a big challenge for the government and the Reserve Bank. Equally, I am conscious of the fact that industry, business and investors gathered here today have had to make very challenging adjustments in these difficult times.

The Chinese have a saying, "may you live in interesting times." I can hardly complain. These have been very interesting times for me, perhaps a bit too interesting. I came into the Reserve Bank when runaway inflation around the world, and here in India, was the overriding concern. Less than a month later, this turned into the biggest global recession of our times with severe financial dislocation and concerns about deflation becoming the global chorus.

Crisis Management around the World

During this period, macroeconomic management, needless to say, has been challenging. The financial crisis called into question several fundamental assumptions and beliefs about economic resilience and financial stability. With all the advanced economies in a synchronised recession, global GDP is projected to contract for the first time since the Second World War. We were lulled into believing that the rewards of the Great Moderation were with us for ever to enjoy until the

Great Unraveling hit us and forced us into this Great Recession.

Governments and central banks around the world have responded to the crisis in an unprecedented show of policy force. The shock and awe of fiscal stimulus and monetary easing is still with us. Importantly, given the nature of the crisis, purely national responses have been supplemented by global efforts. The G-20 group of nations met twice in the last six months. At their April 2009 meeting, the G-20 leaders collectively committed to take decisive, coordinated and comprehensive actions to revive growth, restore stability of the financial system, restart the impaired credit markets and rebuild confidence in financial markets and institutions.

The crisis has forced macroeconomic policy around the world into clearly uncharted territory. Governments and central banks took largely unprecedented fiscal and monetary policy measures to prevent the global recession from turning into a protracted depression.

Some analysts said this was an over reaction. Others criticized the tyranny of the short term compromising medium term sustainability. But received wisdom and mainstream view have been that it was clearly safer to err on doing too much rather than doing too little. Thus the policy response should be seen as an insurance against this risk. But there is no real way of judging whether we are over insuring or underinsuring. If indeed the world has over insured, then there is a risk that all this liquidity has the potential to trigger a bout of undesirable inflation. Conversely, if we have underinsured, then this recession could turn deeper, nastier, and longer. And as we know from experience, there is no way to measure *a priori* whether we have insured right. So policymakers all over the world are perhaps erring on the side of over insuring - keeping financial markets flush with liquidity, providing substantial fiscal support, using the breathing space provided by the policy support to restructure the financial system, and hoping that they can withdraw the liquidity and stimulus as the recovery firms up and before inflationary threats take root.

Notwithstanding the relative calm in recent weeks, the global financial outlook continues to be uncertain. It is not clear that we have seen the end of the emergence of tainted assets, and doubts persist on whether the initiatives underway are sufficient to restore the stability of the financial system. There is continued debate on the adequacy of the fiscal stimulus packages across countries, and their effectiveness in arresting the downturn, reversing job losses and reviving consumer confidence. Many major central banks have nearly or totally exhausted their conventional weaponry of calibrating policy interest rates and are now resorting to unconventional measures such as quantitative and credit easing. Given the erosion of the monetary policy transmission mechanism, there are concerns about when and to what extent monetary response, admittedly aggressive, will begin to have an impact on reviving credit flows and spurring aggregate demand.

India: Crisis Response and Challenge

At home, the impact of the crisis has been deeper than anticipated earlier although less severe than in other emerging market economies. The extent of impact has caused dismay, mainly on two grounds: first, because our financial sector remains healthy, has had no direct exposure to tainted assets and its off-balance sheet activities have been limited; and second, because India's merchandise exports, at less than 15 percent of GDP, are relatively modest. Despite these mitigating factors, the crisis hit India underscoring the rising two-way trade in goods and services and financial integration with the rest of the world.

There have been several comforting factors going into the slowdown. First, our financial markets, particularly our banks, have continued to function normally. Second, India's comfortable foreign exchange reserves provide confidence in our ability to manage our balance of payments notwithstanding lower export demand and dampened capital flows. Third, headline inflation, as measured by the wholesale price index (WPI), has declined sharply. Consumer price inflation too has begun to moderate. Fourth, because of mandated agricultural lending and social safety-net programmes, rural demand continues to be robust.

Both the Government and the Reserve Bank responded to the challenge strongly, and in close coordination and consultation. The Reserve Bank shifted its policy stance from monetary tightening in response to the elevated inflationary pressures in the first half of 2008-09 to monetary easing in response to easing inflationary pressures and moderation of growth engendered by the crisis. The Reserve Bank's policy response was aimed at containing the contagion from the global financial crisis while maintaining comfortable domestic and foreign exchange liquidity. Taking a cue from the Reserve Bank's monetary easing, most banks have reduced their deposit and lending rates.

The Government launched three fiscal stimulus packages between December 2008 and February 2009. These stimulus packages came on top of an already announced expanded safety-net programme for the rural poor, the farm loan waiver package and payout following the Sixth Pay Commission report, all of which too added to stimulating demand.

As the monetary and fiscal stimuli work their way through, and if calm and confidence are restored in the global markets, we can see economic turn around later this year. After averaging nine percent growth over the last four years, economic activity in India has slowed since the last quarter of 2008. The outcomes in recent months have been mixed. While overall industrial production fell again in March, cement and steel production have shown some preliminary signs of upturn. Segments in the automobile sector, particularly two and three wheelers and passenger cars, are showing modest revival of demand. The industrial and business outlook is improving. These signs are not unambiguous—there is as yet no clear sign of export decline reversing the trend, and credit growth continues to be subdued. Taking the evolving global situation and the domestic conditions into account, in our Annual Policy Statement last month, we projected real GDP growth of 6.0 percent for 2009/10. The balance of our assessment continues to support this growth projection.

While the risks from the uncertainties in the global financial markets continue to persist, there are risks on the domestic front too. The challenge is how we manage the recovery. The fiscal and monetary response now on will have to weigh in the state of the economy going forward 6-9 months. If the global recovery takes root and private investment demand revives faster, there could be less of a case for further stimulus. On the other hand, if global financial markets do not stabilize and global recovery does not take hold by the last quarter of 2009, we would realize with the benefit of hindsight, that the domestic policy response should have been stronger.

So, where and how does the economic dilemma fit into the topic of risk management, which is the subject of this summit? It fits in because the context throws up questions about risk management in the macro-economy. How does one hedge against the uncertainty of outcomes of toady's fiscal and monetary policy actions? How does one insure against such risks? Clearly there are no easy ways; if indeed there were, we would not be having this seminar. I will focus on three aspects: monetary policy, fiscal policy, and financial stability to define the contours of uncertainty.

Looking Ahead: Monetary Policy

On the monetary policy front, managing the risk calls for maintaining ample liquidity in the system. The RBI has done so the past six months through a variety of instruments and facilities. And in the April 2009 policy review, we extended the tenure many of these facilities. Some will argue, and rightly so, that this might be sowing the seeds of the next inflationary cycle. And this is exactly the kind of risk one has to grapple with. So while the Reserve Bank will continue to support liquidity in the economy, it will have to ensure that as economic growth gathers momentum, the excess liquidity is rolled back in an orderly manner. It is important to note though that even as the monetary easing has increased liquidity considerably, at the aggregate level this has not been out of line with our monetary aggregates unlike in many advanced countries. As such, the challenge of unwinding will be less daunting for India than for other countries.

The rise in macroeconomic uncertainty and the financial dislocation of last year have raised a related problem. The adjustment in market interest rates in response to changes in policy rates gets reflected with some lag. In India monetary transmission has had a differential impact across different segments of the financial market. While the transmission has been faster in the money and bond markets, it has been relatively muted in the credit market on account of several structural rigidities. However, the earlier acceleration in inflation coupled with high credit demand appears to have added to these rigidities by prompting banks to raise deposits at higher rates to ensure longer term access to liquidity. High deposit rates in turn have not allowed banks to cut lending rates at a faster pace consistent with the growth and inflation outlook. Although deposit rates are declining and effective lending rates are falling, there is clearly more space to cut rates given declining inflation. Making liquidity available in sufficient quantity, as RBI has done, should also help by giving confidence to banks of the availability of funds.

Looking Ahead: Fiscal Policy

The challenge for fiscal policy is to balance immediate support for the economy with the need to get back on track on the medium term fiscal consolidation process. The fiscal stimulus packages and other measures have led to sharp increase in the revenue and fiscal deficits which, in the face of slowing private investment, have cushioned the pace of economic activity.

The first order of economic business for the new government will be the full budget. Given the still soft economy, the pressure to provide more stimulus will persist. While this may help in the very near term, the sustainability of the recovery requires returning to responsible fiscal consolidation. The borrowing programme of the government has already expanded rapidly. The Reserve Bank has been able to manage the large borrowing programme in an orderly manner. Large borrowings by the government run against the low interest rate environment that the Reserve Bank is trying to maintain to spur investment demand in keeping with the stance of monetary policy.

The Reserve Bank will continue to use a combination of monetary and debt management tools to manage the government borrowing programme to ensure its successful completion in a smooth manner. During the first half of 2009-10, planned Open Market Operations (OMO) purchases and Market Stabilisation Scheme (MSS) unwinding will add primary liquidity which will be equivalent, in terms of monetary impact, to reduction of CRR by three percentage points. This should leave adequate resources with banks to expand credit. However, with every percentage point increase in the fiscal deficit, maintaining adequate liquidity in the system becomes that much more difficult. Managing this trade off between our short term compulsions and longer term sustainability will be one of the big challenges going forward.

Looking Ahead: Financial Stability

Beyond monetary and fiscal policies, preserving financial stability is key to navigating these uncertain times. A sound and resilient banking sector, well-functioning financial markets, robust liquidity management and payment and settlement infrastructure are the pre-requisites for financial stability. The banking sector in India is sound, adequately capitalized and well-regulated. By all counts, Indian financial markets are capable of withstanding the global shock, perhaps somewhat bruised but definitely not battered.

But how sure can we be? Here we have some encouraging news. Amidst the din of the financial turmoil and the all-consuming fixation on rate cuts over the last six months, a seminal report on the health of the Indian financial system has received less notice than it deserved.

Committee on Financial Sector Assessment (CFSA)

In March this year, the Government and RBI jointly released the report of the Committee on Financial Sector Assessment (CFSA) that was co-chaired by Deputy Governor Rakesh Mohan and Finance Secretary Ashok Chawla. The report is the culmination of work started in September 2006 to undertake a comprehensive self-assessment of India's financial sector, particularly focusing on stability assessment and stress testing and compliance with all financial standards and codes.

The CFSA owes its origins to the Financial Sector Assessment Program, FSAP for short, that was initiated in 1999 and carried out jointly by the IMF and the World Bank after the Asian crisis. Several countries, including India, participated in this long drawn and resource intensive exercise. This program so far has been conducted by the IMF and the World Bank using experts from around the world to carry out the assessment with participation from the host country.

While India had earlier participated in the FSAP conducted by the IMF and World Bank, to the best of my knowledge, we are first country to make a self assessment of its financial sector in line with the FSAP. This is a remarkable achievement especially as the assessment conformed to the structure and procedure laid down by the IMF, the World Bank and several standard-setting bodies like the BIS, IOSCO and IAIS. As the previous Finance Secretary, I had watched the process first hand. By all accounts, this was a large and complex exercise. But the Government and the RBI remained committed to a rigorous, transparent and unbiased process.

The CFSA followed a forward-looking and holistic approach to self-assessment, based on three mutually reinforcing pillars: financial stability assessment and stress testing; legal, infrastructural and market development issues; and an assessment of the status of implementation of international financial standards and codes. The first pillar is essentially concerned with stability assessment. Taking into account the legal, regulatory and supervisory architecture in India, the CFSA felt the need for involving, and associating closely, all the major regulatory institutions in the financial sector—the RBI, SEBI and IRDA, besides the relevant government departments. Direct official involvement at different levels brought about enormous responsibility, ownership, and commitment to the process, ensuring constructive pragmatism when faced with contentious issues.

Since the assessment required comprehensive domain knowledge in the various technical areas examined, the CFSA initially constituted Technical Groups comprising officials with first-hand experience in handling the respective areas from the regulatory agencies concerned as well as the government to undertake the preliminary assessment and to prepare technical notes and background material in the concerned areas. This ensured that officials who are well-conversant with their own systems and are aware of the existing strengths and weaknesses could identify the best alternative solutions.

To ensure an impartial assessment, the CFSA constituted four external independent Advisory Panels, comprising non-official experts drawn from within the country. These Panels made their assessments after thorough debate and rigorous scrutiny of inputs provided by the Technical Groups. To further strengthen the credibility of this assessment, the Advisory Panels' assessments were peer reviewed by eminent international experts.

The CFSA then drew up its own overview report at the final stage, drawing upon the assessments, findings and recommendations of the Advisory Panels and the comments of the peer reviewers. The assessments and recommendations comprise six volumes. All the six volumes are freely available on RBI's website and I would strongly recommend that you read them. If six volumes are daunting, then read at least the first two volumes, viz., the Executive Summary and the Overview Report.

Overall, the CFSA found that our financial system is essentially sound and resilient, and that systemic stability is by and large robust. India is broadly compliant with most of the standards and codes though gaps were noted in the timely implementation of bankruptcy proceedings.

Of immediate interest, and related closely to the current macroeconomic conditions, the CFSA also carried out single-factor stress-tests for credit and market risks and liquidity ratio and scenario analyses. These tests show that there are no significant vulnerabilities in the banking system. This does not mean that NPAs will not rise in this economic slowdown. NPAs may indeed rise, as the Reserve Bank has pointed out. But given the strength of the banks' balance sheets, that rise is not likely to pose any systemic risks, as it might in many advanced countries.

Risk assessment, however, is a continuous process and the stress tests need to be conducted taking into account the macroeconomic linkages as also the second round and contagion risks. The Reserve Bank intends to formalize this process by setting up an inter-disciplinary Financial Stability Unit to monitor and address systemic vulnerabilities.

India Outlook

Let me now conclude. We are, as I said at the beginning, in uncharted policy territory. The crisis is forcing countries around the world to test the limits of their fiscal and monetary tools. This is true for macroeconomic policy, and I believe it is also true for business policy, which you will be discussing today. Our economy remains fundamentally strong despite the adverse impact of the global financial crisis. With the right mix of macroeconomic policy and corporate strategy, my sense is that, as an economy, we will emerge from this global recession stronger than before.

Once again thank you for this opportunity to share my views. I wish your deliberations all success.

Source:www.rbi.org.in.
© Reserve Bank of India, RBI. Reprinted with Permission.

This speech was delivered by Dr. D. Subbarao, Governor, Reserve Bank of India at the Financial Management Summit 2009 organized by the Economic Times on May 22, 2009 in Mumbai.

Index

Index

SBD/542